Praise for David Shenk's

THE IMMORTAL GAME

"Beguiling. . . . [Shenk's] history has an improvisational dexterity that suits its subject." —*The Weekly Standard*

"Shenk's book possesses an almost inestimable advantage over the many other publications about chess. . . . You can be an utter novice, just a simple wood-pusher, and enjoy the author's engaging prose, honest self-deprecation (he's a lousy player) and the charm of his personal connection with the game." —*The Washington Post*

"Wonderful. . . . A book filled with daring moves and cunning patience." —Stephen J. Dubner, coauthor of *Freakonomics*

"Shenk writes with passion and grace. *The Immortal Game* is a book both for die-hard chess players and anyone who is acquainted with one." —*The Dallas Morning News*

"A bravura demonstration of the art of storytelling." —*The Globe and Mail* (Toronto)

"An enriching and inviting prism through which to view and better understand history in general." —*Albuquerque Journal*

"With the depth and insight of a grandmaster, *The Immortal Game* explores and explains not only the addictive power of chess but its shockingly important, Zelig-like role in the history of humankind." —Stefan Fatsis, author of *Word Freak*

"Everyone, from expert to patzer, will find something to admire about Shenk's investigation into our most-beloved board game." —*The Wichita Eagle*

"Fun, factual, and a good read. . . . Not a reference book to be stored on a shelf [but] a book to be read and enjoyed, and even read again. . . . Buy this book!"
                                                                —*Chess Life*

"A thrilling tour. . . . An engaging, colorful look at a world that blissfully remains black-and-white."
                                                    —*Entertainment Weekly*

"Fascinating. . . . [Shenk] writes about chess history with contagious zest."
                                                        —*The Plain Dealer*

"I loved this book . . . Like a great chess game, this is an achievement that will be talked about for many years to come."
                        —Simon Winchester, author of *The Professor and the Madman*

"Brilliantly conceived. . . . You won't find a more lucid and captivating exploration of [chess]."
                                                        —*The Toronto Star*

"Shenk weaves a masterful tale that all readers can enjoy, no matter how little they know about chess."
                                            —*Milwaukee Journal Sentinel*

"An enjoyable read. . . . We all profit from [Shenk's] late-blooming interest with [chess]."
                                                    —*The Washington Times*

"Shenk's desire to discuss chess as metaphor comes as a refreshing change of pace from the popular abuse of the game's vocabulary."
                                                —*Minneapolis Star Tribune*

"David Shenk takes us millennia back and light years ahead."
                        —Bruce Pandolfini, legendary chess instructor

David Shenk

THE IMMORTAL GAME

David Shenk is a national bestselling author of four previous books, including *The Forgetting* and *Data Smog*, and a contributor to *National Geographic*, *Slate*, *Gourmet*, *Harper's Magazine*, *The New Yorker*, and NPR. *The Forgetting* was hailed by John Bayley as "the definitive work on Alzheimer's," and subsequently inspired an Emmy Award–winning PBS film of the same name. Shenk frequently lectures on health, aging, technology, and talent, and has advised the President's Council on Bioethics. He lives in Brooklyn, New York, with his family.

www.davidshenk.com

ALSO BY DAVID SHENK

The Forgetting

The End of Patience

Data Smog

Skeleton Key
(*with Steve Silberman*)

THE
IMMORTAL
GAME

· · · · · · · ·

A HISTORY OF CHESS

or How 32 Carved Pieces on a Board
Illuminated Our Understanding of War,
Art, Science, and the Human Brain

DAVID SHENK

Anchor Books
A Division of Random House, Inc.
New York

FIRST ANCHOR BOOKS EDITION, SEPTEMBER 2007

The Library of Congress has cataloged the Doubleday edition as follows:
Shenk, David, 1966–
The immortal game : a history of chess / David Shenk.
p. cm.
Includes bibliographical references and index.
1. Chess—History. I. Title.
GV1317.S44 2006
794.109—dc22   2005056025

Anchor ISBN: 978-1-4000-3408-6

Author photograph © Jon Shenk
Book design by Lovedog Studio
Map by Jackie Aher
Photographs on page 244 © 2005 by Ian J. Cohn

www.anchorbooks.com

Printed in the United States of America
10   9   8   7   6   5   4   3   2   1

FOR KURT

CONTENTS

III. ENDGAME
(Where We Are Going)

Caliph Ar-Radi was walking in the country, and stopped in a lovely garden, replete with lawns and flowers. His courtiers immediately began to dilate on the wonders of the garden, to extol its beauty, and to place it above all the wonders of the world.

"Stop," cried the Caliph. "As-Suli's skill at chess charms me more."

—al-Masudi, tenth century

PROLOGUE

THINK OF A VIRUS so advanced, it infects not the blood but the thoughts of its human host. Liver and spleen are spared; instead, this bug infiltrates the frontal lobes of the brain, dominating such prime cognitive functions as problem solving, abstract reasoning, fine motor skills, and, most notably, agenda setting. It directs thoughts, actions, and even dreams. This virus comes to dominate not the body, but the mind.

When eleven-year-old Marcel Duchamp first played chess with his older brothers Gaston and Raymond in their home in the French village of Blainville-Crevon in 1898, the game seemed like a harmless distraction, an interesting way of passing the quiet nights in the Normandy countryside. A quick thinker brimming with charm and confidence, Marcel excelled at most things and was well liked wherever he went. Nurtured by his family's deep artistic roots and following in the path set by his older brothers, he emerged in his late teens as an ambitious cartoonist and painter in Paris.

In just a few years, Duchamp's intense and unusual work began to catch the public eye—mainly for its refusal to settle into a neat classification. He experimented with and quickly passed through the well-established painting styles of Postimpressionism, Fauvism, and Cubism. By his mid-twenties, in fact, he was moving past painting altogether, into an intellectual-aesthetic realm that would come to be known as conceptual art. With his landmark works *Nude Descending a Staircase*, *The Large Glass*, *Fountain* (a "ready-made" urinal), and *LHOOQ* (a postcard reproduction of the *Mona Lisa* doctored with a mustache and goatee),

Duchamp gave a jump-start to the sedate art world and helped inspire the Dada, Surrealist, and Abstractionist movements. Further, his art and ideas anticipated the emergence of Pop Art, minimal art, performance art, process art, and, says biographer Calvin Tomkins, "virtually every postmodern tendency." By age thirty, Duchamp had produced a body of work that would make him perhaps the most influential artist of the twentieth century.

And then chess took over.

"Chess holds its master in its own bonds," Albert Einstein once said, "shackling the mind and brain so that the inner freedom of the very strongest must suffer."

For more than a decade, the checker-square board game with four-inch medieval war figurines had been merely a happy diversion in Duchamp's life. In his teens and early twenties, he had played vigorously with family and friends. He also worked it into a few early paintings. But in his late twenties something happened between Duchamp and chess that transformed the relationship into an addiction, and eventually an obsession. Slowly, over a few years' time, chess moved to the very front of his brain, somehow forcing fundamentals like art, ideas, friendships, and romance to the rear. It was as if these thirty-two inanimate pieces of wood emitted some sort of unseen magnetic or hypnotic power, bending Duchamp's formidable mind to its own will.

Strangest of all, perhaps, was the fact that this transition happened in the midst of career glory. Imagine John F. Kennedy chucking politics in June 1960 in favor of billiards. Popular and intriguing, Duchamp was the toast of art patrons in Paris, New York, and beyond. Now, at his peak, he was turning away from all this. Days that would ordinarily have been filled receiving admiring gallery owners and customers, and late nights that would have included dinner parties and more studio work, instead became packed with one chess game after another (after another, after another). Between games, Duchamp engaged in the silent, monastic study of chess problems—thousands of tricky endgame scenarios labored over by most serious players. In New York, Duchamp joined the Marshall Chess Club near Washington Square Park, playing until all hours of the night. During a two-year stint in Buenos Aires, he constantly sought opponents, studied chess books, and commissioned a set of custom rubber stamps in order to play through the mail with his New York patron and friend Walter Arensberg.

By his early thirties, the transition was complete. Apart from the design of some chess sets, Duchamp was producing virtually no art. He shocked friends by bluntly declaring that he was giving up his old career to become a full-time chess player. "I play day and night," he declared in 1919 (at age thirty-two), "and nothing interests me more than to find the right move."

For hours at a stretch, taking just enough time for meals in between, Duchamp played alone in his apartment, with friends and strangers at cafés, and even in the midst of loud art-world parties. This new life involved not just a reordering of his work and social priorities, he explained to friends, but also his very consciousness. "Everything around me takes the shape of the Knight or the Queen," he said, "and the exterior world has no other interest for me other than its transformation to winning or losing positions."

In 1923 he moved to Brussels to further his studies of the game, and then returned to Paris. There he would work on chess problems all evening long, take a short break at midnight for scrambled eggs at the Café Dome, and then return to his room to work on chess again until about four A.M.

Even true love could not moderate his fixation. In 1927 Duchamp married Lydia Sarazin-Lavassor, a young heiress. On their honeymoon he spent the entire week studying chess problems. Infuriated, his bride plotted her revenge. When Duchamp finally drifted off to sleep late one night, Lydia glued all of the pieces to the board.

They were divorced three months later.

Illustration by John Tenniel, from Lewis Carroll's
Through the Looking Glass and What Alice Found There

THE IMMORTAL GAME

INTRODUCTION

LARGE ROCKS, SEVERED HEADS, and flaming pots of oil rained down on Baghdad, capital of the vast Islamic Empire, as its weary defenders scrambled to reinforce gates, ditches, and the massive stone walls surrounding the fortress city's many brick and teak palaces. Giant wooden *manjaniq* catapults bombarded distant structures while the smaller, more precise *arradah* catapult guns pelted individuals with grapefruit-sized rocks. Arrows flew thickly and elite horsemen assaulted footmen with swords and spears. "The horses . . . trample the livers of courageous young men," lamented the poet al-Khuraymi, "and their hooves split their skulls." Outside the circular city's main wall—100 feet high, 145 feet thick, and six miles in circumference—soldiers pressed forward with battering rams while other squads choked off supply lines of food and reinforcements. Amid sinking boats and burning rafts, bodies drifted down the Tigris River.

The impenetrable "City of Peace" was crumbling. In the fifty years since its creation in A.D. 762, young Baghdad had rivaled Constantinople and Rome in its prestige and influence. It was a wildly fertile axis of art, science, and religion, and a bustling commercial hub for trade routes reaching deep into Central Asia, Africa, and Europe. But by the late summer of A.D. 813, after nearly two years of civil war (between brothers, no less), the enlightened Islamic capital was a smoldering, starving, bloody heap.

In the face of disorder, any human being desperately needs order—some way to manage, if not the material world, at least one's *under-*

standing of the world. In that light, perhaps it's no real surprise that, as the stones and arrows and horses' hooves thundered down on Baghdad, the protected core of the city hosted a different sort of battle. Within the round city's imperial inner sanctum, secure behind three thick, circular walls and many layers of gate and guard, under the luminescent green dome of the Golden Gate Palace, Muhammad al-Amin, the sixth caliph of the Abbasid Empire, spiritual descendant of (and distant blood relation to) the Prophet Muhammad, sovereign of one of the largest dominions in the history of the world, was playing chess against his favorite eunuch Kauthar.

A trusted messenger burst into the royal apartment with urgently bad news. More inglorious defeats in and around the city were to be reported to the caliph. In fact, his own safety was now in jeopardy.

But al-Amin would not hear of it. He waved off his panicked emissary.

"O Commander of the faithful," implored the messenger, according to the medieval Islamic historian Jirjis al-Makin. "This is not the time to play. Pray arise and attend to matters of more serious moment."

It was no use. The caliph was absorbed in the board. A chess game in progress is—as every chess spouse quickly learns—a cosmos unto itself, fully insulated from an infant's cry, an erotic invitation, or war. The board may have only thirty-two pieces and sixty-four squares, but within that confined space the game has near-infinite depth and possibility. An outsider looking on casually might find the intensity incomprehensible. But anyone who has played the game a few times understands how it can be engrossing in the extreme. Quite often, in the middle of an interesting game, it's almost as if reality has been flipped inside out: the chess game in motion seems to be the only matter of substance, while any hint of the outside world feels like an annoying irrelevance.

The messier the external world, the more powerful this inverted dynamic can be. Perhaps that is why Caliph al-Amin, who sensed that his hours were numbered, preferred to soak in the details of his chess battlefield rather than reports of the calamitous siege of his city. On the board he could see the whole action. On the board he could neatly make sense of significant past events and carefully plan his future. On the board he still might win.

"Patience my friend," the caliph calmly replied to his messenger standing only a few feet away and yet a world apart. "I see that in a few moves I shall give Kauthar checkmate."

Not long after this, al-Amin and his men were captured. The sixth Abbasid caliph, victor in his final chess game, was swiftly beheaded.

CHESS LIVED ON. The game had been a prominent court fixture of Caliph al-Amin's predecessor, and would voraciously consume the attention of his successor—and the caliph after that, and the caliph after that. Several centuries before it infected feudal Christian Europe, chess was already an indelible part of the landscape adjoining the Tigris and Euphrates. This simple game, imbued with a universe of complexity and character, demanded from peasants, soldiers, philosophers, and sovereigns an endless amount of time and energy. In return it offered unique insights into the human endeavor.

And so, against all odds, it lasted. Games, as a general rule, do not last. They come and go. In the eighth century, the Irish loved a board game called *fidchell*. Long before that, in the third millennium B.C., the Egyptians played a backgammonlike race game called *senet*. The Romans were drawn to *duodecim scripta*, played with three knucklebone dice and stacks of discs. The Vikings were obsessed with a game called *hnefatafl* in the tenth century, in which a protagonist King attempted to escape through a ring of enemies to any edge of the board. The ancient Greeks had *petteia* and *kubeia*. These and hundreds of other once-popular games are all now long gone. They caught the public imagination of their time and place, and then for whatever reason lost steam. Generations died off, taking their habits with them; or conquering cultures imposed new ideas and pastimes; or people just got bored and wanted something new. Many of the games fell into such total oblivion that they couldn't even make a coherent mark in the historical record.

Try as they might, determined historians still cannot uncover the basic rules of play for a large graveyard of yesterday's games.

Contrast this with chess, a game that could not be contained by religious edict, nor ocean, nor war, nor language barrier. Not even the merciless accumulation of time, which eventually washes over and dissolves most everything, could so much as tug lightly at chess's ferocious momentum. "It has, for numberless ages," wrote Benjamin Franklin in 1786, "been the amusement of all the civilized nations of Asia, the Persians, the Indians, and the Chinese. Europe has had it above 1000 years; the Spaniards have spread it over their part of America, and it begins lately to make its appearance in these States."

The game would eventually pass into every city in the world and along more than 1,500 years of continuous history—a common thread of Pawn chains, Knight forks, and humiliating checkmates that would run through the lives of Karl Marx, Pope Leo XIII, Arnold Schwarzenegger, King Edward I, George Bernard Shaw, Abraham Lincoln, Ivan the Terrible, Voltaire, King Montezuma, Rabbi Ibn Ezra, William the Conqueror, Jorge Luis Borges, Willie Nelson, Napoleon, Samuel Beckett, Woody Allen, and Norman Schwarzkopf. From Baghdad's Golden Gate Palace to London's Windsor Castle to today's lakeside tables at Chicago's North Avenue Beach, chess would tie history together in a surprising and compelling way.

How could a game last so long, and appeal so broadly across vast spans of time, geography, language, and culture? Endurance is not, of course, a magnificent accomplishment in itself, but a compelling sign that something profound is going on, a catalytic connection between this "game" and the human brain. Another sign is that chess was not just played but also integrated into the creative and professional lives of artists, linguists, psychologists, economists, mathematicians, politicians, theologians, computer scientists, and generals. It became a popular and pliable metaphor for abstract ideas and complex systems, and an effective tool through which scientists could better understand the human mind.

The remarkable scope of this game began to infect my own brain after a visit from an old family ghost in the fall of 2002. My mother had sent on some faded newspaper clippings about her great-grandfather, my great-great-grandfather, a diminutive Polish Jew named Samuel Rosenthal who immigrated to France in 1864 and became one of its legendary chess masters. Family lore had it that Rosenthal had impressed and/or somehow secured the gratitude of one of the Napoleons, and had been awarded a magnificent, jewel-encrusted pocket watch. No one in the family seemed to have actually seen this watch, but they'd all heard about it. Four generations down the line, this story, retold to a boy from the Ohio suburbs, was just exotic enough, and just hazy enough, to set the mind racing. I had begged Mom for years to tell me more about the great S. Rosenthal and his lost watch.

As I combed through the records on my mother's mother's father's father's achievements, wondering what spectacular (if still hidden) intelligences had filtered down through the generations, I also became reacquainted with the game itself, which I had not played since high school (and then only a handful of times). Stumbling through a few dozen games with friends at home and with strangers over the Internet, I found that I was just as ambivalent about chess as I'd been twenty years earlier—charmed by its elegance and intrigued by its depth, but also put off by the high gates of entry to even moderately serious play. Graduating from patzer to mere competence would require untold hundreds of hours of not just playing but studying volumes of opening theory, endgame problems, and strategy. Years of obsessive attention to the game might—*might*—eventually gain me entry into reasonably serious tournaments, where I would no doubt be quickly dispatched by an acid-tongued, self-assured ten-year-old. Chess is an ultimately indomitable peak that gets steeper and steeper with every step.

I was also repelled, frankly, by the forbidding atmosphere of unforgiving rules, insider jargon, and the general aggressiveness and unpleasantness that seemed to accompany even reasonably casual play. I recalled one of Bobby Fischer's declarations: "Chess is war over the board," he proclaimed. "The object is to crush the opponent's mind." Fischer was not alone in his lusty embrace of chess's brutality. The game is often as much about demolishing your opponent's will and self-esteem as it is about implementing a superior strategy. No blood is drawn (ordinarily), but the injury can be real. The historical link between top chess play and mental instability stands as yet another intriguing feature about the game and its power. "Here is nothing less," writes recovering chess master Alfred Kreymborg, "than a silent duel between two human engines using and abusing all the faculties of the mind. . . . It is warfare in the most mysterious jungles of the human character."

Still, much to my wife's dismay, I got hooked. It is an intoxicating game that, though often grueling, never grows tiresome. The exquisite interplay of the simple and the complex is hypnotic: the pieces and moves are elementary enough for any five-year-old to quickly soak up, but the board combinations are so vast that all the possible chess games could never be played—or even known—by a single person. Other parlor games sufficiently amuse, entertain, challenge, distract; chess *seizes*. It does not merely engage the mind; it takes hold of the mind in a way that suggests a primal, hardwired connection.

Even more powerfully, though, I became transported by chess's rich history. It seemed to have been present in every place and time, and to have been utilized in every sort of activity. Kings cajoled and threatened with it; philosophers told stories with it; poets analogized with it; moralists preached with it. Its origins are wrapped up in some of the earliest discussions of fate versus free will. It sparked and settled feuds, facilitated and sabotaged romances, and fertilized literature from Dante to Nabokov. A thirteenth-century book using chess as a guide to social morality may have been the second-most popular text in the Middle Ages, after the Bible. In the twentieth century, chess enabled computer scientists to create intelligent machines. Chess has also, in modern times, been used to study memory, language, math, and logic, and has recently emerged as a powerful learning tool in elementary and secondary schools.

The more I learned about chess's peculiarly strong cultural relevance in century after century, the more it seemed that chess's endurance was no historical accident. As with the Bible and Shakespeare, there was something particular about the game that made it continually accessible to generation after generation. It served a genuine function—perhaps not vital, but often far more than merely useful. I often found myself wondering how particular events or lives would have unfolded in chess's absence—a condition, I learned, that many chess haters had ardently sought. Perhaps the most vivid measure of chess's potency, in fact, is the determination of its orthodox enemies to stamp it out—as long ago as a ruling in 655 by Caliph Ali Ben Abu-Talib (the Prophet Muhammad's son-in-law), and as recently as decrees by Ayatollah Ruhollah Khomeini in 1981, the Taliban in 1996, and the Iraqi clergy in post-Saddam Iraq. In between, chess was tamped down:

in 780 by Abbasid Caliph al-Mahdi ibn al-Mansur
in 1005 by Egypt's al-Hakim Bi-Amr Allah
in 1061 by Cardinal Damiani of Ostia
in 1093 by the Eastern Orthodox Church
in 1128 by St. Bernard
in 1195 by Rabbi Maimonides
in 1197 by the Abbot of Persigny
in 1208 by the Bishop of Paris
in 1240 by religious leaders of Worcester, England
in 1254 by King Louis IX of France (St. Louis)
in 1291 by the Archbishop of Canterbury
in 1310 by the Council of Trier (Germany)
in 1322 by Rabbi Kalonymos Ben Kalonymos
in 1375 by France's Charles V
in 1380 by Oxford University's founder William of Wickham
in 1549 by the Protohierarch Sylvester of Russia
and in 1649 by Tsar Alexei

But like the Talmud, like the theory of natural selection, like any organized thought paradigm that humans have found irresistibly compelling, chess refused to go away. Why were sixty-four squares and a handful of generic war figurines so hard to erase from the human imagination? What was it about chess that drew simultaneous devotion and disgust, and sparked so many powerful ideas and observations over many centuries?

This is what I set out to understand, through a close survey of chess's history and a fresh look at the game.

PIECES AND MOVES

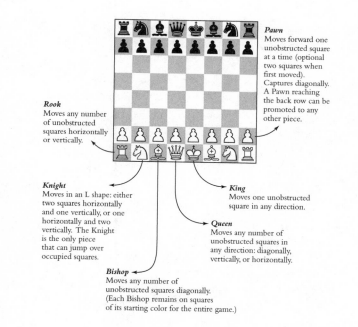

Pawn
Moves forward one
unobstructed square
at a time (optional
two squares when
first moved).
Captures diagonally.
A Pawn reaching
the back row can be
promoted to any
other piece.

Rook
Moves any number
of unobstructed
squares horizontally
or vertically.

Knight
Moves in an L shape: either
two squares horizontally
and one vertically, or one
horizontally and two
vertically. The Knight
is the only piece
that can jump over
occupied squares.

King
Moves one unobstructed
square in any direction.

Queen
Moves any number of
unobstructed squares in
any direction: diagonally,
vertically, or horizontally.

Bishop
Moves any number of
unobstructed squares diagonally.
(Each Bishop remains on squares
of its starting color for the entire game.)

For more details, see Appendix I: The Rules of Chess.

I.

OPENINGS

(Where We Come From)

"UNDERSTANDING IS THE ESSENTIAL WEAPON"

Chess and Our Origins

When Sissa had invented chess and produced it to King Shihram, the latter was filled with amazement and joy. He ordered that it should be preserved in the temples, and held it the best thing that he knew as a training in the art of war, a glory to religion and the world, and the foundation of all justice.

—ibn Khallikan, thirteenth century

STORIES DO NOT EXIST to tell the facts, but to convey the truth. It is said that in ancient India, a queen had designated her only son as heir to the throne. When the son was assassinated, the queen's council searched for the proper way to convey the tragic news to her. They approached a philosopher with their predicament. He sat for three days in silent thought, and then said: "Summon a carpenter with wood of two colors, white and black."

The carpenter came. The philosopher instructed him to carve thirty-two small figurines from the wood. After this was done, the philosopher said to the carpenter, "Bring me tanned leather," and directed him to cut it into the shape of a square and to etch it with sixty-four smaller squares.

He then arranged the pieces on the board and studied them silently. Finally, he turned to his disciple and announced, "This is war without bloodshed." He explained the game's rules and the two began to play.

Word quickly spread about the mysterious new invention, and the queen herself summoned the philosopher for a demonstration. She sat quietly, watching the philosopher and his student play a game. When it was over, one side having checkmated the other, the queen understood the intended message. She turned to the philosopher and said, "My son is dead."

"You have said it," he replied.

The queen turned to the doorkeeper and said, "Let the people enter to comfort me."

The annals of ancient poetry and weathered prose are filled with many such evocative chess stories, stretched over 1,400 years. Over and over, chess was said to have been invented to explain the unexplainable, to make visible the purely abstract, to see simple truths in complex worlds. Pythagoras, the ancient mathematician heralded as the father of numbers, was supposed to have created the game to convey the abstract realities of mathematics. The Greek warrior Palamedes, commander of troops at the siege of Troy, purportedly invented chess as a demonstration of the art of battle positions. Moses, in his posture as Jewish sage, was said to have invented it as a part of an all-purpose educational package, along with astronomy, astrology, and the alphabet.

Chess was also considered a window into other people's unique thoughts. There is the legend of the great medieval rebbe, also a cunning chess player, whose son had been taken away as a young boy and never found. Many decades later, the rebbe was granted an audience with the pope. The two spoke for a while, and then decided to play a game of chess. In their game the pope played a very unusual combination of moves that to any other opponent would have been astonishing and overpowering. But the strange combination was not new to the rebbe; he had invented it, in fact, and had shared it only with his young son. The pope, they both instantly realized, was the rebbe's long lost child.

And there are hundreds—maybe thousands—more. Hearing these stories, we care less about whether they are completely true and more about what they say. Myths, said Joseph Campbell, "represent that wisdom of the species by which man has weathered the millenniums." Chess myths, in particular, tell us first that chess goes way, way back, and that it has always been regarded not just as a way to pass the time, but also as a powerful tool for explanation and understanding. While chess is ostensibly about war, it has for 1,400 years been deployed as a metaphor to explore everything from romantic love to economics. Historians routinely stumble across chess stories from nearly every culture and era—stories dealing with class consciousness, free will, political struggle, the frontiers of the mind, the mystery of the divine, the nature of competition, and, perhaps most fundamentally, the emergence of a world where brains often overcome brawn. One need not have any passion for the game itself to be utterly captivated by its centuries of compelling tales, and to appreciate its importance as a thought tool for an emerging civilization. Chess is a teaching and learning instrument older than chalkboards, printed books, the compass, and the telescope.

As a miniature reflection of society, it was also considered a moral guidepost. Yet another myth has chess invented to cure the cruelty of Evil-Merodach, a vile Babylonian king from the sixth century B.C. who murdered his father King Nebuchadnezzar and then disposed of his body by chopping it into three hundred pieces and feeding the pieces to three hundred vultures. Desperate to curb the brutality of his new leader, the wise man Xerxes created chess in order to instill virtues and transform him into a just and moral ruler: Here is how a king behaves toward his subjects, and here is how his grateful subjects defend their just king . . .

Separately, each chess myth conveys a thousand truths about a particular moment in time where a society longed to understand something difficult about its own past—the source of some idea or tool or tradition. Taken together, they document our quest to understand—and explain—abstraction and complexity in the world around us. The paradox of illuminating complexity is that it is inherently difficult to do so without erasing all of the nuance. As our developing civilization faced more intricate facts and ideas in the early Middle Ages, this was a fundamental challenge: to find a way to represent dense truths without washing out their essence. (This ancient challenge is, of course, also very contemporary, and, as we will see, makes chess fundamentally relevant in the Age of Information.)

WHEN AND HOW and why was chess invented? The very oldest chess myths point toward its actual origins. One story portrays two successive Indian kings, Hashran and Balhait. The first asked his sage to invent a game symbolizing man's dependence on destiny and fate; he invented *nard*, the dice-based predecessor to backgammon. The subsequent monarch needed a game which would embrace his belief in free will and intelligence. "At this time chess was invented," reads an ancient text, "which the King preferred to nard, because in this game skill always succeeds against ignorance. He made mathematical calculations on chess, and wrote a book on it. . . . He often played chess with the wise men of his court, and it was he who represented the pieces by the figures of men and animals, and assigned them grades and ranks. . . .

"He also made of this game a kind of allegory of the heavenly bodies (the seven planets and the twelve zodiac signs), and dedicated each piece to a star. The game of chess became a school of government and defense; it was consulted in time of war, when military tactics were about to be employed, to study the more or less rapid movements of troops."

King Balhait's wide-ranging list of the game's uses has a connecting thread: chess as a demonstration device, a touchstone for abstract ideas. The reference to "mathematical calculations" is particularly noteworthy, as math comes up over and over again in many of the oldest chess legends. One tale, known as "The Doubling of the Squares," tells of a king presented with an intriguing new sixty-four-square board game by his court philosopher. The king is so delighted by chess that he invites the inventor to name his own reward.

Oh, I don't want much, replies the philosopher, pointing to the chess-board. *Just give me one grain of wheat for the first square of the board, two grains for the second square, four grains for the third square, and so on, doubling the number of grains for each successive square, up to the sixty-fourth square.*

The king is shocked, and even insulted, by what seems like such a modest request. He doesn't realize that through the hidden power of geometric progression, his court philosopher has just requested 18,446,744,073,709,551,615 (eighteen *quintillion*) grains of wheat—more than exists on the entire planet. The king has not only just been given a fascinating new game; he's also been treated to a powerful numbers lesson.

This widely repeated story is obviously apocryphal, but the facts of geometric progression are real. Such mathematical concepts were crucial to the advancement of technology and civilization—but were useless unless they could be understood. The advancement of big ideas required not just clever inventors, but also great teachers and vivid presentation vehicles.

That's apparently where chess came in: it used the highly accessible idea of war to convey far less concrete ideas. Chess was, in a sense, medieval presentation software—the PowerPoint of the Middle Ages. It was a customizable platform for poets, philosophers, and other intellectuals to explore and present a wide array of complex ideas in a visual and compelling way.

The game, in reality, was not invented all at once, in a fit of inspiration by a single king, general, philosopher, or court wizard. Rather, it was almost certainly (like the Bible and the Internet) the result of years of tinkering by a large, decentralized group, a slow achievement of collective intelligence. After what might have been centuries of tinkering, *chatrang*, the first true version of what we now call chess, finally emerged in Persia sometime during the fifth or sixth century. It was a two-player war game with thirty-two pieces on a sixty-four-square board: sixteen emerald men on one end and sixteen ruby-red men on the other. Each army was equipped with one King, one Minister (where the Queen now sits), two Elephants (where the Bishops now sit), two Horses, two *Ruhks* (Persian for "chariot"), and eight Foot Soldiers. The object was to capture, trap, or isolate the opponent's King.*

Chatrang may have been an import from neighboring India, where a similar game was known as *chaturanga*—and that game may have been a much older import from neighboring China. The game probably evolved along the famous Silk Road trading routes, which for centuries carried materials, information, and ideas between Delhi, Tehran, Baghdad, Kabul, Kandahar, and China's Xinjiang Province. On the Silk Road, merchants transported cinnamon, pepper, horses, porcelain, gold, silver, silk, and other useful and exotic goods; they also inevitably blended customs picked up from various locales. It was the information highway of the age. No doubt many other games were invented and transported by the same roving merchants. But there was something different about *chaturanga* and *chatrang*. In a critical departure from previous board games from the region, these games contained no dice or other instruments of chance. Skill alone determined the outcome. "Understanding [is] the essential weapon" proclaims the ancient Persian poem *Chatrang-namak* (The book of *chatrang*), one of the oldest books mentioning the game. "Victory is obtained by the intellect."

This was a war game, in other words, where ideas were more important and more powerful than luck or brute force. In a world that had been forever defined by chaos and violence, this seemed to be a significant turn.

It is clearly no coincidence that *chaturanga*'s emergence happened

---

* The moves in *chatrang* were very similar to but not exactly the same as in modern chess; overall the pieces were far less powerful, making the game significantly slower. Modern flourishes like castling and en passant capture did not exist. But, strikingly, the Horse in sixth-century *chatrang* advanced in exactly the same two-squares-up, one-square-over maneuver as today's Knight. The *Ruhk* also moved exactly the same as the modern Rook. The Foot Soldier nearly perfectly mirrors the modern chess Pawn, moving forward one square at a time, capturing other pieces diagonally, and getting promoted to Minister—the predecessor to the Queen—upon reaching the back row.

around the same time as India's revolutionary new numeral system, rooted in the invention of the number zero. Zero as a concept had been used on and off for centuries, but it was the Indians who formally adopted zero both as a number (as in 5−5=0 or 5×0=0) and as a place-holder (as in "an army of 10,500 men"), and who explored it deeply enough to allow for the development of negative numbers and other important abstractions. India's decimal arithmetic was the foundation of the modern numeral system, which served as a critical building block for the advancement of civilization.

The new numeral system was a great breakthrough. But who or what could effectively convey it, in all of its nuance, to others? In the centuries to follow, chess carried the new math across the world. "Chess was the companion and catalyst for the cultural transfer of a new method of calculation," writes Viennese historian Ernst Strouhal. The early Islamic chess master al-Adli mentioned using a chessboard as an abacus—that is, as a tool to perform calculations based on the new Indian numerals. The Chinese and Europeans later used the chessboard in exactly the same way. In medieval England, accounts were settled on tables resembling chessboards, and the minister of finance was given the playful title "Chancellor of the Exchequer." A twelfth-century text explains how the reference was doubly apt:

> Just as, in a game of chess, there are certain grades of combatants and they proceed or stand still by certain laws or limitations, some presiding and others advancing: so, in this, some preside, some assist by reason of their office, and no one is free to exceed the fixed laws; as will be manifest from what is to follow.
>
> Moreover, as in chess the battle is fought between Kings, so in this it is chiefly between two that the conflict takes place and the war is waged,—the treasurer, namely, and the sheriff who sits there to render account . . .

Chess also turned up in a late-twelfth-century Cambridge manuscript as a game that "thrives in the practice of geometry," and in Dante's

Paradiso ("And they so many were, their number makes / More millions than the doubling of the chess"). Chess, like any great teaching tool, didn't *create* these sublime notions and complex systems, but helped make them *visible*. Math and other abstractions were just slippery notions floating in the air; chess, with its simple squares and finite borders, could represent them in a visual narrative played out on a tiny, accessible stage. Chess could bring difficult notions to life. Understanding, just as the ancient text said, was the essential weapon.

THE IMMORTAL GAME

Move 1

THERE WAS NO CHESS at all in my childhood home or
school life. Growing up in the 1970s, we played cards, checkers,
Monopoly, Atari—*games*. To the extent that I ever thought about
chess, which was very little, it seemed like an absurd amount of effort—much more exertion than the pleasure it would give back. "I
hate it and avoid it because it is not play enough," Montaigne com-
plained about chess in the sixteenth century. "It is too grave and serious a diversion; and I am ashamed to lay out as much thought and
study upon that as would serve to much better uses." Replace
"ashamed" with "too lazy," and you have, in a nutshell, my attitude
toward chess for my first seventeen years.

Later, in high school, I developed a taste for more complexity, risk,
confrontation. I fancied myself a young intellectual—told friends that
I was a nonconformist. Still, chess didn't enter my orbit until a friend
insisted that I learn it during our senior year. That I did, and pro-
ceeded to play a score of games with him over a few weeks' time. It
must have made a powerful impression. I never got very good, but I
did briefly surrender my mind to chess consciousness. To this day
(twenty years distant), I have a clear memory of sitting in the back of
a tourist bus on a spring school trip to Washington, D.C., my mind
vaguely wandering through a chess game I'd recently played, and
then strangely—involuntarily—imagining myself as a chess Knight
and examining my possible moves: from where I sat in the bus, I
could move up two rows and over one seat to the right or left, or up
one row and over two seats . . .

It was a creepy feeling, this sensation that chess could redefine how I saw the outside world. I stopped playing chess shortly thereafter, at least partly due to this strange event. (Imagine my sense of déjà vu twenty years later when I read from Marcel Duchamp's letter to a friend: "Everything around me takes the shape of the Knight or the Queen. . . .") Without any family encouragement or group of chess friends, I dropped the game, found other things to do with my time, and didn't happen to run across it again until my mid-thirties.

Was I avoiding chess out of fear—or due to a lack of innate ability? Or was it simply that I had a full life and I never found myself in a chess-playing crowd? One thing seems certain: falling into chess is rarely a casual affair. Whether you're five or thirty-five, the game tends to repel those who aren't attracted to its particular brand of strenuous mental effort. Serious converts to the game usually have some powerful motivation—perhaps unknown to them—for investing in the game at a particular time in their lives.

In the late summer of 2002, something—I wasn't quite sure what—brought me back to the game. Was it the need for an emotional escape pod from 9/11 and the expectation of another New York attack? Was it a primal desire to forge a connection with my semifamous ancestor? Or was it just a simple need to carve out some leisure time with friends? Kurt, an old college pal who had also never really played before, proclaimed in solidarity that he, too, would take up the game. One small problem was that Kurt lived in Chicago and I lived in Brooklyn. We agreed to try a little experiment: every day at noon, we would convene online for a short, timed game.

We were both pretty lousy, of course, though Kurt seemed consistently one beat quicker than I was; under time pressure, he could still make reasonably well-considered moves, while I frequently choked. It seemed obvious to me that Kurt's well-oiled, methodical mind would soon leap past my neural cobwebs and we would no longer be well matched. My only hope was to seek some expert help. At the Brooklyn Public Library, I dove into some beginner guides by

Bruce Pandolfini and others. I read about openings, tactics, and strategy, and learned to avoid some of the very dumbest moves.

Many of the books and Web sites also featured guided tours through celebrated chess games from history. Like football teams studying films of old games, the astute player could potentially pick up a lot of strategic insight by following these legendary contests. "When one plays over a game by a fine technician," declared chess author Anthony Saidy, "one receives a sense of rightness and the impression that the master has penetrated very deeply indeed into the workings of the chess pieces."

One contest in particular, from the mid-nineteenth century, immediately captured my imagination: the legendary Immortal Game, a game so surprising, so brilliant and full of life, that it drew the admiration of everyone from novices to the game's greatest champions. After 150 years, the game continued to fascinate and amaze the global chess community.

The Immortal Game grabbed me at first not for its blindingly brilliant moves—what did I know from great chess?—but for its human drama. This was supposed to be a forgettable practice game, a throwaway. No one, least of all the two players, had any idea that they were about to produce one of chess's all-time gems, a game some would consider the most remarkable ever played.

ADOLF ANDERSSEN VS. LIONEL KIESERITZKY
JUNE 21, 1851
LONDON

1. e4*
(White King's Pawn to e4)

It began commonly enough. Adolf Anderssen, playing White, moved his King's Pawn forward two squares. (White always moves first in chess, and in doing so carries an advantage that is roughly akin to

---

* Standard notation, the universally accepted scheme for conveying chess moves, is crisply efficient, but so abstract that it takes some getting used to. Only the barest minimum of necessary information is conveyed for each move:

• The move number: 1. to indicate White's move; 1. . . . to indicate Black's.
• The symbol of the piece being moved: K for King, Q for Queen, B for Bishop, R for Rook, and N for Knight. Pawns are indicated by the absence of a piece symbol.

serving in tennis. The first to move not only gets to decide on the early trajectory of a game; he also gets a head start in the development* of his pieces. In master-level chess, where the games are often so close that one single move makes all the difference, White's tiny head start is often conclusive.)

Lionel Kieseritzky responded with exactly the same move, mirroring White's move by pushing *his* King's Pawn forward two squares.

1. . . . e5
(Black King's Pawn to e5)

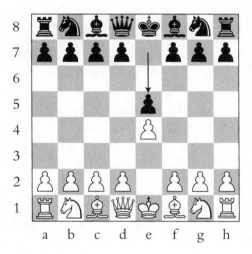

The King's Pawn *opening*—a very popular opener then and probably the most popular still—has both players jockeying right away for the

---

• The grid location of the piece's destination (a6, c3, etc.).

• Other symbols to indicate special action: × for capturing a piece; + for check; ++ for checkmate; O-O for castling on the Kingside of the board; O-O-O for castling on the Queenside.

* *Development*: Activating the pieces by taking them out of their starting positions to more active and effective squares.

center of the board, a strategic asset, and making room for the Queen and/or King's Bishop to come out early. It was a quiet beginning for a casual game, held at Simpson's Grand Divan Tavern, the smoky men's club and chess café on the Strand boulevard in London.

These were two of the greatest chess players in the world at the time, but very few people were likely watching this throwaway practice game—the real action was a mile away at the St. George's Chess Club at Cavendish Square, where Anderssen, Kieseritzky, and fourteen other world-class players were competing in chess's first-ever true international tournament.

Kieseritzky, a former math teacher from Estonia, had traveled from Paris, where he dominated the chess scene at the Café de La Régence, giving lessons and playing games for five francs an hour. His specialty was defeating lesser players even after removing one or more of his pieces at the game's start. (This is known as "giving odds." Playing without one of your Knights, for example, is giving Knight odds.) In 1849 Kieseritzky had founded his own chess journal, naming it *La Régence* after his favorite haunt. In 1851 he traveled to London as one of the leading favorites to win the tournament.

The German-born Anderssen, also a math professor, was known for both his expert play and his spirited chess problems, which in 1842 he had collected in a book called *Aufgaben für Schachspieler* ("Problems for Chessplayers"). Serious problemists and serious players know how very different their tasks are from one another—much like the highly distinct worlds of musical composition (Beethoven) and performance (Yo-Yo Ma). But Anderssen appeared to cross over effortlessly from one world to the other, becoming increasingly interested in chess play and, in 1848, forcing a leading player, Daniel Harrwitz, into a five-game-to-five-game draw. It was a startling accomplishment for a problemist not previously thought to possess world-class playing skills, and it earned Anderssen his London invitation. Still, in 1851 he was given little chance to do well among the London field of sixteen, the rest of the world's top players arriving from St. Petersburg, Budapest, Berlin, Paris, and London itself for the three-round, seven-week tournament.

This was a gathering of chess talent never before seen, and aficionados expected the games to be proportionately exciting—bold, counterintuitive, theory-busting. They anticipated a caliber of chess that people would talk about for centuries to come. What no one could possibly have foreseen, as the tournament captured so much attention and raised so many expectations, was that the real triumph would occur down the street, away from all the lights and the gawkers.

HOUSE OF WISDOM

Chess and the Muslim Renaissance

"ACQUIRE KNOWLEDGE," the Prophet Muhammad commanded his followers. ". . . It guideth us to happiness; it sustaineth us in misery; it is an ornament amongst friends, and an armour against enemies."

Understanding is the essential weapon. Victory is obtained by the intellect . . .

Chess and Islam were born about the same time—chess out of a regional need to understand complex new ideas, and Islam out of the Arabs' desperate need for discipline, intelligence, and meaningful community. In the year 612, Muhammad ibn Abdullah, a prosperous merchant from Mecca deeply troubled by the splintered, selfish nature of Arab society, emerged as the Prophet Muhammad with divine instructions on how to unite and transform his people. He called his new belief system *Islam*, meaning "peace through surrender to God." In its essence, Islam was a strict code of ethics requiring subservience to the community and compassion toward the poor. It quickly helped Arab tribes end their constant blood feuds and create an all-powerful supertribe based not on family connection but on shared ideology and security. Islam made Arabia an instant superpower. Within two decades of Muhammad's death in 632, the new Muslim Empire controlled Persia, Syria, Egypt, and pieces of North Africa.

In Persia the Muslims encountered *chatrang*, the bloodless new war game which relied solely on players' intellect. Chess and Islam complemented each other well: a new game of war, wits, and self-control serving a spirited new religious and social movement organized around the same values. "The [board] is placed between two friends of known friendship," wrote ninth-century poet Ali ibn al-Jahm. "They recall the memories of war in an image of war, but without bloodshed. This attacks, that defends, and the struggle between them never languishes."

Lacking the *ch* and the *ng* sounds in their speech, Arab Muslims changed *chatrang* into *shatranj*, and quickly made the game their own. As if invented by Muhammad himself, the game seemed to speak directly to the new Muslim ideals—and found its way into the progressive rhetoric of the day. "The skilled player places his pieces in such a way as to discover consequences that the ignorant man never sees," wrote the poet al-Katib. ". . . Thus he serves the Sultan's interests, by showing how to foresee disaster."

Records show that *shatranj* quickly became woven into the fabric of the new Muslim culture. A list of prominent players of the seventh, eighth, and ninth centuries includes caliphs, lawyers, immigrants, intellectuals, and even young girls. It's also clear that the game soon transcended mere play for its Islamic adopters. "I keep you from your inheritance and from the royal crown so that, hindered by my arm, you remain a Pawn (*baidaq*) among the Pawns (*bayadiq*)," wrote the poet al-Farazdaq in the late seventh century. The caste implications of chess quickly captured the popular imagination, with the array of pieces seen as a microcosm not just of a fighting army but also more generally of human society, with its all-important monarch, its privileged nobility, and its expendable peasants. A chess set was not, in and of itself, social commentary, but with its crystal clear labeling of society's constituent parts, it did strongly *invite* social commentary. Already the game was an indelible part of the Islamic landscape.

Even with its broad resonance, though, chess was not immune to controversy. From the very first exposure to the game, there had been a serious and recurring question as to whether chess was allowable un-

A Guide to Shatranj
(Islamic Chess), circa a.d. 700

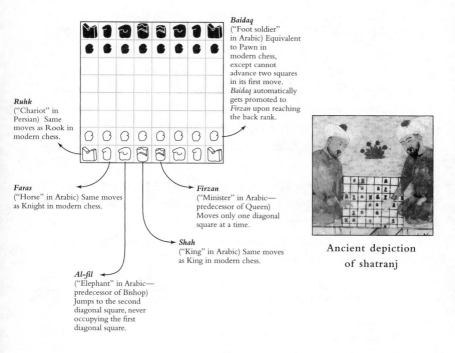

Ruhk
("Chariot" in Persian) Same moves as Rook in modern chess.

Baidaq
("Foot soldier" in Arabic) Equivalent to Pawn in modern chess, except cannot advance two squares in its first move. *Baidaq* automatically gets promoted to *Firzan* upon reaching the back rank.

Faras
("Horse" in Arabic) Same moves as Knight in modern chess.

Firzan
("Minister" in Arabic—predecessor of Queen) Moves only one diagonal square at a time.

Shah
("King" in Arabic) Same moves as King in modern chess.

Al-fil
("Elephant" in Arabic—predecessor of Bishop) Jumps to the second diagonal square, never occupying the first diagonal square.

Ancient depiction of shatranj

Other differences from modern chess

- The board was not yet checkered.
- Stalemating the opposing King resulted in a win for the player delivering stalemate. (In modern chess, stalemate results in a draw.)
- Capturing all of the opponent's pieces except the King also counted as a win, provided that one's own King could not be left alone on the very next move.
- There was no castling option (wherein the King essentially changes places with one of his Rooks—to be explained in detail in Chapter 3).

der Islamic law. The Koran—the sacred text of revelations received by Muhammad—did not mention chess by name, but did explicitly outlaw the use of both "images" and "lots." The prohibition of *images* was aimed at eliminating any sort of idol worship, and was instituted broadly against any directly representational art or sculpture. *Lots* included gambling of any kind. Since chess play at the time quite often involved wagers—indeed, one ancient story from India portrayed young players betting their own fingers in games, cutting them off on the spot after a loss, cauterizing the wounds, and continuing to play—many first- and second-generation Muslims considered the game altogether tainted and plainly illegal. Others regarded chess as having no purpose other than recreation, and thus falling into the category of official disapproval (though not strict prohibition).

But chess did have a purpose, a deadly serious one, according to many proponents at that time. It not only broadly sharpened the mind, but also specifically trained war strategists for battle. "There is nothing wrong in it," proclaimed Muhammad's second successor, the pious and austere Caliph Umar ibn al-Khattab. "It has to do with war."

Eventually, a general consensus found the game acceptable in the Islamic world under certain conditions:

no wagering
no interference with religious duties
no displays of anger or improper language
no playing in public
no representational pieces

This last item came out of the Koran's prohibition against images. It is said that Ali ibn Abu Talib, Muhammad's cousin, son-in-law, and the fourth caliph (*caliph* means "deputy of the prophet"), passed by a game in progress one day and asked, disapprovingly, "What *images* are these upon which you are gazing so intently?" By Indian and Persian tradition, chess pieces had vividly represented the mechanics of war, depicting tiny soldiers, elephants, chariots, horses, and so on. Islamic law forced a complete reconception of chess's aesthetics. Muslim craftsmen abstracted the explicit Persian figures into elegant, hand-carved, cylindrical or rectangular stones with subtle indentations, bumps, and curves to symbolize a throne or a tusk or a horse's head.

Ceramic chess set from twelfth-century Iran

They created symbols, that is, of symbols. The severe abstraction made the game acceptable to most religious authorities.

BY THE BEGINNING of the ninth century, the game had also spread farther westward, to the Byzantine capital of Constantinople. In 802 the new emperor Nicephorus employed chess terminology to convey a threat to Caliph Harun ar-Rashid at his Baghdad palace:

> The empress into whose place I have succeeded looked upon you as a Rook and herself as a mere Pawn; therefore she submitted to pay you a tribute more than the double of which she ought to have exacted *from* you. All this has been owing to female weakness and timidity. Now, however, I insist that you, immediately on reading this letter, repay to me all the sums of money you ever received from her. If you hesitate, the sword shall settle our accounts.

In life, as in chess, a rash player can too easily become caught up in the excitement of a single bold move and thus be utterly blind to his opponent's obvious and devastating response. The caliph, a chess player himself, did not repay or reverse the flow of the tribute. Instead, his army marched on and laid siege to Nicephorus's army at Heracleia, forcing him to succumb to the same tribute arrangement as his predecessor.

Caliph ar-Rashid, both a warrior and an intellectual, ushered in the first true Islamic Renaissance—which later became the impetus for the European Renaissance. Acting on the Prophet's direct wishes, ar-Rashid made acquisition of knowledge a central Islamic mission. Centuries of books from all over the world were translated into Arabic, including the pantheon of Greek philosophy. Greek medical knowledge was incorporated into the first true Islamic hospital. Islamic literature bloomed, sparking *The Arabian Nights* and other great works. In 832 ar-Rashid's son, Caliph al-Ma'mun, completed the spectacular House of Wisdom in Baghdad, which quickly became one of the world's great libraries. Important advances were made during this period in chemistry, astronomy, agriculture, architecture, and engineering. Mathematicians applied spherical trigonometry and the new science of algebra to all sorts of worldly observations, including a more precise calculation of time, latitude and longitude, the earth's surface area and circumference, and the location of the stars.

Both father and son were chess fanatics; both employed top chess players and personally competed against them. Chess to these early enthusiasts wasn't just idle fancy, a means to pass the many leisurely hours on the throne. They also recognized a direct connection between chess and the intellectual vitality they were trying to nurture in their expanding empire. "A Muslim philosopher has maintained that the inventor of chess was a [believer] in the freedom of will," wrote medieval Islamic historian al-Mas'udi (appropriating the earlier Indian legend), "while the inventor of nard was a fatalist who wished to show by this game that man can do nothing against fate." In the history of intellectual progress, the embrace of free will over fate was a critical step. The realization, both personal and institutional, that people could help shape their own destiny helped lay the foundations of all modern science, philosophy, economic development, and democratic culture. Chess may have helped fertilize the concept, and certainly helped some people comprehend it.

With such weighty associations, chess from the very beginning was intuitively understood by Muslims to be more than a game, and its most expert players to be engaged in more than simple recreation. Chess was a paradigm that you could legitimately spend your whole life studying. From the earliest centuries of the recorded history of the game, there is evidence of a small academic/professional class of players who studied openings, devised endgame problems, wrote about strategic approaches (now known as chess theory), and towered above all challengers. In the Islamic world, these top players were known as *aliyat*, the "highest of ranks," the grandmasters. *Aliyat* were said to be able to see an astonishing ten moves ahead, much deeper than the second skill class, the *mutaqaribat*.

In the entire ninth century there were just five *aliyat*, each succeeding the other as the strongest known player. The first two, Jabir al-Khufi and Rabrab, competed against one another in the presence of Caliph al-Ma'mun. The caliph was a serious player who insisted that his subordinates play him at their top strength. He was also humble enough to understand his deep limitations. "Strange," he once remarked, "that I who rule the world from the Indus in the east to the Andalus in the west cannot manage thirty-two chessmen in a space of two cubits by two."

A few years after al-Ma'mun's death in 833, the strongest player yet emerged: the apparently unbeatable al-Adli. Possibly of Turkish descent, al-Adli dominated the game for much of his lifetime and also wrote chess's first in-depth book of analysis, *Kitab ash-shatranj* (The book of chess), circa 840. In his book he defined the five classes of skill and introduced the very first chess problems. Most of these problems were lost forever with copies of his manuscript, but some survive—thanks to the many medieval Arabic books which quoted his.

One particular al-Adli problem is still highly accessible to any modern chess player, because it includes only Kings, Rooks, Knights, and Pawns—pieces that have exactly the same moves in modern chess as they did in ancient *shatranj*.

Originally from al-Adli's *Book of Chess* (circa 840)

It is White's turn, and the challenge is for White to checkmate* Black in just three of his own moves.

(Do what I did: Pause book. Gnash teeth. Sleep on it. Gnash further. Give up.)

Al-Adli's solution, as is common in elegant chess problems, lies in the counterintuitive sacrifices that White must make to win in so few moves. Major sacrifices can puzzle players because so much of a chess player's energy is ordinarily directed toward *protecting* his or her pieces. But that's precisely what makes a sacrifice so beautiful to watch. Intuition and expectation is confounded, and an opponent's reality flips upside down when he sees what has happened.

In modern chess notation, the solution is: 1. Nh5+ Rxh5 2. Rxg6+ Kxg6 3. Re6++.

In plain English:

---

* *Check*: An attack on the opponent's King, which can be answered by capturing the attacking piece, interposing a piece, or moving the King to an unattacked square.

Checkmate: An attack on the opponent's King that cannot be countered and from which the King cannot escape—thus handing victory to the attacker.

First, the White Knight moves two squares forward and one square to the right, settling on the last vertical column—called a file—and putting Black in check.

Black has what looks like not only an easy way out of this problem, but also a major gain: he can capture the White Knight with his Rook.

After Black takes this irresistible bait, White sets up what looks like another preposterous sacrifice: he moves one of his Rooks up the penultimate file to capture the Black Knight, again putting the Black King in check.

The Black King follows this by capturing the White Rook, once again escaping check.

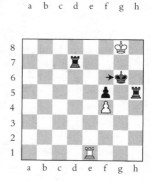

But—surprise—White then moves his other Rook forward five squares. The Black King has no escape. *Checkmate.*

It was a classic chess problem: maddeningly obtuse and impossibly simple at the same time. "It should be understood," Vladimir Nabokov would write many centuries later, "that competition in chess problems is not really between White and Black but between the composer and the hypothetical solver . . . so that a great part of a problem's value is due to the number of 'tries'—delusive opening moves, false scents, specious lines of play, astutely and lovingly prepared to lead the would-be solver astray."

Some problems were more agonizing than others. One in particular, from the ninth-century master as-Suli, was apparently unsolvable. "There is no one on earth who has solved it unless he was taught it by me," he wrote. Indeed, the problem was so impenetrable it came to be known as "as-Suli's Diamond." His solution, if ever published, was lost forever. After as-Suli's death, his Diamond chess problem went unsolved for over a thousand years.

But that didn't stop people from trying. The bedrock ethic for chess enthusiasts would forever be entwined with the ethic of the Muslim Renaissance. Knowledge, said the Prophet, "guideth us to happiness; it sustaineth us in misery; it is an ornament amongst friends, and an armour against enemies."

THE IMMORTAL GAME

Move 2

IN RETROSPECT, BRILLIANT ACHIEVEMENTS often seem preordained. But they are, of course, impossible to schedule or predict. Improvisational musicians talk about the ethereal feeling they occasionally experience where everything suddenly seems to click into place and the music soars way beyond what they had even thought possible. The anticipation of the next magic moment can single-handedly drive a performer to keep playing night after night, year after year.

So it is with chess. Dedicated players who tread through hundreds and then thousands of games find that the vast majority of them, while often interesting, are not revelatory. But every once in a while, often when it is least expected, a pair of players stumble into a game of true grace and beauty, danger and cunning, temptation, treachery, and surprise after surprise after surprise.

This is precisely what happened to Adolf Anderssen and Lionel Kieseritzky at the Grand Divan on June 21, 1851: they sat down for a casual game and fell into a once-in-a-lifetime event. And that un-expectedness, that surprising brilliance and beauty, is precisely what makes the Immortal Game such a great game to dissect, move by move. Anyone, experienced chess player or not, can look at each move and watch the slow transformation from mere possibility and complete uncertainty to tentative exploration, provocation, risk, and finally triumph. Following the game carefully, one can not only learn the rudiments of the game and its phases, but more importantly can also see how chess comes to life. Through this game, one can imbibe the very spirit of the game.

But one has to be patient. The road to brilliance can for a long while appear exceedingly common. Move 2 for Anderssen (White) was to slide the King's Bishop Pawn ahead two squares.

2. f4

(White King's Bishop Pawn to f4)

Also known as the King's Gambit, this was one of the most popular second moves in the mid-nineteenth century. A gambit, in chess, is an offer from one player to give up a piece (usually a Pawn) in return for some possible strategic or tactical advantage. (The word *gambit*, from the Italian *gambetto*, "a tripping up of the heels," has been a part of the chess lexicon since 1561.)

The concept of the strategic opening, wherein the players scrupulously lay the groundwork for later phases of the game, goes back at least as far as the ninth-century grandmasters of *shatranj*, who gave colorful names to various opening sequences in their books of analysis:

- Pharaoh's Stones ("Abu'l-Bain played it")
- The Torrent ("Abu Shahara the elder used to begin with it")
- The Sheik's Opening ("Na'im used to begin with it")

Today, the *Oxford Companion to Chess* lists 1,327 opening combinations, ranging from two to eleven moves long, some with evocative names like the Sicilian Variation, the Anti-Meran Gambit, and the Queen's Indian Defense. They are a part of every serious chess player's toolkit—"as necessary to the first-rate player," declared the American transcendentalist minister and chess aficionado M. Conway in the *Atlantic Monthly* in 1860, "as are classifications to the naturalist. They are the venerable results of experience; and he who tries to excel without an acquaintance with them will find that it is much as if he should ignore the results of the past and put his hand into the fire to prove that fire would burn."

These were words of sour, firsthand experience, no doubt. For myself, as I took up the game again, I preferred to put my hand straight into the fire. I *did try* to pay some attention to my chess-beginner books from the library. But I found overwhelmingly that my interest was in *playing* chess, not studying it, which to me meant diving straight into the game and sparring with my opponent piece for piece. The concept of strategic, long-range planning felt as foreign to me as it might feel to a puppy to be asked to control her bladder. I was a chess warrior! I moved pieces in surprising ways! Standard openings be damned—I tried to throw my opponent off guard. After a particularly strange move, I would congratulate myself for my bravery; then, not losing a moment, I would plan something even more surprising for the next move. If the whim struck, I sacrificed a Pawn—not for any particular strategic advantage, but just to make sure that we kept playing the game according to my terms.

For fun, I did try to understand the four Rosenthal Variations, the opening sequences named after my great-great-grandfather that were included in the *Oxford Companion*. But I couldn't understand their logic at all. I hoped that one day it would just come to me.

2. . . . e×f4

(Black King's Pawn captures White Pawn on f4)

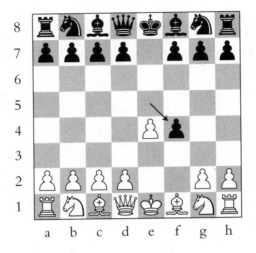

Sacrifice accepted. Kieseritzky (Black), in his response, elected to play the King's Gambit Accepted by capturing the White Pawn. (When a player ignores this particular gambit and moves another piece instead, the opening is known as the King's Gambit Declined.)

Already, Kieseritzky was up by one Pawn. A lost Pawn may not seem like much to the chess outsider, but later on in the game it can easily become the difference between night and day, crushing defeat and glorious victory—partly due to the Pawn's ability to defend other pieces, and partly because of the Pawn's potential to be promoted to Queen if it reaches the last rank. No serious player ever gives up a Pawn lightly.

On the other hand, because Black accepted the gambit and took the Pawn, White now had uncontested control of the center of the board. Such control is critical (I eventually learned) because it establishes which army will have the freest movement from one side of the board to the other. Kieseritzky undoubtedly knew he would have to fight back for the control he'd just willingly given up. At the moment, though, he thought the extra Pawn was worth the risk.

3. THE MORALS OF MEN AND THE DUTIES OF NOBLES AND COMMONERS

Chess and Medieval Obligation

DESPITE APPEARANCES TO THE CONTRARY, the rolling, uneven dunes on the west coast of the Isle of Lewis, about fifty miles west of the Scottish mainland, are not ancient burial mounds. They're natural formations, configured over thousands of years by the shifting water table and the terrific sea winds howling off the Atlantic.

But the dunes do have their powerful secrets, as an unsuspecting island peasant learned one day in the spring of 1831. At the base of a fifteen-foot sandbank near the south shore of the Bay of Uig, the interior was somehow exposed, and with it a nearly seven-hundred-year-old crypt. Our unwitting archaeologist stumbled into an ancient and cramped drystone room, six feet or so long and shaped like a beehive, with ashes strewn on the floor. The tiny room was filled, impossibly, with dozens of shrunken *people*: tiny lifelike statuettes, three to four and a half inches high, some stained beet-red and the rest left a natural off-white. The long hair, contoured faces, and proportionate bodies were eerily vivid, even animated, with wide-eyed, expectant expressions, battle-ready stances, and a full complement of medieval combat equipment and apparel. Hand-carved from walrus tusk and whale teeth, they wore tiny crowns, mitres, and helmets; held miniature swords, shields, spears, and bishop's crosiers; some rode warhorses.

They were chess pieces, a total of seventy-eight figurines comprising four not-quite-complete sets:

eight Kings (complete)
eight Queens (complete)
sixteen Bishops (complete)
fifteen Knights (one missing)
twelve Warders (as Rooks, four missing)
nineteen Pawns (forty-five missing)

No one living at the time had ever seen anything like them. The ornamentation had a medieval gothic quality that lent the pieces an ancient and even mythic aura. Experts pronounced them Scandinavian, probably mid-twelfth century, probably carved near the Norwegian capital Trondheim some seven hundred miles away by sea, where a drawing of a strikingly similar chess Queen was later discovered. Norway was a long way off, but the link did make historical sense. The Isle of Lewis had been politically subject to the Kingdom of Norway up to 1266, and the local bishop held allegiance to the powerful Archbishop of Trondheim.

These weren't nearly the oldest chessmen discovered—1150 put them somewhere in the middle of the chess chronology. But their abundance, origins, artistry, and superb condition made them among the most important cache of ancient pieces yet found. The modestly endowed Society of Antiquaries of Scotland tried immediately to buy them for display in Edinburgh, but before they could raise the funds, bigger fish swam in. A wealthy Scottish collector somehow plundered eleven of them for his private collection, and the British Museum in London bought the rest—sixty-seven pieces for eighty guineas (equivalent to £3,000 or roughly U.S. $5,000 in today's currency).

The museum immediately recognized not only the pieces' unique importance in the history of chess, but more importantly their profoundly palpable connection to life in the Middle Ages. "There are not in the museum any objects so interesting to a native Antiquary as the objects now offered to the trustees," wrote the museum's keeper of antiquities, Edward Hawkins, as he presented the pieces for the first time. The Lewis Chessmen were a priceless link to the past, and would become a signature draw at the museum.

There they now sit, sealed in a new glass crypt in the British Museum's Gallery 42. Anyone can visit them.

King   Bishop   Knight

The Lewis Chessmen

"When you look at them," suggests curator Irving Finkel, "kneel down or crouch in such a way that you can look through the glass straight into their faces and look them in the eye. You will see human beings across the passage of time. They have a remarkable quality. They speak to you."

WHAT DO they say? The story of how chess migrated from the Golden Gate Palace in Baghdad to the remote Isle of Lewis, and how the pieces morphed from abstracted Persian-Indian war figurines to evocative European Christian war figurines, is an epic that underscores the enormous transfer of culture and knowledge in the Middle Ages from the East to the West. It also heralds an important shift in chess's role as a thought tool. In medieval Europe, chess was used less to convey abstract ideas and more as a mirror for individuals to examine their own roles in society. As Europe developed a new code of social morality, chess helped society understand its new identity.

The depth of chess's role in the Middle Ages is not necessarily a story that was destined to be told. But for the perseverance of a single British scholar, much of the detail would likely have remained indefinitely buried under the sandbank of time. Fortunately, such doggedness was second nature to Harold Murray, thanks to the peculiar circumstances of his youth. In 1879, when Murray was eleven, his father, James Murray, a self-educated son of a Scottish tailor with a passion for language, began what would become easily the most exhaustive and most revered publishing project in the history of his own native English: the *Oxford English Dictionary*, which aimed to parse out the precise meaning, origin, and historical trajectory of every English word in general use. Harold, James's eldest son, was one of the most prolific contributors to the *OED*'s first edition, cataloguing an astounding 27,000 quotations. By the time Harold graduated with honors from Oxford University's Balliol College, he closely shared his father's intense historical curiosity, attachment to precision, and zeal for the unearthing of origins. He also inherited the family passion for languages: James Murray was fluent in twenty-five; Harold knew at least twelve, including Icelandic, Old Middle German, Early Anglo-Saxon, Medieval Latin, and Sanskrit.

On top of all this, Harold had a special love for numbers, games, and puzzles, an appetite for anything that would challenge the mind. He displayed unusual powers of concentration. In school he excelled at mathematics. This potent combination of interests paved an inevitable road to chess and to its elaborate history. Harold picked up the game at age twenty, playing with his younger siblings and cousins. From the start, he studied tried-and-true strategies, and was the kind of player who stuck to a handful of opening moves that felt comfortable and worked. "I have seen no reason to abandon a style of play which is generally successful against the players I meet," he wrote. He made rich chess friendships, won more than his share of games, and even sometimes played blindfolded or against several people at once.

After leaving Oxford to teach at preparatory schools, Murray broadened his commitment to the game as a school club coach. But the best way to make his personal mark on chess, he realized, was through a massive excavation of its history. No book had rigorously sought to establish the true origins of the game, trace the early history, and then bring it up to the present. The challenge of writing the definitive history of chess, spanning 1,300 years and dozens of languages, was monumental. Even with all the resources at Oxford's Bodleian Library, tracking a thousand-year-old chess migration across continents and religions and cultures was like trying to find and track a bird without any homing device. But for the trained son of James Murray, it was suitably proportional, a fitting family task. Harold Murray set out in 1897 "to investigate . . . the invention of chess; and to trace the development of the modern European game from the first appearance of its ancestor." This impossible job would consume much of his energy for the next sixteen years, and become his life's one great work.

One of Murray's first chores was to learn Arabic and immerse himself in the early days of Islam. He documented how the Muslims took to chess, wrestled with its legality and propriety, and plugged it into their intellectual and territorial ambitions. Then he traced the Islamic geographic expansion, and chess's.

Following Muhammad's death in 632, the empire grew at a staggering pace, expanding into Persia, Palestine, Syria, Iraq, Egypt, Nubia, Libya, Morocco, Cyprus, Sicily, and parts of Spain, Portugal, Turkey, Afghanistan, India, and China. By 900, Muslim armies controlled an uninterrupted stretch of land and sea from the Himalayas all the way across North Africa and into Spain.

So also went Islamic culture. In 1005 the Egyptian ruler al-Hakim tried to outlaw chess and ordered the burning of all chess sets in his territory. But it was too late to stop the game's march across North Africa. Murray discovered references to Muslim players in Cairo, Tripoli, Sicily, Sijilmasa, Fez, Seville, and Córdoba.

The game may have enjoyed its European debut in 822, having been introduced to the emir of Córdoba, Abd-al-Rahman II, by an outcast

Muslim Empire
circa 900

Persian Muslim nicknamed Ziriab. A onetime slave, Ziriab had trained
in Baghdad with the legendary musician Ishaq at the court of Harun ar-
Rashid. Then he became too good at his job: after Ziriab had the au-
dacity to outshine his mentor in the presence of their caliph, Ishaq
stepped in to protect his ground. "Jealousy is the oldest human evil,"
Ishaq warned Ziriab. "No one is immune to it, not even I. There is not
room enough at this court for both of us. You can choose between two
things. Either you stay here and I'll have you killed, or you go so far
away from here that I'll never hear of you again. If you choose this, I'll
give you the [travel] money." Thus began an epic journey, wives and
children in tow, across North Africa, into Morocco, and finally across
the Strait of Gibraltar into Muslim Spain. When he arrived in Córdoba,
this unwitting ambassador from Baghdad brought an early glimpse of
the Islamic enlightenment. Famous for the sounds of his gut-stringed

lute, Ziriab also dazzled Emir Abd-al-Rahman II and friends with re-
finements in cooking, fashion, hygiene, home decor, and recreation.
Baghdad's favorite new board game of symbolic warfare was apparently
an instant hit in Spain. The very next emir, Mohammed I, was personally devoted to the game.

Meanwhile, chess also made its way into Italy via Sicily. Bands of
Muslims from modern-day Spain, Tunisia, Libya, and Egypt attacked
and eventually conquered Sicily in the ninth century. The new Sicilians
modeled their city of Bahl'harm (modern-day Palermo) on glorious
Baghdad. These same groups also tentatively occupied areas on the
Italian mainland near Naples and Rome. Not long after this, the poet
and expert chess player Muhammad ibn Ammar was said to have saved
the Islamic Kingdom of Seville from attack by winning a game of chess
against the Christian King Alfonso VI of Leon and Castile. They played
a chess game, that is, in lieu of clashing in a real war.* Whether this was
fact or legend, the mere suggestion of replacing bloody conflict with a
board game contest foreshadowed a crucial advance in civilization: the
replacement of violent struggle for resources with nonviolent competition.

In between the long, brutal Muslim-Christian battles, scholars, spiritual figures, and even sovereigns exchanged a voluminous quantity of
customs and knowledge. "It is a paradoxical but well-established fact,"
reports historian Richard Eales, "that even in the period of the Crusades
more new learning came to the West from the Muslim 'enemy' than
through eastern Christian civilization. This was true not only of science
and mathematics, some of which, like chess, originated in India, but also of
classical literature. The Aristotelian texts which were to revolutionize
European philosophy were first translated into Latin in the twelfth century
from Arabic, and the main translating centers were in areas of cultural co-

---

* The same story is also told of the Croat Svetoslav Surinj, who, in 1271, was said
to have won the right to rule the Dalmatian towns on the Adriatic by beating the
Venetian Peter II in a chess match.

existence: Spain and Sicily, and to a lesser extent the Latin states founded in Palestine by the Crusaders.*

The importance of this massive transfer of knowledge cannot be overstated. Through much of the twentieth century, historians taught that Western civilization passed directly from Greece and Rome to Europe. But in fact the Islamic Renaissance was a critical middle ground for much of the knowledge that would make the European Renaissance possible.

Tracking chess's migration is also a way of tracking the larger transmission of knowledge. Records show chess spreading to a Swiss monastery by 997; to northern, Christian-controlled Spain by 1008; to southern Germany by 1050; and to central Italy by 1061. Everywhere the game appeared in Europe, it seemed to take root quickly. By the early twelfth century it was ubiquitous, so ensconced in the culture of medieval chivalry that it was listed as one of seven essential skills for every knight (along with riding, swimming, archery, boxing, hawking, and verse writing).

Not surprisingly, the game had a few distinctive European modifications by then. The Elephant, an animal largely foreign to Europe, was replaced by the Bishop—except in France, where that piece became *le fou* (the jester or fool)—and the King's Minister was replaced by the Queen.† The board, which had been divided into sixty-four monochrome squares (as shown in the tenth-century illustration on page 31), now saw the introduction of dark and light checkered squares—not out of any vital necessity, but simply to make movements easier for the eye

---

* The medieval French historian Robert de St. Remi reported in the early twelfth century that participants in what came to be known as the First Crusade relied on chess as one of their chief diversions between battles. It was a rich irony that, in the midst of a real war against the Muslims, the Christian Crusaders relaxed by playing a war game that Muslim culture had nurtured and delivered to them.
† The very first mention of the chess Queen occurs in the ninety-eight-line elegiac poem "Verses on Chess," found in the Einsiedeln monastery and dated reliably back to the 990s. Historian Marilyn Yalom speculates that the shift from

to track. Since Christianity has no prohibition against representational images, the design of chessmen also slowly moved back toward more literal imagery. Finally, the game's name shifted from the Arabic *shatranj* to the Latin *ludus scacorum* ("the game of the chessmen"), and from there to the Italian *scacchi*, the French *eschecs*, the German *schachspiel*, the Dutch *schaakspel*, the Icelandic *ska'ktafle*, the Polish *szachy*, and the English *chess*.

Europe's kings personally embraced the game as sultans, caliphs, and emirs had before them. The medieval historian Alexander Neckam reported on a battle, in 1110, for control over Gisors, in Normandy, where the French King Louis VI suddenly found himself seized by an enemy knight.

"The king is taken," shouted the knight.

"Ignorant and insolent knight," replied the king. "Not even in chess can a King be taken."

The spread continued. By 1200 or so, the game was established in Britain and Scandinavia. The Lewis Chessmen had been carved in Norway, and the game was utterly adored in Iceland. It was an unstoppable force—not simply because people loved the game, but also because it served a function. "There was a *demand* for a game like chess from its earliest appearance," suggests Richard Eales, "a demand sufficient to change it from an oriental curiosity into a regular feature of noble and courtly life."

The proof is in how thoroughly chess became woven into the fabric—and literally tiled onto the floor—of Christian medieval European society. In the twelfth century a mosaic artist laying the floor of the San Savino Basilica in Piacenza, Italy (about forty-five miles southeast of Milan), used tiny black and white tiles to illustrate a dramatic philosophical divide. In the lower left corner he depicted a dice game in progress;

Minister to Queen was probably inspired either by the powerful German Queen Adelaide, wife to King Otto I (they later became emperor and empress of the Holy Roman Empire), or by the next queen and empress, Theophano, wife to Otto II, the son of Otto I and Adelaide.

in the lower right-hand panel he conjured a chess scene—probably chess instruction rather than an actual game.

Mosaic floor
in San Savino Basilica

Notice the correct number of squares on the board, and the differentiation of the pieces. Such a detailed, familiar chess landscape rendered at such an early date demonstrates how quickly the game had become embedded into the European medieval consciousness. And in a house of worship, no less. There was no explicitly religious iconography in the mosaic, but its church setting was no accident. The panels presented a sharp moral sermon about one of mankind's great existential choices in the Middle Ages. The dice game, explained art historian William Tronzo, "represents the state of man's life in which he commits himself to the unstable forces of the world. Captivated by them, life becomes lawless and chaotic.

"On the right [where chess is located], man orders his world with intelligences and virtue and imbues it with law and harmony."

For moralists of the day, dice and chess nicely symbolized these opposing choices—just as it had for the earlier Islamic historian al-Mas'udi. Dice, the older game, represented a consciousness resigned to a world dominated by fate; chess stood for the new empowerment, the idea of making one's way in the world based on one's own effort and ability. The juxtaposition even became embedded into twelfth-century Italian law, which prohibited dice but allowed chess because the game depended "on one's own talents. One is not entrusted to the powers of fortune."

Implanting chess into basilica floors and even into legal doctrine, though, was just a prelude. One century later, a monk from the nearby coastal city of Genoa produced what would become by far the most influential chess book of all time. Whereas San Savino's mosaic never left the ground and was probably meant to be seen by only a few hundred pairs of eyes, the text penned by Dominican monk Jacobus de Cessolis in the halls of San Domenico Basilica, about one hundred miles away from San Savino, traveled great distances. Shortly after its inception around 1300, Cessolis's potent work spread far beyond Italy, having an impact on all of Europe as virtually no other piece of writing in the Middle Ages did. As if carried by an interpretive wind, the Latin manuscript was eventually transformed into eighteen separate versions and translated into Italian, French, English, German, Dutch, Swedish, and Czech. "No other work of medieval times was so much copied," concluded Harold Murray. "Its popularity . . . must have almost rivaled that of the Bible itself."

A chess book almost as popular as the Bible? Obviously Cessolis was speaking to something much greater than a board game. And so suggests the book title: *Liber de moribus hominum et officiis nobilium ac popularium sive super ludo scacchorum* (The book of the morals of men and the duties of nobles and commoners—or, On the game of chess). The work was actually a collection of sermons about how each person should act in society. Cessolis was concerned with nothing less than the clarification and refinement of social norms. In chess, he found a superb model, a near-literal miniaturization of medieval society. Each chess piece could be correlated to a distinct social ranking—starting with the obvious correlations of the King, Queen, and Knight. Rooks represented the King's emissaries in his scheme. To each of the eight Pawns, Cessolis assigned a different peasant-class profession:

Tillers of the earth
Metal workers
Tailors and notaries
Merchants and money changers
Physicians and apothecaries
Tavern and hotel workers
City guards
Couriers

Further, Cessolis was almost comically specific in describing how the powers and restrictions of each piece matched the rights and responsibilities of that piece's human counterpart:

> When the *queen*, which is accompanied unto the *king*, beginneth to move from her proper place, she goeth in double manner . . . she may go on the right side and come to the square before the *notary*. . . . Secondly on the left side where the *knight* is. And thirdly indirectly unto the black point before the *physician*. And the reason why is for as much as she hath in her self by grace the authority that the *rooks* have . . . she may give and grant many things to her subjects graciously. And thus also ought she to have flawless wisdom.
>
> —From a fifteenth-century English translation of Cessolis

Cessolis also included a practical guide for playing the game, encouraging his audience to experience the symbolism in action. It was the right sermon about the right game at the right time. After many centuries with little real intellectual progress, the twelfth century had seen an "early Renaissance" with a vast increase in literacy, the birth of the great northern European universities, and important intellectual contributions from Peter Abelard, St. Bernard, and John of Salisbury, among others. All of this eventually fueled a seismic shift into a new political consciousness in the noble class. *Liber de moribus* used the chess metaphor to help individuals track their evolving relationship to society, and its popularity marked a real turning point. "Before the *Liber*," argues University of Massachusetts medievalist Jenny Adams, "the predominant metaphor for the state was the human body, which represented types of people as parts subordinate to the body as a whole. . . . If the head [i.e., the King] of a body decided that the body should walk, the feet would have to follow. By contrast, the chess allegory imagines its subjects to possess independent bodies in the form of pieces bound to the state *by rules* rather than biology. If the chess King advances, the Pawns are not beholden to do the same."

This new consciousness did not, of course, alter the fundamental class division between the tiny noble minority and the serf majority—a division that the Middle Ages had inherited from the older Mediterranean society. But it did change the way that those divisions were enforced. Throughout the twelfth and thirteenth centuries, feudal society developed an elaborate legal justification for itself, enabling what Adams calls a "shift from physical to non-physical coercion." Knights, shopkeepers, farmers, and other classes now felt a moral and legal responsibility to the state. They had more physical control of their own actions, but were mindful of their role in society, and of being watched by others. Cessolis's use of the chess metaphor modeled this dynamic beautifully. "A Knight playing the game cannot move himself anywhere but must act according to [his legal moves]," says Adams. "Failure to do so will place both his own body and his community in jeopardy. Nor will this failure be hidden but exposed publicly on the board. . . . If one can see one's own 'self' on the board, other players can see one's own 'self' too."

Enabling people to see themselves on the board would turn out to be the second great metaphorical contribution of chess over the centuries, after chess's capacity for demonstrating enormous complexity. Would the intellectuals of the Middle Ages have been able to understand themselves without chess as social mirror? Undoubtedly. But in chess's absence, something like chess would have had to be invented—something universal that could symbolize the dynamic rudiments of society. Metaphor—the art of symbolic comparison—is not an optional accessory, but a vital cultural necessity that dates back to the very earliest points in human communication. A substantial degree of everyday language is built on top of it. Metaphor helps us organize our thoughts and at the same time frees us from previous contextual restraints. So much about the experience of living is intangible. To understand these intangibles, we need choice comparisons and symbols to help frame our thinking, and expand those frames, to make more and more sense of what we see, hear, and feel—and to convey that understanding to others. Aristotle considered symbolic metaphor a tool so powerful that he urged the state to regulate its use. Slaves, he warned, should not be permitted to utilize it.

One particular use of symbolic metaphor is to help us navigate complexity by reducing it to simpler, more manageable concepts. Chess is a powerful reducing agent. It can reduce a whole battlefield or city or planet down to sixty-four squares. And yet, within that simplistic frame, chess retains its active quality; like a snow globe, it shrinks things down, but retains its dynamic essence.

MORALITY AND POLITICS were not the only things being transformed in medieval Europe. Influential medieval poets were also busy inventing the notion of romantic love, and using chess to convey it.

Strange as it might seem, the Western conception of romance did not much exist before the twelfth century. So-called courtly love was an invention of medieval poets who at first imagined it—rather narrowly by today's standards—as a knight's unrequited crush on a noblewoman who was unable to return the affection. Gradually, the romantic ideal evolved to become more of a mutual matter, and to spread beyond the ruling class.

Many epic romantic poems from the late twelfth century onward struggled to adequately articulate this new ideal of overt intimacy and to reconcile such expression with other social obligations. Indeed, the game of chess began to come in handy as a courting ritual. Young men and women played each other as an excuse for romantic intimacy—this in an age where physical privacy was otherwise almost nonexistent.

Chess became ubiquitous in romantic medieval poetry. In the Carolingian romance *Huon de Bordeaux*, the strikingly titled *Les échecs amoureux* (The chess of love), Jacques de Longuyon's *Voeux du paon*, Chaucer's *Book of the Duchess*, and many others, chess served to advance romantic plots and to symbolically depict feudal figures and rules.

Players, meanwhile, tinkered with the game—and in some cases contaminated it outright. The changes should not have been such a surprise considering the surrounding social turbulence. A five-hundred-year-old Persian/Islamic game was now stumbling into a very different world—or, more accurately, an array of different worlds. In contrast with the relatively unified Islamic Empire, Europe was a collection of separated fragments with different languages, customs, political realities, and thick cultural and physical barriers. The Continent was slowly being brought together into a more unified spiritual-political hegemony under increasingly powerful kings and the Church, and it was sharing more ideas and culture through the development of cities and universities; but it remained relatively balkanized until the Renaissance in the fourteenth and fifteenth centuries.

Thus chess, now with many different names, was also essentially many different local games—called *assizes*. It was as if the game had been shot out of Arabia like a shotgun shell, scattering similar but distinct fragments all across the Continent. The so-called *Lombard assize* allowed the King an extended leap over other pieces, as well as permitted the King and Queen to move together for their first move. England had two separate sets of rules for a short game and long game. In Germany, four of the eight Pawns were allowed the double-square initial move. Iceland accelerated changes in the endgame and placed enormous emphasis on the *higher* and *lower* forms of checkmate. "It took time for a happy improvement discovered perhaps in Spain to reach Germany,

England or Iceland," writes Murray, "and all the modifications did not commend themselves to players in other countries."

Eventually, the game would take on a pan-European character. But for the first few centuries, citizens of the Middle Ages seemed to be more enamored of the game's social carriage than its intellectual ferocity. A review of problem sets and games from these early centuries in Europe shows that competition was not fierce. There were no grandmasters, no provocative analysis, no organized competitions. "The general standard of play," says Richard Eales, "was not high." The fragmented, struggling Europe needed the game's iconography, its metaphoric power, and its infectious playfulness—but not its grueling rigor. Real life was wearing and grueling enough.

In this transitional period, chess in some areas took on a very strange temporary association with, of all things, dice. While dice was being starkly contrasted with chess in sermons, it was also mingling with chess play in some European play as a new rescue from what many considered the game's unbearable sluggishness. "The wearingness which players experienced from the long duration of the game when played right through [is the reason] dice have been brought into chess, so that it can be played more quickly," a player from the Castile region of Spain explained in 1283.

Even with the many assizes, this was still essentially the same game as *shatranj*, with the Pawns' initial two-square move not yet universally accepted, and the Bishop and Queen severely constrained. The weak pieces made it a much slower game than modern chess.

The slow pace had suited Muslims just fine, but from a European point of view, says Harold Murray, "the game was long in coming to a point, and the tactics of the prolonged opening play were by no means easy to discover." To speed up the game, alternative versions had emerged wherein one die would be thrown before each move to determine which piece would be played:

If it landed on "1," the player would move a Pawn.

If on "2," a Knight.

If on "3," a Bishop.

If on "4," a Rook.

If on "5," the Queen.

If on "6," the King.

From the standpoint of the moralists who saw chess and dice as opposites, this was a perplexing development: fate had been invited into humanity's great symbolic arena of skill and free will. Essentially, it pitted chess in a cultural battle against itself. Dice, declared Murray, "ruins the real entity of chess."

Like Europe itself, the game was crying out for consolidation.

THE IMMORTAL GAME

Move 3

SITUATED ON LONDON'S ANCIENT aristocratic boulevard known as The Strand, Simpson's Grand Divan was a distinguished center of drinking, dining, and leisure in the mid-nineteenth century. Men with some time to spare would gather here to smoke cigars, read the newspaper, talk politics, and play chess. For one shilling and sixpence (equivalent to nine U.S. dollars today), a patron would be furnished with coffee, a cigar, and unlimited access to a chess table. Howard Staunton, the great English champion who helped popularize the game and was organizing the 1851 international tournament, had actually learned how to play chess in the Divan years earlier. So it was a very natural place for two would-be competitors, Anderssen and Kieseritzky, to meet for practice play on one of their days off from formal competition.

Move 3 was, of course, still far too early in the game for any onlooker to detect anything extraordinary. This, so far, was thoroughly typical nineteenth-century chess. Having moved two Pawns and opened up space for the development of his major pieces, Anderssen now began to develop them, first by moving his King's Bishop out three diagonal squares.

3. Bc4
(White King's Bishop to c4)

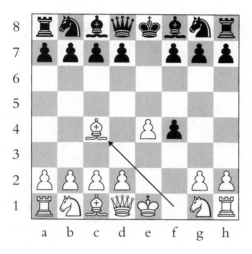

This move strengthened White's hold on the center of the board and put pressure on Black's inherently weak f7 Pawn—weak because the only piece defending it is the King. (Anderssen's early moves suggested that White might be planning a Kingside* attack.)

---

* *Kingside*: The side of the board closer to the King's original square, as opposed to the Queenside.

3. . . . Qh4+

(Black Queen to h4; check to the White King)

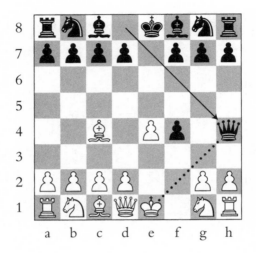

Kieseritzky (Black) responded with his own attack, taking advantage of a glaring breach in the defenses of the White King. He swept his Queen all the way out to the edge of the board and put White in check.

This wasn't checkmate, or anything close. The utility of this particular early check is that it forces White to move his King, thereby eliminating his ability to castle.* White's King was now permanently relegated to the center, easier prey for a later attack.

---

* Castling is a onetime defensive and offensive move wherein the King essentially changes places with one of his Rooks. Castling must occur before either the King or the Rook in question has moved, and cannot occur while a King is in check. The move itself involves shifting the King over two squares toward the Rook, and then moving the Rook to the other side of the King, on the adjacent square. (Today, the consensus is that castling should be accomplished by move 12 or so, unless the player has something special up his sleeve or forgoes the castle in order to take advantage of a terrible blunder by the opponent.)

Anderssen, the underdog, had now lost a Pawn *and* the ability to castle. Had he already stumbled?

On the other hand, with his aggressive Queen move, Kieseritzky had also opened up an important vulnerability of his own by exposing his Queen to attack, which could soon force him to use valuable moves to retreat or reposition her. In chess, getting caught in a retreat can be a very dangerous thing. It risks turning over all momentum and control to one's opponent. The best-laid plans, along with assorted hopes and curiosities, can quickly disappear into a how-did-I-get-here? cloud of disconnected Pawns, pinned Knights, and a helpless, unprotected King.

Both players had already begun offensive maneuvers and also taken some calculated risks. It would take many more moves to see who had made the better gamble.

4. MAKING MEN CIRCUMSPECT

Modern Chess, the Accumulation of Knowledge, and the March to Infinity

IN THE FIFTEENTH AND SIXTEENTH centuries, a cluster of charismatic and powerful queens emerged in Europe: Catherine of Aragon, Isabella of Castile, Mary Tudor, Elizabeth I, Catherine de Médicis of France, Queen Jeanne d'Albret of Navarre, and Mary, Queen of Scots.

By no coincidence, chess players all across the Continent discovered during the very same period that their game had been transformed. Gone were the regional assizes with assorted rules and pieces of varying strengths; gone was the corruption of dice; gone was the agonizing sluggishness. Now there was a new, faster, more universal game, with three significant rule changes:

- Each Pawn could now move either one or two squares in its first move.*
- Bishops could now move any number of unobstructed squares diagonally.

---

* The optional two-square Pawn move had actually been around for a few centuries in some assizes, but it wasn't standardized until around 1475, when the Bishop and Queen changes were also widely introduced.

- An exceptionally powerful Queen was now endowed with the combined powers of the Rooks and the newly strengthened Bishops, able to move any number of unobstructed squares in any direction: diagonally, vertically, or horizontally.

If Otto I's Queen Adelaide had likely been the original inspiration for changing the piece from Minister to Queen in the tenth century, the substantial boost in the Queen's power appears to have been inspired by Isabella, who for decades in the latter half of the fifteenth century reigned over the Castile and León regions of Spain in an extraordinary cosovereignty arrangement with her husband, King Ferdinand. Both rulers were avid chess players. One legend has it that Ferdinand was himself right in the middle of a chess game when Christopher Columbus approached the court with his plan to sail west in search of the Indies; at that moment, victory came to Ferdinand on the chessboard, putting him in such a good mood that he quickly approved Columbus's request.

Isabella was the personification of new female power, equally admired and feared. She helped unite Spain, reorganized the kingdom's finances, and instigated the Spanish Inquisition. It simply cannot have been happenstance, argues historian Marilyn Yalom, that in the same country at the exact same time several influential chess authors proposed a new chess Queen with unprecedented powers on the board. "A militant Queen more powerful than her husband had arisen in Castile; why not on the chessboard as well?" Yalom writes in her book *Birth of the Chess Queen*. "This may have been the thinking of those players from Valencia who endowed the chess Queen with her extended range of motion. Perhaps they even hoped to win favor from the Queen by promoting the chess Queen. Yet it is just as likely that those Valencian players *unconsciously* redesigned the Queen on the model of the all-powerful Isabella."

Such was the dynamic, symbiotic relationship between chess and its adopted continent—game and society reflected and influenced another, like a painted portrait and its subject. The new, faster, more intellectually challenging chess echoed not just the rise of female power, but also a culture in transformation. A renaissance was taking place. Europe was slowly becoming a more frenetic, curious society.

It was the age of humanism, the printing press, Leonardo da Vinci, and Erasmus. "This Century, like a golden age," declared Italian philosopher Marsilio Ficino in 1492, "has restored to light the liberal arts, which were almost extinct: grammar, poetry, rhetoric, painting, sculpture, architecture, music . . . has joined wisdom with eloquence, and prudence with the military art. . . . [and] invented the instruments for printing books." Echoing these changes, the new chess was a much quicker game, giving it a higher-octane feel and making it an emblem of the emerging age of knowledge. Whether by accident or design, the Renaissance itself was reflected in the new, more engaging format of the game, which quickly became the universal standard. Modern chess was born.

Just looking at static pieces on the board, the enormity of the shift would have been impossible for a casual observer to appreciate. The chessboard, after all, was exactly the same. The pieces were exactly the same. Their arrangement was exactly the same. Looking at the board through a snapshot, there was no indication that anything at all had changed. But in animated motion and in the mind's eye of the player, it was a different matter. Seasoned players realized all too well that with the tweaking of a few pieces' powers of motion, it was an entirely new game. It was much faster and more aggressive in that the Queen and the Bishops could now move into threatening positions within just a few moves. (One opening sequence emerged which allowed Black to checkmate White in two moves.)* And it was vastly more complex because at any given time, each player had many more move choices—and had to anticipate more responses from the opponent. Suddenly, there were vastly more possibilities of play from the very start. Now the game was not only fast, it was also nearly infinite.

Nearly infinite? There's a suspicious phrase, to be sure. How could something be *nearly* infinite? It's like calling a tumor *almost* malignant. But such is the deceptive power of geometric progression, a method of

---

* Checkmate in two moves: 1. f3 e5 2. g4 Qh4++

numerical increase that leaps forward not by addition (10 + 10 + 10 = 30) but by multiplication (10 × 10 × 10 = 1,000). Geometric progression is one of the foundational principles of all mathematics, helping to advance understanding of everything in nature that grows or spreads, from human population to financial investments to nuclear fission. Its manifestation in chess, which can be easily explained but is not ordinarily intuited, is one of the particulars that make the game so fascinating to mathematicians—and so intriguing to players.

It all starts out so simply: In the first move, White is limited to twenty options:

Each Pawn can move either one or two squares on its first move. 8 × 2 = 16 possible moves.

Each Knight is restricted to two possible first moves. 2 × 2 = 4 moves.

(The Rooks, Bishops, King, and Queen are all blocked and have no chance of moving on the first move.)

Black has the same twenty possible moves with his first response.

But with chess, the number of legal moves is only a small part of the equation. Because while there are only forty possible first moves per pair of players, there are actually *400* possible board positions inherent in those moves. That's because for every one of White's twenty moves, Black's response can lead to twenty separate positions. If White moves his Pawn to a3: Black can move Pawn to a6, or Pawn to a5, or Pawn to b6, or Pawn to b5, or Pawn to c6, or Pawn to c5, or Pawn to d6, or Pawn to d5, or Pawn to e6, or Pawn to e5, or Pawn to f6, or Pawn to f5, or Pawn to g6, or Pawn to g5, or Pawn to h6, or Pawn to h5, or Knight to a6, or Knight to c6, or Knight to f6, or Knight to h6.

If White moves his Pawn to a4, Black can move Pawn to a6 or Pawn to a5 . . .

If White moves his Pawn to b3, Black can move Pawn to a6 or Pawn to a5 . . .

—and so on up to 400 distinct positions. To the outsider, the distinctions among all of these early board positions may seem negligible, but the seasoned chess player knows from hard-won (or rather hard-*lost*) experience that every such variation is critically distinct, that the dynamics of the game depend entirely on the exact position of the pieces. Just as an infinitesimal change in the interaction of H_2O molecules will change their structure from water to ice, the movement of any Pawn just one square forward can drastically alter the course of a hard-fought chess game.

Think of it as chess chemistry: each player moving just once can yield any one of 400 distinct chess "molecules," each with its own special properties.

In the second move, the number of possible chess molecules shoots up almost past belief: for every one of those 400 positions, there are as many as 27 options that each player has for a second move. It's not quite so simple a calculation as with the first move, but the total number of distinct board positions after the second complete move (two moves per player) is—you'll have to trust the number crunchers on this—71,852. After just two moves each, the power of geometric progression is already bearing down hard on both players. Already, it is nearly impossible for any human to track all the possible chess molecules.

After three moves each, the players have settled on one of approximately nine million possible board positions.

Four moves each raises it to more than 315 billion.

The game has barely started and already we're into the hundreds of billions of game sets. From there, it's not so difficult to imagine how easily the number of discrete board positions spirals into the stratosphere as the game winds on. The total number of unique chess games is not literally an infinite number, but in practical terms, the difference is indistinguishable. It is truly beyond comprehension—"barely thinkable," as one expert puts it—and beyond human or machine capacity to play through them all. The estimated total, in scientific notation, is 10^{120}.

With all the zeros laid out, that's *1,000,000,000,000,000,000,000, 000,000,000,000,000,000,000,000,000,000,000,000,000,000,00 0,000,000,000,000,000,000,000,000,000,000,000,000,000,000, 000,000* games.

(In conversational English, it is a thousand trillion trillion trillion trillion trillion trillion trillion trillion trillion trillion games.)

By way of comparison, the total number of electrons in the universe is, as best as physicists can determine, 10^{79}. A chessboard, bizarre as it sounds, is pregnant with vastly more possibility.

Thus the unsettling term *near-infinite* is not inappropriate. Of course there's no such thing in the literal sense (perhaps a physicist or mathematician will correct me on this point), but in subjective human reality, the phrase fits. In the same way that a near-death experience purports to give a taste of death without the victim actually dying, chess's expanse skims close enough to infinity for players to peer over the ledge and envision the fall.

WITH THE new uniform rules, quicker pace, and near-infinite possibility, chess in the sixteenth century not only reclaimed much of its earlier intellectual character. It also gained an even wider social currency. On separate paths, the game and the metaphorical tool each became so entrenched in the culture that "chess" seemed to take on two distinct identities. Among an emerging class of fervent players, it was a supremely hard-fought contest that required intense study and that taxed and stretched minds as never before. For many others, it was an increasingly useful social and symbolic device, diverting idleness, brokering romance, settling feuds, and even aiding diplomacy.

It came in handy, for example, in the tense atmosphere of the English throne room in the early months of 1565. The young Protestant queen, Elizabeth I, who had ruled for six years, was rightly worried about the

ambition of her Catholic cousin Mary, Queen of Scots. Indeed, Mary
had already asserted her right to the English throne, and many agreed.
Owing to the voiding of the marriage between Elizabeth's father, Henry
VIII, and her mother, Anne Boleyn, some considered Mary's claim
(through her mother, Henry's older sister) the stronger one.

The question of the day was who Mary would now choose for a husband, and whether that marriage would give her the leverage to capture
the English crown. This was a life-and-death matter for Elizabeth, and
she worried about it constantly. Her biggest concern was Mary's suitor,
the dashing nineteen-year-old Lord Henry Stewart Darnley, who was
himself of considerable royal lineage. Knowing this union would be particularly threatening, Elizabeth maneuvered instead to pair Mary with
the Earl of Leicester, one of Elizabeth's closest confidants (and report-
edly Elizabeth's lover).

On such highly sensitive matters, one had to be especially careful
with one's remarks. One useful way to address the monarch was to talk
around things, to speak metaphorically. An indirect comment could
safely be ignored, deflected, or redirected. There was much less of a
chance of exposure and humiliation. And yet, while the risk was low,
the potential benefits were high; a well-placed analogy could make precisely the point intended and help facilitate an intimate rapport.

Enter chess, the popular game of political symbols. In a visit during
this delicate period, the French ambassador Paul de Foix carefully relied
on the game as an icebreaker. Conveniently, Elizabeth was playing chess
as Foix was escorted into the chamber.

"This game," offered the ambassador, motioning toward the chessboard, "is an image of the works and deeds of men. If we lose a Pawn
it seems a small matter; but the loss often brings with it that of the whole
game."

"I understand you," replied the queen. "Darnley is only a Pawn, but
he may checkmate me if he is promoted."*

---

* Mary and Darnley did wed, with fateful results. Their son, James, succeeded
Elizabeth after her death in 1603. (James, incidentally, was not a fan of chess. "I

Notion conveyed; rapport intact. Chess's allegorical clout, its ability to symbolize a wide variety of social and political situations, was reaching a new summit. The game was now approaching the end of its first millennium. It had been an extension of sixth-century Indian warfare and mathematics, a seventh-century Persian cultural mainstay, a useful thought tool for the eighth-century Muslim warrior-philosophers, a favorite occupation of the ninth- and tenth-century Spanish Muslims, and a social mirror for the knights, kings, and clerics of medieval Europe in the eleventh through fourteenth centuries. Now, as society became more enlightened, the game's metaphoric use mushroomed, moving in several directions at once. It became, says Oxford University's William Poole, the "Renaissance symbol of courtly, aristocratic entertainment, even of sexual equality." What stands out, he says, is its breadth, its "metaphorical richness in many different spheres of reference." A small sampling:

- In 1550 Saint Teresa of Ávila used chess extensively in her text *The Way of Perfection* as a tool to explore the dynamics of prayer and contemplation.
- In 1595 English courtier Sir Philip Sidney used the game to discuss the function of names.
- Cervantes used it to discuss issues of inequity in *Don Quixote* in 1615.
- The English playwright Thomas Middleton, in his 1624 play *A Game at Chess*, satirized the failed marriage negotiations between Prince Charles, the son of England's James I, and Donna Maria, the sister of Philip IV of Spain.

Physically, most chessboards were no larger than a couple of square feet, but inside the Elizabethan mind the game's scope was vast.

---

thinke it ouer fond," he remarked just before becoming the English king, "because it is ouerwise and Philosophicke a follie. . . . [it] filleth and troubleth mens heads with as many fashious toyes of the playe, as before it was filled with thoughts of his affaires.")

Surveying the chess scene in 1614, English writer Arthur Saul marveled at the "many morall mysteries that this Game secretly contayneth."

How could one game symbolize so many different entities, structures, relationships, notions? It largely came down to the fact that chess had been designed as a symbol to begin with. Out of the box, it came furnished with a wide variety of generic attributes that lent themselves to an even wider variety of metaphorical applications: chess was a *battle* between two groups, each *stratified* by social ranking, *contesting for dominance* over a *finite* piece of geography, interacting in a *dynamic so complex* it seemed to take on a life of its own, each army *manipulated by a player*, battling each other with *wits rather than brawn*, employing both *tactics* (short-term planning) and *strategy* (long-term planning), in a game that could *never truly be mastered*.

It was a long list of attributes, any combination of which could help fuel particular metaphors. Anyone in need of a dynamic symbol to explore and convey elements of war, competition, hierarchy, political power, battle for resources, control by a higher power, meritocracy, the nature of thought, futility, abstract movement, complexity, or infinity had a choice vehicle standing by for metaphoric flight. (Such conditions would also keep chess perpetually relevant. In the twenty-first century, political cartoonists would still use chess to depict global struggles; business schools, law firms, technology consultants, and the U.S. Army would adopt the chess logo to convey an emphasis on strategic thinking; journalists would use it as shorthand for complex and unpredictable social dynamics—and so on.)

Occasionally, the game itself sufficed as a powerful rhetorical device without needing to turn it into a metaphor. In his landmark *Essay Concerning Human Understanding*, published in 1689, English philosopher John Locke used chess to help establish his epistemology of empiricism, arguing that each human mind begins as a blank slate and becomes informed principally by experience and the senses.*

---

* Locke's empiricism was in contrast to the rationalism of René Descartes, the vastly influential French mathematician and philosopher from earlier in the same

From "Place relative to particular bodies"

Thus a company of chess-men, standing on the same squares of the chess-board where we left them, we say they are all in the same place, or unmoved, though perhaps the chess-board hath been in the mean time carried out of one room into another; because we compared them only to the parts of the chess-board, which keep the same distance one with another.

From "Place relative to a present purpose"

. . . but when these very chess-men are put up in a bag, if any one should ask where the black King is, it would be proper to determine the place by the part of the room it was in, and not by the chess-board.

In conjuring up the image of chessmen resting in a bag, Locke was reverting to a popular centuries-old metaphor that spoke to questions of moral and political equality. "The whole world is like a chess-board," one thirteenth-century document had declared. ". . . The society of this chess-board are men of this world, who are all taken from a common bag . . . and when they have finished the game, just as they come out of one place and one bag, so they are put back in one place, without a distinction between the King and the poor Pawn."*

The chess–life comparison was clear. On the board (i.e., in life), each chess piece (person) had his own particular standing. But after the game (upon death), all the pieces (people) would be thrown into the bag (the afterlife) and would be equal forevermore. The board–bag contrast was

---

century who founded modern philosophy, famously declaring, "I think, therefore I am." "Descartes's rationalism was designed to shake our faith in our senses and, instead, place reasoning and logic at our core," explains Williams College professor of philosophy Steven Gerrard. "Locke's empiricism argued for just the opposite: all knowledge must begin with our humble senses."

★ This treatise came to be known as the *Innocent Morality*, named after its purported (and not implausible) author, Pope Innocent III.

invoked often in medieval works—usually emphasizing that the King was just as likely as not to end up near the bottom of the bag after he died. It seemed intended at first as a conservative reinforcement of social order, in that it encouraged peasants not to seek to climb above their lower ranks during life and assured them that salvation and moral justice would be theirs in the afterlife. But the image could also be seen as—inadvertently—planting the seeds for the later revolutions of equality and democracy: if peasants and kings were equal in death, where was the legitimacy in the arbitrary rules that made them unequal in life?

Such was perhaps the greatest paradox of chess over the many centuries: it was on the one hand an icon of the status quo, a favorite of rulers and of traditional moralists seeking to reinforce social obligations; and yet, at the very same time, it was also inherently an agent of change. Any tool that encourages new ways to think is inherently subversive because it challenges the intellectual status quo. Chess, as James Rowbothum suggested in 1562, couldn't help but "make men circumspect not onelye in playing this game, but also comparing it to a publick gouernement."

Making men circumspect is exactly what metaphors do for us in every century. Through them, we see the world in new and different ways. We gain insight into ourselves and our relationships. We get access to new ideas and creative solutions to problems. We progress.

THE IMMORTAL GAME

Moves 4 and 5

ON ANY GIVEN TURN, chess will usually offer a player many choices—very often *too* many—but one particular scenario is always beyond a player's control. When in check, one must immediately escape it, if possible.

So it was that Anderssen (White), in his move 4, had no choice but to move his White King one square to the right, the only relatively safe option. (There are only three legal moves here, and the other two quickly get White into even deeper trouble.)

4. Kf1
(White King to f1)

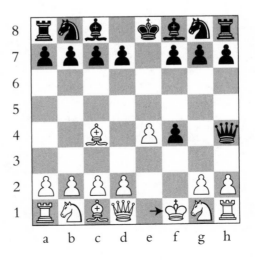

With that move, Anderssen had now lost his ability to castle, and thus his King was stuck on his weakened Kingside, quite vulnerable to attack.

He'd been there before, though. Anderssen and Kieseritzky had both seen this exact position before. Among the tens of millions of sequences possible in a three-and-a-half-move chess game, these two players had effortlessly tangoed into a most familiar arrangement. For that matter, so had thousands of others, going back at least as far as a published analysis of this position by the Spanish priest Ruy Lopez in 1561. In a game of almost limitless possibility, Anderssen and Kieseritzky seemed somehow to be playing their game from memory, or dictation. Why?

The answer has to do with chess's most elemental truth: that it is a game of knowledge and understanding as much as wits.

After the explanation of chess's near-infinite quality, an outside observer might find this hard to understand. With so much fluidity in the game—a near-infinite number of ways to win and a near-infinite number of ways to lose—a newcomer might reasonably assume (as I certainly did) that chess is mostly a game of quick thinking. Since a game is won or lost on a player's ability to outmaneuver an opponent's pieces, and since it is surely impossible to memorize or analyze even a tiny fraction of all the possible board configurations, one would naturally expect most games to go to the sharpest—or deepest—thinker, the player able to see the furthest ahead.

Fortunately, the game turns out to be a lot more interesting than that. It is not limited to the moment-by-moment calculation and creativity of players, but subject also to a broader—and ever-growing—understanding of the game's dynamic principles and distinct phases: *opening, middlegame, endgame*. Like rabbinic scholars poring over the Talmud, serious chess players are constantly interpreting and reinterpreting well-worn chess truths and rendering them into inventive new modes of play.

First, they come to understand and respect the fundamentals. All seasoned players, for example, appreciate the critical importance of fighting right from the beginning for control of the four center squares. Control of the center gives a player control over the most active part of the chessboard. Rooks, Bishops, and the Queen need passage through the center in order to be most effective. Knights are able to put pressure on many more squares at once from center positions. Losing complete control of the center can quickly lead to a drastic power imbalance where the opponent dominates much of the board and forces you into a cramped position with limited options. (And then the slaughter begins.)

Early development of the back rank pieces—Knights, Bishops, Queen, and Rooks, roughly in that order—is also vital. A delay will inevitably yield board control to the opponent.

These are *strategic* considerations—long-range, whole-game thinking, as opposed to *tactical* play, which is the shorter-range, move-by-move maneuvering with tricky combinations. Good chess requires both strategic and tactical thinking, particularly in the opening phase of the game, where a single clumsy move can leave a player so disadvantaged he is almost fated to lose. Consequently, there is no limit to the attention serious players give to the science of openings. They approach every game with enough knowledge to play competitively against a wide range of opening variations. But most also concentrate on a few favorites, so that they may sharpen their knowledge of at least some limited approaches to the game.

4. . . . b5

(Black Queen's Knight Pawn to b5)

For his fourth move, Kieseritzky (Black) played another reasonably well-studied move of the day—Pawn to b5, offering it as a sacrifice to White's Bishop. This so-called Bryan Countergambit (a countergambit is a gambit offered by Black)—named for the nineteenth-century American player Thomas Jefferson Bryan, who had extensively analyzed and advocated its use—was less familiar than the previous moves, but still no wild gamble on Kieseritzky's part. In fact, it had been very productive for him in the past, helping him win important games in 1844 and 1847. The Bryan Countergambit aims to knock White's Bishop off its controlling center square.

Adventurous players like Bryan liked to comb over openings from the past and tinker with new possibilities, a chess ritual going back to the birth of the modern game, circa 1475, after which serious players had no choice but to reassess old ideas and habits in light of the game's new chemistry. The path was forged by the wealthy Spaniard Luis Ramirez Lucena (pronounced Loo-THAY-na), the son of a diplomat working under Isabella and Ferdinand. In 1497 Lucena wrote *E arte de axedrez* (The art of chess), the first chess guide ever produced by a printing press and the first to include analysis of modern openings. (The book was dedicated to Isabella and Ferdinand's son, Prince Juan.)

Lucena had played chess throughout Europe and had witnessed firsthand the transition to the more agile and difficult game. In his book he carefully explained the new rules, and explored eleven sample openings from the new game—"all the best games I have seen played by players in Rome and all Italy, France and Spain, and which I have been able to understand myself." By modern standards, his observations are judged painfully dim, but it was a start, and the new custom of intensive opening analysis endured. Lucena was followed by a somewhat more sophisticated work from the Portuguese apothecary Pedro Damiano in 1512, and an even wider-ranging treatise by the Spanish priest and chess legend Ruy Lopez in 1561. It was Lopez, in fact, who introduced the King's Gambit.

5. B×b5
(White Bishop captures Black Pawn on b5)

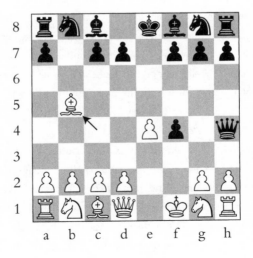

Now Anderssen accepted the Bryan Countergambit, taking Kieseritzky's Pawn on b5. Why? In part it was for the gain in material—in accepting the gambit he captured a Pawn and was now even in that respect with Black. It was also Anderssen's least bad option. Chess is rarely a game of ideal moves. Almost always, a player faces a series of difficult consequences whichever move he makes. In contemplating declining the gambit, Anderssen had to consider either the sacrifice of his Bishop (not desirable) or the retreat of the Bishop to a less advantageous square. In the latter case he also risked turning over the momentum to Black by allowing him to continue to develop his Queenside pawns.

The Bryan Countergambit wouldn't weather all that well in later years as it fell prey to sharper and more rigorous analysis. In the serious chess world, all opening sequences must withstand exhaustive scrutiny, as players probe for weaknesses. The most durable schemes then spawn ultraspecialized books—books that focus on a single opening variation. For example:

Easy Guide to the Bb5 Sicilian, by Steffen Pedersen
The Chigorin Queen's Gambit, by Angus Dunnington
The Fianchetto King's Indian, by Colin McNab
The Modern French Tarrasch, by Eduard Gufeld
Nimzo-Indian Defence: Classical Variation, by Ivan Sokolov
Petroff Defense, by Gyozo Forintos and Haag Ervin
Play the Benko Gambit, by Vaidyanathan M. Ravikuma
Play the Caro-Kann, by Egon Varnusz
Play the Evans Gambit, by Tim Harding and Bernard Cafferty

These are not books I rushed to buy. I wanted nothing to do with rehearsed openings. To me, studying them was like memorizing numbers in a phone book; it was mind-numbing and devoid of all meaning. I strongly preferred to plunge blindly into the chaotic thrill of an unrehearsed game and fend for myself. I wanted not to be a chess scholar but a chess player, enjoying the moment-to-moment challenges in each game.

Then I started losing, and kept on losing—even to my friend Kurt, who started beating me consistently even though we had taken up the game at the same time. One crucial difference in our play was that Kurt, while not studying openings intensely, did at least have the discipline to stick to just a very few. That way he could closely monitor what worked and what didn't. Kurt was establishing a repertoire in order to win more games. I was still playing on instinct, playing only in the moment.

An impressive string of crushing defeats helped clarify my thinking, leading me eventually to understand that my aversion to openings and chess theory severely limited my potential as a player. Playing well requires study—period. There are more and less sophisticated ways to play the game, and those unwilling to face up to the reality of chess knowledge will be consigned forever to be ineffective, ignorant underachievers. (Understanding this hard truth didn't amount to acting on it, but it was at least a good first step.)

In this way chess serves as a useful microcosm of human progress. Civilization is built on learned lessons from past achievements and mistakes. In physics, mathematics, medicine, engineering, legal theory, and so on, success is defined as improving upon the knowledge of our forebears. A young physician of the twenty-first century does not begin her career with the same understanding of bone, blood, tumors, and hygiene as Hippocrates or Benjamin Rush or Louis Pasteur. Regardless of her own capacity, she is miles ahead of her predecessors. Her judgments are built on top of a mountain of past medical experience.

Chess works the same way. One learns from past play; one does not start from scratch. Every notable game is entered into the historical record, studied by humans—and now computers—until it becomes an essential part of the foundation of knowledge that future games will be built on. In not wanting to study openings, I was the equivalent of an unenlightened medieval cleric ranting against intellectual discovery.

Humbling, to be sure. But, to be honest, that still didn't make me want to study opening theory.

5. . . . Nf6
(Black Knight to f6)

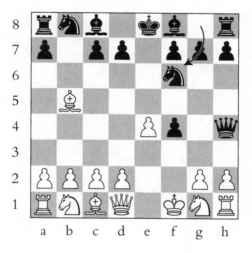

Kieseritzky followed his countergambit with another effort at controlling the center, this time bringing his Knight out to f6, which put pressure on two center squares—one of them occupied by an unprotected White Pawn. Now White would have to defend his Pawn, and would have to worry about the potentially imminent move of Black Knight to g4, which would set up the White King for a quick checkmate with the Queen moving to f2.

Kieseritzky probably felt reasonably good about his position at this point. So far, this friendly game perfectly mirrored, move for move, a game from seven years earlier—a game he had won (against a different opponent). Then again, he also knew that he was playing a master tactician, and that anything could happen. They were just getting started.

II.
MIDDLEGAME

(Who We Are)

Chess is a great, worldwide fact. Wherever a highway is found, there, we may be sure, a reason existed for a highway. And when we find that the explorer on his northward voyage, pausing a day in Iceland, may pass his time in keen encounters with the natives; that the trader in Kamtschatka and China, unable to speak a word with the people surrounding him, yet holds a long evening's converse over the board which is polyglot . . . the game becomes authentic from its universality.

—M. Conway, Atlantic Monthly, 1860

5. BENJAMIN FRANKLIN'S OPERA

Chess and the Enlightenment

ALONG WITH JUST ABOUT everyone else in the American colonies, Benjamin Franklin wanted to avoid war against King George III's soldiers if at all possible. But in 1774, anyone could plainly see that armed conflict was coming on fast. Boston had just held its rebellious Tea Party, which was followed by five British imperial maneuvers that the colonists termed the Intolerable Acts. Under the command of General Thomas Gage, the British military was tightening its control over local government, legal procedures, and civil order—all of which, of course, only caused the colonists to chafe even more. Slowly but surely, both sides seemed headed toward a bloody and world-altering battle.

Franklin, who by this time was an accomplished publisher, scientist, entrepreneur, and postmaster, had also emerged as one of the colonies' most effective diplomats. He had spent most of the previous twenty years, and all of the previous ten, in London and Paris and moved easily among European circles of power. Yet his true allegiance was never in question, and as the tension ramped up and he reinforced his loyalties to America, the British crown was moved to relieve him of his post as deputy postmaster general of the colonies (a position based in London). Franklin wore the dismissal with pride. "Intending to disgrace me," he wrote to a friend, "they have done me honour. . . . I am too much attached to the interests of America, and an opposer of the measures of Administration. The displacing me is therefore a testimony of my being uncorrupted."

By late 1774 the hostility toward America was so uncomfortable in London that Franklin realized it was time to return home to Philadelphia. War seemed imminent, at which point his physical safety would be in jeopardy. Franklin still hoped for reason and peace to prevail, but no longer believed he could help bring it about. His loyalty to America had caused his personal reputation in England to plummet; London papers labeled him an "old snake," a "veteran of mischief," and a "grand incendiary." The invective made it virtually impossible for any influential British politicians to meet publicly with Franklin without risking serious damage to their own careers. Franklin wisely prepared to head home.

Then chess intervened. Just as he was set to leave, Franklin received a surprise invitation to play a single game with the prominent socialite Lady Howe at her comfortable London home. He put his departure on hold.

Political rhetoric had been exhausted between the two sides, but here was a symbolic contest in which colonists and Brits could still publicly engage without personal risk. The surprise chess invitation in London didn't have any overt diplomatic connotations at the start—and it didn't have to for Franklin to accept. He loved the game that much. Homesick after many years abroad, worn out from the public flagellation, and in considerable personal danger, Franklin nevertheless could not say no to a set chessboard. "The Game of Chess is not merely an idle amusement," he would later declare. "Several very valuable qualities of the mind, useful in the course of human life, are to be acquired or strengthened by it. . . . For Life is a kind of Chess, in which we have often points to gain, and competitors or adversaries to contend with." Among other motives, this was Franklin's way of admitting his outsized lust for the game. He played it whenever he could, traveling with his own miniature set (one of the very first known to exist in the colonies). Franklin wrote about chess; sermonized with it; used it to make new friends, flirt with women, and bully opponents. He scouted constantly for worthy adversaries in Philadelphia, London, and Paris, and studied all available books on strategy. Much as it had already been for so many in the past, the game became a sort of intellectual and moral whetstone for Franklin. He relied on it to continually sharpen his thinking and clarify his values. In his essay "The Morals of Chess," published in 1786, he asserted that the game improved a person's

- *Foresight*—looking ahead to the long-term consequences of any action
- *Circumspection*—surveying the entire scene, observing hidden dynamics and unseen possibilities
- *Caution*—avoiding haste and unnecessary blunders
- *Perseverance*—refusing to give up in dim circumstances, continually pushing to improve one's position

He was also captivated by chess's metaphorical resonance—so taken, in fact, that he was willing to bend the rules if it suited some moral or mischievous purpose. During a game one day in France in the midst of the American struggle for independence, his French opponent maneuvered into an attack position and put Franklin in check. Franklin replied with a blatantly illegal move: he ignored the check and moved an unrelated piece.

His astonished opponent naturally objected. *Cannot you see, sir, that your King is in check?*

"I see he is in check," Franklin impishly replied. "But I shall not defend him. If he was a good King, like yours, he would deserve the protection of his subjects; but he is a tyrant and has cost them already more than he is worth. Take him, if you please. I can do without him, and will fight out the rest of the battle *en republicain*."*

★ Thomas Jefferson tells a similar story: "When Dr. Franklin went to France on his revolutionary mission, his eminence as a philosopher, his venerable appearance, and the cause on which he was sent, rendered him extremely popular. For all ranks and conditions of men there, entered warmly into the American inter-

In that one playful remark, Franklin brilliantly encapsulated the democratic revolution. America was breaking from a long tradition of autocratic rule, and no longer had any need for the king. Defending the American colonies by day and playing chess at night, it was impossible for Franklin not to look at the board and project onto it his nation's own political circumstances. Democracy was itself an abstract concept. No one could *see* democracy, hold it in a hand, turn it around on a table to observe, share, and discuss. The most anyone could do was try to represent it in words and laws. With chess, democracy could (temporarily) take on a concrete, if much simplified, shape. One could lift the King off the board to make a point, or simply ignore his existence. In doing so, one would be giving life to an abstract notion—making it communicable. (Inspired by Franklin's comment and more broadly by the democratic revolution, American chess designers subsequently produced various "democratic" sets, with a President in the place of a King, and so on. But the medieval European iconography continued as the universal standard.)

Franklin was a unique figure, but in his devotion to chess in the eighteenth century he was merely one of a crowd. Chess was, quite simply, *the* recreation of choice for key constituents of the scientific and cultural awakening now known as the Enlightenment. The game inspired and fascinated such thinkers as Voltaire, Jean-Jacques Rousseau, the encyclopedist Denis Diderot, and the philosopher Gottfried Wilhelm Leibniz, among others. "In the Age of Reason, the moves of the pieces were like the conclusions of syllogisms," write expert players and chess authors Larry Parr and Lev Alburt. Perhaps more than in any previous age, the internal logic of the game itself became intertwined with the thinking of its leading proponents. The same spirit of thought guided these thinkers

est. He was therefore feasted and invited to all the court parties. At these he sometimes met the old Duchess of Bourbon, who being a chess player of about his force, they very generally played together. Happening once to put her king into prise, the Doctor took it. 'Ah,' says she, 'we do not take kings so.' 'We do in America,' says the Doctor."

as they calculated chess moves and as they worked through philosophical problems: search, test, doubt, search again, test again, doubt, and on until the best course of action wiggled to the top.

So it was, then, that chess games were often entangled within great meetings and important conversations. "He seldom goes to bed till daybreak, drinking coffee almost every half hour, and playing at chess," a close observer wrote of Voltaire in 1767. "Next day he is never visible till noon, and then disagreeably so. . . . His house is a receptacle for all foreigners; and, as every such visitor strains his genius to entertain him, no wonder, by such a quick succession of all the several inhabitants of the four quarters of the world, that Voltaire has such an universal knowledge of mankind."

The line was often indistinguishable between the game of chess and the ideas it helped fertilize. In 1754 the Jewish philosopher Moses Mendelssohn and the Lutheran dramatist Gotthold Lessing met over a chessboard and quickly became regular opponents, good friends, and indispensable colleagues. Lessing later modeled the lead character in his play *Nathan the Wise* on Mendelssohn. The play itself includes much chess, which Lessing used both to facilitate and to drive the dialogue between the enlightened Muslim sultan Saladin and his sister Sittah. Lessing and his friends considered chess to be a useful metaphorical tool in their quest to promote social tolerance.

Chess could help this cause in two substantial ways. First, the interaction of the actual pieces offered a sophisticated comment on social stratification and the true nature of power. While at first the different pieces appeared to be severely unequal, any seasoned player knew that each had strengths to be reckoned with. Pawns, particularly working together, could hold their own and even sometimes dominate a region of the board. The lesson from this was that each member of a society has particular virtues, regardless of social rank.

Second, as a game won or lost purely on skill, chess offered as level a playing field as one could find in society. Indeed, it was the epitome of meritocracy, an arena where advancement was procured solely on the basis of skill. Judging people on their contributions to society rather than their inherited wealth, race, or religion was at the root of the campaign for social tolerance. The mutual respect between the bourgeois Lessing and the impoverished Jew Mendelssohn served as a public example for all to follow. Mendelssohn's last written work, in fact, was an intellectual defense of Lessing. The message of religious tolerance that spilled out of their friendship would reverberate for centuries.

As much as chess inspired Benjamin Franklin's thinking, it also scratched some sort of personal itch. He seemed to need to play it. Though he didn't become acquainted with chess until young adulthood—comparatively late—he made up for lost time by studying incessantly, continually working to improve his game and never missing an opportunity to play. His correspondence was riddled with references to casual games with friends. In Philadelphia in his middle years, he became more and more frustrated by the dearth of skilled opponents. Admirers frequently worked to pair him with good players, and though the game was popular among the American elite, including John Adams, John Quincy Adams, James Madison, James Monroe, and Thomas Jefferson,* accomplished chess players were a rare find. Perhaps the best player in all the colonies, Franklin was in some ways too strong for his own good. In 1752 he reported to a friend in Europe: "Honest David Martin, Rector of our Academy, my principal Antagonist at Chess, is dead, and the few remaining Players here are very indifferent, so that I have now no need of Stamma's Pamphlet [an advanced chess guide], and am glad you did not send it."

---

* Of Jefferson, a friend wrote: "He was, in his youth, a very good chess-player. There were not among his associates, many who could get the better of him. I have heard him speak of 'four hour games' with Mr. Madison. Yet I have heard him say that when, on his arrival in Paris, he was introduced into a Chess Club, he was beaten at once, and that so rapidly and signally that he gave up all competition. He felt that there was no disputing such a palm with men who passed several hours of every evening in playing chess."

In London and Paris, accomplished players abounded, and Franklin happily found himself just one of the crowd of chess aficionados. (The vastly superior chess scene there was probably not inconsequential in Franklin's spending so many years of his later life abroad.) But even in London, Franklin was always pleased to find someone new to play with. Bad timing notwithstanding, he was enthusiastic about Lady Howe's invitation.

On his first visit to her home, in late 1774, the two played several games together and enjoyed each other's company. They quickly arranged for a return visit, which featured more good chess, along with some stimulating talk. At first Lady Howe steered Franklin into a discussion of mathematics; then, abruptly, she switched to politics.

"What is to be done with this dispute between Britain and the colonies?" she blurted out. "I hope we are not to have civil war. They should kiss and be friends." Going further, she then asked Franklin bluntly if he was still willing to play a part in some sort of reconciliation.

Franklin replied that he was willing, and added that he still thought it achievable with the right interlocutors. "The two countries have really no clashing interests to differ about," said Franklin, with a diplomat's optimism. "It is rather a matter of punctilio, which two or three reasonable people might settle in half an hour."

Two cerebral individuals sat together over a symbolic game of war imagining alternative ways to settle a red-hot conflict. The scene called to mind the ancient notions that chess could assist warriors in understanding combat, and perhaps replace it. It also spoke to the psychological compulsion that many players felt. "Viewed in terms of psychoanalytic theory," psychologist Norman Reider writes, "the invention of chess expressed the triumph of secondary process thinking over the primary process. Actual warfare [is replaced by] a struggle which is organized, controlled, circumscribed and regulated."

The irony was probably not lost on Franklin at the time. But his notes reflect that he still didn't understand that his casual banter during that second meeting with Lady Howe was any more consequential than their symbolic moves on the board.

The shift occurred when Franklin entered Lady Howe's home for the third time, on Christmas Day, 1774. This time Franklin was surprised to find Lord Howe, Lady Howe's influential brother, waiting to meet him. Lord Howe represented a collection of moderates who, like Franklin, hoped to avert a collision between the crown and the colonies. He put it to Franklin directly: Would Franklin be willing to enter one final secret negotiation to avert war? Franklin agreed to take part—and now likely realized that chess had been a diplomatic tool all along. It would continue to play an important role: under cover of social chess games, Lord Howe and Franklin embarked on a secret two-month project. Publicly, Franklin kept visiting Lady Howe's home to play chess. Once inside, however, they schemed on how to prevent a real war.

The chess intrigue worked perfectly; the diplomacy failed miserably. After much discussion, it became apparent that Lord Howe and his group could not win enough government support to stop the momentum toward war. Franklin was finally forced to give up. He left for America on March 20, 1775.

His boat trip lasted six weeks; the spark of war did not take even that long. Two weeks before he landed, in the early morning of April 19, the Revolutionary War began with Paul Revere's midnight ride and the battles of Lexington and Concord.

A year later, after helping to draft the Declaration of Independence, Franklin, now aged seventy, traveled to Paris to negotiate treaties and secure a critical military alliance. There, he was thrilled to be surrounded by an overwhelming abundance of top-quality chess players. "I rarely go to the operas at Paris," Franklin said in designating chess as his cultural priority. "I call *this* my opera." He played whenever he could with colleagues and admirers, including games in the boudoir of his friend Anne-Louise Boivin d'Hardancourt Brillon de Jouy as she took exceptionally long baths.

CHESS PLAY was exploding. Throughout Europe and Russia, crowds packed chess cafés to play friends and strangers. Men and women of means, leisure, and intellectual ambition played chess just as princes and knights had centuries earlier, but now many aspired to excel at it. Much of the surging popularity and higher quality of play was due directly to the Italian master Gioacchino Greco's new popular style of chess guide. In the early seventeenth century, Greco had become the first chess instructor to chart out entire games in order to demonstrate the trajectory of various openings. That led to a dramatic public breakthrough. In the same way that *National Geographic* magazine made anthropology more accessible to a wider public in the twentieth century, Greco's full-game illustrations gave the seventeenth-century public a tangible hold on what a strategic chess game could look and feel like. The English poet Richard Lovelace later paid tribute to Greco's games (as published by the Englishman Francis Beale in 1656):

Men that could only fool at fox and geese
Are new made polititians [sic] by thy book*

With Greco's chess guides, the restless energy of the Enlightenment, and an increase in available leisure time, all of Europe now had a growing chess culture. In France, the mix was particularly combustible. Greco's games were published there in forty-one separate editions, and chess became a vital part of the Parisian landscape, played avidly in just about every café in the city.

Around 1740, the most ambitious players in Paris began to gather daily at Café de la Régence, a dingy bistro on the rue Saint-Honoré near the Louvre. Chessboards there were rented by the hour, with a higher fee at night to pay for the candlelight. The Régence quickly became not just the most popular chess café in France, but the undisputed center of the chess universe. Improbably, it stayed that way for a long

---

* "Fox and Geese" was another popular board game of the era, in which one player represents a flock of geese trying to restrict the movement of the other player's lone fox. "Polititians" refers, simply, to chess and the way all chess players pretend to direct political (or military) action on the chessboard.

time. "The Régence represents the sun, round which the lesser spheres of light revolve," reported the English chess author and collector George Walker a century later, in 1840. "It is the centre of civilised Europe, considered with regard to chess. As Flanders in days of yore was the great battle-ground . . . at which nations engaged in the duello, so for above a hundred years has this café served as the grand gladiatorial arena for chess-players of every country and colour."

Part of the electric quality of the Régence in its early years was conferred by the presence of M. de Kermur Sire de Légal, a superb chess instructor and without question the best player in Paris. His standing was such that the Régence's management put him on the payroll in order to keep him there. Then, in 1743, a teenaged musician named François-André Danican Philidor, who had been taking lessons from Légal, began beating him. Word quickly spread of a genuine new chess phenomenon.

In Paris, Holland, and London, Philidor dazzled opponents and onlookers. He had an extraordinary memory, and in 1744 (at age eighteen) shocked the world by playing two games simultaneously while blindfolded. This was not nearly a historical first. Dating all the way back to Sa'id Bin Jubair in 665, a small number of players had played blind throughout the centuries. But for citizens of the eighteenth century, who had little knowledge of previous blind play, it was new and astounding—such an astonishing combination of memory and mental acrobatics that even Philidor's mentor Légal refused to attempt it in public. In response to Philidor's reality-defying display, which he repeated seven years later with *three* players, and many times after that, the public didn't know whether to be impressed or horrified. Philidor, it was said, was "risking his sanity in such a dangerous pursuit."

In another dramatic episode, young Philidor managed to humiliate perhaps the world's most famous chess authority. Phillip Stamma was a Syrian-born player who had tantalized Europe with promises of unearthing ancient chess secrets from the Islamic world. His books of 1737 and 1745 were highly sought after by serious players of the day—including Thomas Jefferson and Benjamin Franklin. But when Stamma met Philidor in London in 1747, the Syrian fell short. Philidor beat him eight games to one, with one draw.*

Ironically, it was Philidor's style of play—not Stamma's—that truly hearkened back to the ancient days of the slower, more strategic *shatranj*. It turned out that his remarkable memory was not his most important asset. Philidor's real secret weapon was his fundamentally different way of looking at the board. "Pawns," Philidor declared, "are the very soul of the game." It was a brilliant piece of counterintuition. Philidor suggested that the Pawns, which at first glance seemed so powerless as to be expendable, could, working in concert with one another, actually exert more influence than any single piece on the board. He made Pawn structure a priority above all else, putting Pawns into diagonal arrangements to defend one another and supporting them from behind with the more prominent pieces. Slowly, his formidable Pawn fence would then creep up the board, squeezing the opponent's pieces on the other side and placing some Pawns in strong contention for promotion at the back row. Implemented correctly, this flexible strategy could defuse virtually any brilliant tactical combination wielded by an opponent.

By coincidence, Philidor's Pawn revolution came just as lasting egalitarian ideals were coming into play in the real world. John Locke had proposed that all men are created equal, with God-given "natural rights" of life, liberty, and property, and that governments should exist only "with the consent of the governed." The American Revolution would soon be the living embodiment of these ideals. This chess–life concurrence could not have been lost on figures such as Jean-Jacques Rousseau, avid chess player and author of the famous declaration "Man is born free but everywhere he is in chains." Along with Voltaire, Rousseau frequented the Café de la Régence and called chess one of his "expedients." In a self-deprecating remark that highlighted the distinction between chess intelligence and other types of intelligence, Rousseau said: "I became acquainted with M. de Légal, M. Husson, Philidor,

---

* The official score was eight games to two, because Philidor had offered that any draw should count as a win for Stamma.

and all the great chess players of the day, without making the least improvement in the game."

In his memoirs, Rousseau used chess to demonstrate his conviction of speaking truth to power. On one occasion, Rousseau bragged, he not only had the opportunity to play France's Prince de Conti, but also displayed the courage to beat him: "Notwithstanding the signs and grimace of the chevalier and the spectators, which I feigned not to see," he later wrote, "I won the two games we played. When they were ended, I said to him in a respectful but very grave manner: 'My lord, I honor your serene highness too much not to beat you always at chess.' This great prince, who had real wit, sense, and knowledge, and so was worthy not to be treated with mean adulation, felt in fact, at least I think so, that I was the only person present who treated him like a man, and I have every reason to believe he was not displeased with me for it."

Voltaire and Rousseau were not the only shining lights of the age that visited the Café de la Régence. The chess center also afforded a brief encounter between Benjamin Franklin and his chess hero Philidor. Arriving at the Régence one day in 1781 with a copy of Philidor's book, Franklin was quickly ushered to the sacred table, where the author's signature was procured. Afterward, finding Philidor otherwise engaged, Franklin quickly excused himself.

"François!" exclaimed proprietor Jacques Labar. "You just autographed your book for the American Ambassador!"

At which point, Philidor raised his head for the first time and remarked, "That's funny, I never knew that he was a chess player."

THE IMMORTAL GAME

Moves 6 and 7

MANY SERIOUS CHESS PLAYERS talk about chess largely in artistic terms, comparing brilliant games to masterful paintings or great symphonies. But they do acknowledge one key difference. "It is a pity," says Anthony Saidy, "that, unlike music or painting, chess requires of the viewer an initial period of instruction before revealing its aesthetic quality."

A pity indeed for all of us chess novices—since many of us long to at least appreciate superb chess even if we don't have a realistic hope of ever attaining it.

Fortunately, there is another route to true chess appreciation, separate from the rote memorization of openings, tactics, and strategies. It is to study the history of play—not just legendary encounters like the Immortal Game, but also how an array of many different well-played games fit within the various styles of play introduced over time: the evolution of chess play. Since chess is largely a game of knowledge built on past experience, there is a demonstrable arc to its progress, dating back to the beginning of the modern game, circa 1475. Each era learns from past eras, and develops a new level of sophistication.

This idea of chess's stylistic evolution was introduced to me by Nicholas Chatzilias, a young, Brooklyn-based chess instructor whom I met one day while looking into the New York–based program Chess-in-the-Schools. Over a sandwich near an elementary school in Sheepshead Bay, I shamelessly name-dropped my famous chess ancestor, Samuel Rosenthal, and immediately got a bright-eyed look in response. "You're related to *him*?" he said. "I teach some of Rosenthal's games in my chess club."

I asked how games over a century old could be useful in chess instruction today. Chatzilias explained how the games from different eras fit together like links in a chain. Studying a sequence of them in context, we can understand not only the collective knowledge of chess, but also how that knowledge coalesced over time. It's the same reason we study the history of anything. Any knowledge is an accumulation of experience and can give off a harsh glare if suddenly imparted all at once as though it were divine revelation. Better to understand it as an organic entity, with a rich and glowing life history.

Chatzilias suggested I pick up a copy of Anthony Saidy's *The March of Chess Ideas*, which I did immediately. That book runs through the four great eras of chess play: Romantic, Scientific, Hypermodern, and the New Dynamism. Hoping to understand them all, I approached them in chronological order; for one simply cannot understand a later style without understanding its predecessors. The first period, Romantic play, stretched all the way from 1475 to the 1880s, and was characterized by swashbuckling attacks, clever combinations, and a relative lack of long-term planning. Romantic chess was almost all tactics (short-term maneuvering) and very little strategy (long-term planning). It was chess as hand-to-hand combat.

I was glad to know about the Romantic school of chess, because it fit well with how *I* wanted to play—attack, trick, surprise, attack again. It turns out that Romantic chess is the style *every* novice player wants to play, because it is innocent fun and because we simply don't know any better. It is also how great chess masters played for centuries—because *they* didn't know any better. In a game that presented trillions upon trillions of possibilities, effective strategic planning was simply too difficult to intuit; instead, it took hundreds of years to evolve. Even after Philidor, in the mid-eighteenth century, had proven the virtue of his Pawn strategy, contributing the first real inkling of a more holistic, strategic approach to the game, the

Romantic school continued on for more than another century. The great Romantic masters steadily cooked up more and more dastardly tactical tricks to try and outmaneuver one another.

Looking back now, the Immortal Game stands as the pinnacle of Romanticism. It was one of its greatest monuments; its winner would forever be known as the Romantic school's all-time great practitioner. Both Anderssen and Kieseritzky knew of Philidor's legacy, of course. But like all great players of their era, they fundamentally ignored his major ideas and stuck to the Romantic style—good, quick, exciting, tactical chess, ingenious combinations and attacks.

In his next-to-last opening move, Anderssen (White) developed his Knight to f3.

6. Nf3
(White Knight to f3)

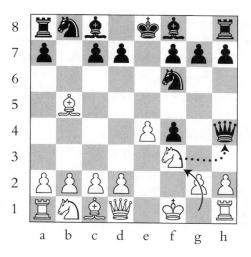

This packed a particular punch because it developed a piece, put pressure on two center squares, and attacked the Black Queen—all at the same time.

The Knight attack forced the Black Queen to retreat to h6.

6. . . . Qh6
(Black Queen to h6)

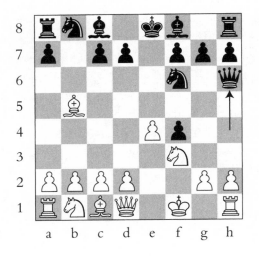

Saving his Queen was a necessary move for Black, of course, but also a wasted one. Kieseritzky accomplished absolutely nothing else, and he hadn't even completely removed his Queen from danger. He would soon be forced to save her again. Meanwhile, Anderssen was developing at a healthy pace, and with every move getting something else accomplished.

On the other hand, Kieseritzky may have liked his position at this point, because if he could regain the offensive he had many provocative possible moves. He hoped it would soon be his turn to start vexing White.

7. d3
(White Queen's Pawn to d3)

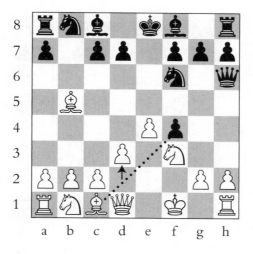

White then moved to protect his Pawn on e4 by moving his Queen's Pawn forward one square to d3. This was also a nice developing move, which allowed White's Bishop to put some pressure on the Black Pawn on f4.

7. . . . Nh5
(Black Knight to h5)

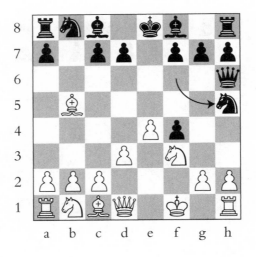

Black responded with a decidedly nondeveloping move: Knight to h5.* Thus middlegame began. If the opening moves in each chess game are a coy dance, a limbering up, some tentative steps in the ring where one takes a few pokes at one's opponent to flush out his soft spots, the next phase of the game is something else altogether. The middlegame is full-on combat, thorny, dense, and unpredictable. "Play the opening like a book, the middle game like a magician, and the endgame like a machine," Viennese player Rudolf Spielmann would later advise. Even the most experienced players, familiar with hundreds of opening combinations, do not know for sure where they are headed in the middlegame, and must rely on intuition when they get there. This is where mere *billions* of game possibilities become

---

* This was not a developing move because that Knight had previously been moved out of its starting position—it had already been developed. Rather than developing his other Knight, or a Bishop or a Pawn, Black moved the King's Knight a second time.

trillions upon trillions, and every player confronts distinct chess molecules that they have never seen before and will never see again.

It is also the leap into the wide-eyed thrill of the game. Now so many pieces are in play that anything can happen. For master or novice, it is often a glorious place to be: no more waiting around on the beach; now you are smacking against high, crashing, erratic ocean waves. Is that a life raft headed your way, or a saw-toothed shark? For a short time during the middlegame it may be impossible to tell, and that's much of the fun.

(It may not last long. Soon the thrill may decay into emptiness and dread, with a gnawing feeling that your opponent has a much keener understanding of where the game is heading, and has probably already bested you. Yes, you can feel his cold shadow now, even if you can't yet see it. You are falling inexorably into his invisible trap. Though it looks like the game is more or less even, you are actually already drawing your final few full breaths.)

In a conventional twenty-first-century game, the players do not usually arrive at the middlegame until somewhere around move 10 or 12, and the arrival is most often signaled by both sides castling for safety. By then, most or all of the Bishops and Knights have been developed, and the hypercomplex interplay of threats and counterthreats can begin.

Rigid definitions of chess's stages cannot, of course, begin to capture all the spectacular variation and the creative possibility inherent in the game. They are nevertheless useful, pointing to some unavoidable realities. In a competitive chess game, development is crucial. Failing to develop one's pieces as efficiently as possible in the opening moves is like neglecting to vaccinate young children. Death isn't *certain*, but you can expect to face serious trouble. An undeveloped position quickly cedes board control to the opponent, and forces one to play a defensive game with fewer and fewer decent options.

Looking back at the start of this particular middlegame, some modern experts would turn down their noses at Kieseritzky's 7. . . . Nh5, regarding it as reckless. In making this attacking move, Black was passing up the opportunity to consolidate his position—to develop his major pieces and protect his King by castling.

That judgment, however, was only worthwhile in the context of twenty-first-century knowledge, which included an extensive catalogue of weaknesses and how they could be exploited. This body of knowledge made the modern chess expert far superior to past experts, but only because they stood on a mountain of understanding. In 1851, 7. . . . Nh5 was thought to be a strong attack move, threatening . . . Ng3+, which, if he achieved it, would end up winning a Rook and inflicting all sorts of damage.

In the context of the time, this game was still wide open.

6. THE EMPEROR AND THE IMMIGRANT

Chess and the Unexpected Gifts of War

TOWARD THE END OF the eighteenth century, the Café de la Régence chess den in Paris saw daily visits from an ambitious young lieutenant named Napoleon Bonaparte. "He played the openings badly," reported British chess writer George Walker in 1840, "and was impatient if his adversary dwelt too long upon his move. . . . Under defeat at chess, the great soldier was sore and irritable."

Napoleon never became a great chess player, but he played passionately his entire life, and took the game everywhere—to battles in Egypt, Russia, and across Europe, sparring constantly against his aides and top generals. "Even at the height of his great campaigns, when he was making mincemeat of the best generals in Europe," offer British writers Mike Fox and Richard James, "he took time off to get thrashed by his own generals over the chessboard." While his skill level did not improve much over time, his proportion of victories did: after he assumed supreme power, his underling opponents frequently found it inconvenient to win. Later, when Napoleon was powerless and exiled to the tiny island of St. Helena, he probably found the competition somewhat stiffer. In any case, he continued to play. The conqueror who had once controlled a large portion of the world was reduced to fighting the rest of his wars on sixty-four squares. (His isolation seemed even more pitiable when it was learned, more than a century later, that an elaborate escape plan had been delivered—but never quite *revealed*—to the exiled emperor. The plan's instructions were embedded in an ivory chess set which was given to Napoleon, but the French officer ordered to disclose the hidden plans had died on the voyage. Napoleon played chess on the special board for the rest of his life without knowing its true significance.)

Napoleon is regarded as one of history's great military geniuses, able to outmaneuver his opponents with a combination of clever tactics and sound strategy. It is no real surprise to learn that this brilliance did not carry over to the conceptual geometry of the chessboard. But what about influence in the other direction? Did Napoleon's countless hours over chess's war board help him with his real-war planning? Napoleon apparently thought so. "He was even wont to say," wrote Walker, "that he frequently struck out new features relatively to a campaign, first suggested by the occurrence of certain positions of the pieces on the chessboard."

This echoed other comments and legends over the game's long span, chess having been a close companion to military commanders from the legendary Indian King Balhait, to Caliph Harun ar-Rashid in the eighth century, to the eleventh-century Norman king William the Conqueror (reported to have broken a chessboard over a French prince's head after a frustrating game), to the fourteenth-century Turkmen Mongol conqueror Tamerlane (who once named a newly conquered town "Shahrukhiya," after a potent chess move that simultaneously attacked an opponent's King and Rook), to Frederick the Great of Prussia, to World War II's George Patton, to Desert Storm's Norman Schwarzkopf.

How, though, could an abstract game with no connection to real weapons, real soldiers, or real terrain be of any use to commanders facing actual battle conditions?

Obviously, a board game with thirty-two symbolic pieces is far removed from the unpredictable grit and gruesome blood salad of war. But that very removal, ironically, is what makes the game a highly relevant and constructive tool. We all take in a surprising amount of practical knowledge from abstraction: abstract reasoning, according to many experts, is what defines human intelligence. By removing ourselves from the morass of functional detail, we can isolate goals, tactics, strategies, patterns—meaning. "Truly practical men give their minds free play about a subject without asking too closely at every point for the advantage to be gained," wrote John Dewey in his 1910 landmark book *How We Think*. "Exclusive preoccupation with matters of use and application so narrows the horizon as in the long run to defeat itself. . . . Power in action requires some largeness and imaginativeness of vision."

So it is with military chiefs charting a course of battle. Reducing an expansive, chaotic battlefield to a handful of symbolic elements gives generals "free play" in war—an opportunity to explore notions of pacing, mobilization, positioning, and surprise, without having to worry about the immediate practical application. In the same way that a painter might sit for an hour in front of a Monet for inspiration, even though she intends to paint a different subject in a completely different style, chess is an ideal reflection pool for war planners. It inspires in them Dewey's "largeness and imaginativeness of vision."

For all of his countless hours of chess concentration, Napoleon may not have been able to show much progress on the chessboard, but he was probably correct in thinking that he'd had a much more significant payoff on his larger battlefields. High-ranking war commanders, after all, are not the sort of people who like to waste time.

The chess–war connection would continue straight into the twenty-first century, with researchers exploiting the game in new ways. In South Australia, analysts from the national Defence Science and Technology Organisation devised an exhaustive computer analysis of chess games in which they examined three key variables:

material (number of pieces per player)
tempo (number of moves allowed a player each turn)
search depth (number of moves ahead)

How would a chess game be affected if these fundamentals were slightly altered? What would happen, for example, if one player had more material but the other side was allowed to make two quick moves in a row? Or if one player could make multiple moves versus the opponent's ability to analyze five moves ahead instead of three? The researchers also wanted to know how the game would be affected if they took away some of the information, making certain pieces invisible to the opponent in some games. "There's all sorts of anecdotal evidence that there are certain factors in warfare that are [more] important," explained Greg Colbert, a mathematician on the Australian team. "But even today there's debate over what really counts. How important is stealth over tempo, or tempo over numerical strength? That's what we wanted to find out."

It was an effort to systematically gain from chess the type of insights into war that human generals had been extracting intuitively for centuries. And it appeared to pay off. One conclusion by the Australians was that a combination of deep searching and increased tempo easily overwhelmed an opposing force with significantly greater material. (Interestingly, this would also turn out to be true for the Immortal Game.) Some of the telling data happened to come in just as the United States was planning its 2003 invasion of Iraq, researchers recalled. "We watched with great interest the dialogue between General [Tommy] Franks, who wanted to use more material, and [Secretary of Defense] Donald Rumsfeld, who wanted a fast tempo and lighter units," Australian researcher Jason Schulz said. "In the end, there was a compromise. But a relatively fast tempo did really gain a very decisive, rapid advantage in Iraq."

NAPOLEON'S CONQUESTS eventually fizzled, his short-lived empire shriveled, and he died in exile in 1821. Meanwhile, his old chess haunt, the Café de la Régence, continued to bustle as Europe began to enjoy the real fruits of the Industrial Revolution. The broad shift from agricultural to factory work in the nineteenth century initially left workers with no additional leisure time; conditions were gruesome and hours were all-consuming. Eventually, though, regulations and the labor movement forced factories to adopt more humane hours, creating a large new class of people with some leisure time; chess and other activities were there to fill in the gap. While the game still attracted the aristocracy, it also reached deeply into the growing European middle class.

The expansion was especially evident in England. From 1824 to 1828, the British public became fascinated with a five-game, four-year contest between the Edinburgh Chess Club and the London Chess Club (Edinburgh won). That event fed interest in accessible and inexpensive books such as William Lewis's *Chess for Beginners* (1835) and George Walker's *Chess Made Easy* (1836). Thereafter, regular chess columns sprung up in European and American newspapers, and the game began to creep into not just erudite but also popular literature. "Kitty, can you play chess?" Alice asks at the start of Lewis Carroll's *Through the Looking Glass and What Alice Found There* (his second *Alice* book). "Now don't smile, my dear, I'm asking it seriously. Because, when we were playing just now, you watched just as if you understood it: and when I said 'Check!' you purred! Well, it *was* a nice check, Kitty, and really I might have won if it hadn't been for that nasty Knight, that came wriggling down among my pieces."

Chess was moving swiftly beyond the chattering classes now, deep into the madding crowd. "The din of voices shakes the roof as we enter," George Walker reported of his 1840 visit to the Café de la Régence.

Can this be chess?—the game of philosophers—the wrestling of the strong-minded—the recreation of pensive solitude—thus practised amid a roar like that of the Regent's Park beast-show at feeding time! Laughter, whistling, singing, screaming, spitting, spouting, and shouting,—tappings, rappings, drummings, and hummings, disport in their glory around us. Have we not made a blunder, and dropped into the asylum of Charenton?

Walker was in the right place. And though other chess cafés weren't quite as pulsating as the Régence, high-quality chess could now be found in Berlin, Warsaw, Vienna, Moscow, Rome, London, and elsewhere. Travel and long-distance communication were cheaper and easier than ever, and the international chess community now mingled regularly. Leading players from all over Europe established closer contact with one another with every passing decade, constantly testing and refining their most ambitious ideas. The better the communication, the farther and faster chess theory was able to advance. In this respect, chess mirrored social and industrial progress: ideas and cultures colliding, blending, improving.

In the mid-nineteenth century, a number of top players, among them Austrian masters Ernst Falkbeer and Wilhelm Steinitz, emigrated to London, helping to transform that city into a full-fledged rival to Paris as the chess capital of the world. All of this inspired *Illustrated London News* chess columnist Howard Staunton in 1851 to organize the world's first true international tournament in London—timed to coincide with a major international fair in the same city.

In this era of play, stamina was vital. With no time controls in place—they would come into use about a decade later—a single game could easily last ten hours or more. Championship chess play therefore required a fertile mix of intellectual prowess, personal charisma, and outright staying power. "Comfort is not particularly high," Adolf Anderssen wrote in a letter from the 1851 tournament. "Chairs and tables are small and low; all free space next to the players was occupied by a [recording assistant]. In short there was not a single place where you could rest your weary head during the hard fight. For the English player, more comfort is not required. He sits straight as a poker on his chair, keeps his thumbs in his waistcoat pockets, and does not move until he for an hour has [surveyed] the chessboard. His opponent has sighed hundreds of times when the Englishman eventually moves his piece."

Perhaps stamina came naturally to my ancestor Samuel Rosenthal, raised as he was in an impoverished Jewish ghetto in the thick forests of

northeast Poland. Jews had lived in Poland at least as far back as the
fourteenth century, under varying degrees of persecution. Chess had
been around at least three hundred years before that, brought back from
a Crusade by Polish knights. In 1103 the knight Pierzchala is said to
have checkmated the Duke of Mazovia with a Rook, earning a new es-
tate and a Rook-laden crest. (To this day, chessboards, Knights, and
Rooks appear on dozens of ancient family crests across Europe.) In 1564
a mock-epic poem, *Chess,* parodied the style of Homer and Virgil in de-
tailing a heroic chess battle with a "wooden army." The six-hundred-
line poem reveals, among other things, how well steeped the Polish
literate class was in the game.

Sandwiched between Germany, Prussia, Hungary, Slovakia, Lith-
uania, and Russia, Poland succumbed many times over the centuries to
foreign rule. Napoleon "liberated" Poland in 1806 but lost it to the
Russians in 1813. Poles chafed constantly under the Russian yoke
throughout the nineteenth century. In 1863, when Rosenthal was
twenty-six, a major Polish revolt against Russian rule left the Jews
squeezed even tighter than usual. By this time, Rosenthal had moved
150 miles southwest to Warsaw (also under Russian control), where he
studied law and played a lot of chess at the popular cafe Pod
Dzwonnicą ("Under the Bell Tower"). He joined the popular uprising
of 1863, was persecuted after its failure, and left Poland the following
year. Joining many others fleeing through Germany to France (following the path of earlier Polish émigrés, including Frédéric Chopin), he
settled in Paris and quickly became a fixture at the most famous chess
café of all.

It wasn't long before he had taken over the place. Rosenthal's young
competitors in Warsaw had been among the very sharpest in Europe,
and he brought to Paris a stamina and consistency that immediately
overwhelmed most of his native French competitors. He won the
Régence's championship in 1865 and repeated his triumph in 1866 and
1867. As the new dean of French chess, he began drawing invitations
to the leading international tournaments. He represented Paris in

Baden-Baden in 1870, in Bonn in 1877, and in London in 1883, where he twice defeated the great champion Wilhelm Steinitz.* In 1884–85, Rosenthal led a Paris team against Vienna in a two-game correspondence match that lasted twenty months. (For his effort, Rosenthal was presented with a spectacular engraved gold pocket watch—the watch that entered our family lore.) In 1887 he was awarded, by the Spanish queen regent, the Charles III Order for his contributions to chess.

With his public displays, café and tournament wins, magazine columns, and private tutoring, Rosenthal was said by Wilhelm Steinitz to be one of the few chess players in the nineteenth century who made a nice living from chess. It didn't hurt that he mentored some of the leading public figures in France—Prime Minister Pierre Tirard, the society portraitist Raimundo de Madrazo, and the powerful French banking family Pereire. His star pupil was Prince Napoleon, a nephew of Napoleon Bonaparte. The relationship brought into striking contrast the young immigrant and the chess-obsessed emperor: two serious chess players, habitués of the very same chess café (if decades apart). One astonished the world with his military prowess but could not—try as he might—duplicate that success on the chessboard. The other made chess his *only* battlefield, forcefully embracing the military metaphor.

Perhaps with Bonaparte in mind, Rosenthal pushed the chess–war comparison to its limit. He wrote:

> Both soldiers and players, regardless of their talent, must know a certain theory and certain principles. Indeed, his theory resembles ours. Isn't it true that it teaches him to conduct his troops on a battlefield,

---

* "Steinitz has been known to grieve much when he has lost at chess," wrote H. E. Bird in 1893. "At Dundee, for example, in 1866 after his defeat by De Vere his friends became alarmed at his woe and disappearance. Again, after his fall to Rosenthal in a game he should have won at the Criterion in 1883, news were brought that he was on a seat in St. James' Park quite uncontrollable."

according to established rules, to reassemble at the opportune moment, to have them converge at a determined point, in the briefest span of time? Shouldn't he try to make the others attack him there where he is the strongest, to change fronts when the opponent attacks him at his vulnerable point, to manage his soldiers' lives for the ultimate moment? . . .

I could make an infinite number of comparisons, for the two are sisters: the path one follows, the method one uses to succeed in chess, are absolutely identical to those that the greatest commanders recommend.

Was Samuel Rosenthal one of chess's "greatest commanders"? Yes and no. Though for three decades he was considered about the best player in France (he "reigned supreme as the leader of Parisian chess," reported the *Chicago Tribune* after his death) and was considered one of the top two dozen players in the world, and though he managed to beat legendary players like world champion Wilhelm Steinitz, Russian champion Mikhail Tchigorin, Polish sensation Simon Winawer, and even Adolf Anderssen in a number of individual games, he never won a major international tournament and was never considered a real contender for the world championship. He captivated the French public, but could not make a permanent mark in chess history. Today he is remembered only by historians and by players who study past masters. A number of his games are included in noted books of analysis, and his own book of analysis on the London tournament of 1900, *Traité des échecs et recueil des parties jouées au tournoi i international de 1900* (a brittle, yellowed author's copy of which was passed down to his youngest granddaughter—my grandmother—and then to me) has been judged by competitive players to be remarkably insightful.

Perhaps just as important as his play was his insistence that chess and war are "sisters." His words frankly do not carry the same eloquence as those of Benjamin Franklin, but in his own way Rosenthal did advance a critical point about chess's social consequence. He was echoing not just Franklin, who had described chess as battle without bloodshed, but many other observers over the years, including twelfth-century Jewish scholar Abraham ibn Ezra, who wrote of the game:

All slaughter each other
Wasting with great wrath each other
    . . . with yet no bloodshed.

As useful as chess may have been to war commanders throughout the ages, it perhaps has been far more useful in bringing the discipline of war to the rest of us. Chess, along with other ancient competitive sports, helped to introduce the concept of nonviolent rivalry. It helped us—and helps us still—crystallize the concept of war without bloodshed. Chess, a game of war, teaches peace.

Civilization today would be lost without the option of bloodless war. The free market depends on it. All politics and diplomacy rest on it. Science, academia, and mediated culture all thrive because of it. The institutions that today give support to our complex and rich world of ideas are sustained first and foremost by brutal, yet bloodless, competition. This is a legacy of chess—not just that it helped train warriors in their art but, more importantly, that it helped transport that same all-out competitive spirit into a peaceful sphere. "For Life is a kind of Chess," declared Benjamin Franklin, "in which we have often points to gain, and competitors or adversaries to contend with."

THE IMMORTAL GAME

Moves 8 and 9

THE ROMANTICS LOVED TO ATTACK, and their games were thrilling to watch. In due course, their style would be made ob-solete. Other inventive players would come along and devise more whole-game, strategic styles that would suffocate the impatient, merely tactical player. But until then, the best players in the world played what they knew.

In this game, Kieseritzky (Black) was setting up for a devastating attack on Anderssen's Kingside. His Queen was already in position. He'd already taken one of Anderssen's Pawns on that side, and he had disabled Anderssen's ability to castle. Finally, in move 7, he had put his Knight on h5, threatening Knight to g3 in the next move, which would simultaneously check White's King and attack his Rook. Kieseritzky knew what he was doing. He'd done this before.

Anderssen, of course, had no choice but to respond.

8. Nh4
(White Knight to h4)

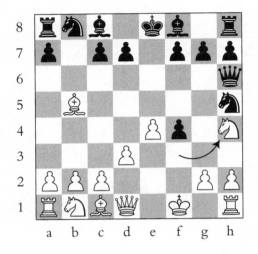

By moving his Knight to h4, Anderssen was able to blunt the attack. If Black now moved Knight to g3, White could safely capture with his Pawn on h2 without exposing his Rook on h1 to capture by the Black Queen.

But White's smart defense couldn't yet blunt Black's offense. He had another attacking move in store.

8. . . . Qg5

(Black Queen to g5)

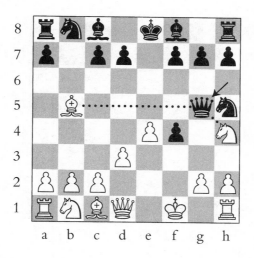

Kieseritzky moved his Queen to g5, simultaneously threatening Anderssen's Bishop and his Knight. Attacking two pieces at once is called a fork, and is highly desirable for obvious reasons. It is often inevitable that the opponent is going to lose one piece or the other.

9. Nf5

(White Knight to f5)

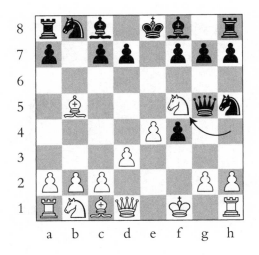

But Anderssen had the perfect defense. In an almost uncanny turn, his only real move here—maneuvering his Knight to the f5 square, not only simultaneously protected both the threatened Knight and the threatened Bishop, but was also an attacking move that he had planned for some time. The f5 square is known as a very strong place for the White Knight, for obvious reasons: it puts the Knight one move away from a possible check.

It looked like dumb luck, but this sort of good fortune happens routinely to players who carefully plan their moves. A move that effectively combines necessary defense with desirable offense is commonly referred to as "gaining a tempo." The player has gained in one single move what might have ordinarily taken two or more moves to accomplish. The concept of tempo is one of the most important in chess.

Anderssen had already gained several tempi in this game, while Kieseritzky had lost a few. That said, Kieseritzky might still have felt pretty good about his position. The simple fact was that the White

Kingside was in a shambles. If Black could find the time to develop some more pressure on the Kingside, he'd be in a strong position to win.

9. . . . c6
(Black Pawn to c6)

Kieseritzky then issued another threat to Anderssen's Bishop by pushing his c Pawn one square forward. He believed he was gaining a tempo here, forcing Anderssen into a defensive posture while making a simple developing move himself. In the next move, Anderssen's response would indicate whether he agreed that he had just lost some of his momentum.

CHUNKING AND TASKING

Chess and the Working Mind

AS MUCH AS FOR HIS playing skills, Samuel Rosenthal was admired for his teaching, his writing, and his showmanship. "Sitting on his chair, blindfolded and motionless," recalled an adoring obituary, "he appeared petrified in his extraordinary thinness. Only his stirring lips

Samuel Rosenthal, the author's great-great-grandfather,
in a simultaneous display in Paris, 1891

would indicate his next move." Even without the blindfold, Rosenthal put on phenomenal public displays, as captured here in an 1891 Paris drawing by the French artist Louis Tinayre.

Such demonstrations electrified the public, but were no longer the otherworldly oddity that they had been a century earlier in Philidor's time. A number of chess masters now took part in blindfold games—so many, in fact, that as a group they attracted the attention of a young French psychologist named Alfred Binet, who was curious to understand the cognition behind them. How on earth did these players juggle memory and analysis so well? In the 1890s, as part of what would ultimately emerge as a career-long dedication to the definition and measurement of human intelligence, Binet was trying to understand the dynamics of memory. He became fascinated by blindfold chess players and their awesome displays of visual memory. Exactly how did they do it?

The conventional wisdom at the time, endorsed by Binet, was that strong visual memory was based in photographic-type recall. It appeared that great chess players somehow had a highly advanced ability to form mental pictures of chess pieces and boards and to preserve those pictures in their minds. They had, Binet theorized, an extraordinary "inner mirror," which would forever reflect back to them, move by move, every successive configuration of the board. This notion was supported by more than two thousand years of memory literature and science that depicted memory as being visually based. The ancient Greeks, with no printing press and no pen and ink, had developed the art of mnemonics—mental tricks that relied on visualization to remember large amounts of detail. Typically, a mnemonist would "deposit" difficult-to-remember information into imagined compartments, seats, or rooms.

Now Binet wanted to determine how such memory tricks actually worked. Inspired by the work of the British anthropologist Francis Galton, he had developed a passion for exploring the healthy working mind, as opposed to the pathology of mental illness. The blindfold chess study was one of his first as assistant director of the Laboratory of

Physiological Psychology at the Sorbonne. His subjects included the accomplished chess masters Stanislaus Sittenfeld, Alphonse Goetz, Siegbert Tarrasch, and the dean of French chess, Samuel Rosenthal. In Binet's laboratory, they were questioned intensively about what they "saw" when they played chess blindfolded. The results were surprising and instructive. Binet was humbled to find that his "inner mirror" theory did not pan out. Astounding chess memories, he learned, did not resemble a collection of photographic snapshots. They were much more abstract than that, more geometric, and more *meaningful*.

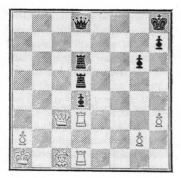 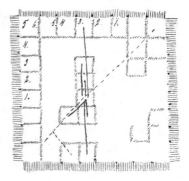

An actual chess position (left) used in the 1890s Binet study, alongside a hand-drawn rendering by the master player Stanislaus Sittenfeld of how, with eyes closed, he pictured the position in his mind.

The intricate chess positions, it turned out, were not stored in chess masters' brains as distinct photolike snapshots, but as a more abstract set of integrated patterns—like a musician's chords or a computer programmer's code. What looked like a chaotic field of data to the nonexpert was to the expert a coherent, meaningful song. "I grasp it as a musician grasps harmony in his orchestra," offered French master Alphonse Goetz. "I am often carried to sum up the character of a position in a general epithet . . . it strikes you as simple and familiar, or as original, exciting and suggestive."

In the mind of Goetz and the other chess masters, each portion of every game triggered impressions, feelings, and observations as meaningful to them as pieces of a car engine are to a mechanic, or as cloud formations are to a meteorologist. In these players' minds, there were no sterile boards or carved wooden chess figurines—only evocative configurations that were familiar or somehow resonant. Ultimately, it wasn't even the chess positions themselves that they were warehousing so much as the impressions they sparked. "It is the multitude of suggestions and ideas emanating from a game," concluded Binet, "which makes it interesting and establishes it in memory."

This insight was not inconsistent with long-standing visual notions of memory, but it provided a key clarification: visual memory operated not by recording a multitude of snapshots, but by encoding information in a meaningful context. It turned out that mnemonics was not so much visual as it was *meaningful*. Great chess players, then, were not simply finely tuned camera-computers, adept at acquiring and processing visual data with superlative efficiency. Rather, Binet's study proved their craft to be supremely human—a combination of resonant feelings, meaningful experiences, and rich memories. Studying chess memory proved that abstract thought and memory were fully entangled with human feeling.

A further surprising revelation of the Binet chess study was the degree to which photographiclike recall of visuals could actually hamper visual memory. "Some part of every chess game is played blindfold," explained leading German player Siegbert Tarrasch in a letter to Binet explaining his thought process. "The sight of the chessman frequently upsets one's calculations." This comment echoed the sentiment of other top players. What they remembered was not a tactile reproduction of the pieces on the board, but rather an abstract sense of each piece's properties and movement. In fact, it was the mediocre players striving to recall actual pieces on a board who inevitably fell short. Binet's photographic theory had not only been wrong; the truth was quite the opposite.

Binet's observations marked the first stage in a century-long effort by scores of psychologists and cognitive scientists to understand how great chess players think—and to incorporate those lessons into other areas of cognition research. Justifiably proud of his pioneering discovery, Binet was also humbled at the study's conclusion by how much more there was to understand about memory and thought. "Though we search and examine in the most minute details," he wrote, "we cannot comprehend with precision the complexity of intellectual activity."

He was impressed, too, by the degree to which chess turned out to be a model for the mind's intricacy. "The blindfold [chess] game," Binet observed, "contains everything: power of concentration, scholarship, visual memory, not to mention strategic talent, patience, courage, and many other faculties. If one could see what goes on in a chess player's head, one would find a stirring world of sensations, images, movements, passions and an ever changing panorama of states of consciousness. By comparison with these our most attentive descriptions are but grossly simplified schemata."

Binet's original hypothesis might have been wrong, but his insight of chess as a powerful lens into the workings of the mind was astoundingly prescient. In fact, it gave birth to a century of chess investigation that would substantially help rewrite our understanding of the human mind. In the ensuing few decades, a few researchers followed up on Binet's important work. But it wasn't until 1946 that Dutch psychologist (and master chess player) Adriaan de Groot picked up where Alfred Binet had left off fifty years earlier. De Groot published a study called *Thought and Choice in Chess*, which investigated the skills, speed, style, and articulation of four separate skill levels of the chess player—from grandmasters to ordinary club players. Among his conclusions, de Groot startled the cognitive world with the observation that great players did *not* actually calculate significantly more or faster than lesser players. They also did not have better memories for raw data. Instead, they recognized more patterns more quickly, so as to make more relevant calculations and therefore better decisions.

With his work, de Groot helped to invent a new field of study—cognitive science—that aimed to systematize and deconstruct the thought process. Cognitive science was created by members of older, more established disciplines—psychology, neurology, linguistics, sociology, and anthropology. It was inherently interdisciplinary, a recognition that better understanding of the mind could be gained only through a steady dialogue among experts from these disparate fields. Chess was considered an essential tool of the new field, allowing researchers to study how the mind works as a machine, combining memory, logic, calculation, and creativity.

In 1973 Carnegie Mellon psychologists William Chase and Herbert Simon published two landmark works that built on de Groot's chess work and that introduced one of the most important cognitive concepts in the twentieth century: a new understanding of memory called "chunking."

Chunking is a memory technique used by all human beings to convert a collection of details into a single memory. Phone numbers, for example, are stored not as ten separate numbers but in three easy chunks: 513-555-9144. Remembering ten unrelated items in the right order is difficult; remembering three is no problem. The same technique applies to reading words, music, or any other complex array of symbols—including chess positions.

Chess, in fact, helped Chase and Simon formulate their theory in the first place. In their experiment they assembled three groups of chess players: *masters* (among the top twenty-five players in the nation); *experienced players* (ranked in the eighty-fifth percentile); and *novices* (who had spent little or no time studying the game). Each group was asked to:

1. Reproduce a particular board position after viewing it for five seconds.
2. Study an entire twenty-five-move chess game and recall a series of different positions from the game.

Based on their reading of de Groot's work, Chase and Simon hypothesized that chess skill depended largely on what players already knew—as opposed to how much new data they could remember. The data fit the hypothesis. Superior players did not have intrinsically faster or better memory skills, but their vastly deeper, broader, and better-organized store of chess knowledge allowed them to recognize patterns faster and to form chunks quicker and more reliably. Their brains were not necessarily any faster than other brains; through much work, they had tuned them to be more *efficient*.

Chunking was a landmark discovery, one of those ideas so brilliant it immediately seemed obvious. But for cognitive scientists working with chess, it was only just the beginning. Chase and Simon declared chess to be the drosophila, or fruit fly, of cognitive psychology. Just as the fruit fly was the ideal laboratory model for heredity—the right genetic complexity, quick to reproduce, physical traits easily manipulated by genetic tinkering—so chess was for the study of the human mind. Its attributes were particularly suitable for scientists seeking to unlock questions about decision making, attention, and consciousness.

Others have since concurred. "Just as biologists need model organisms to explore genetics," writes the University of Waterloo's Neil Charness, "so too do cognitive scientists need model task environments to study adaptive cognitive mechanisms. Chess playing provides a rich task environment that taps many cognitive processes, ranging from perception, to memory, to problem solving." In a 1992 study, Charness exhaustively reviewed chess's impact on the field. The list of contributions was overwhelming. Among other areas, chess had shone light on the superiority of internal over external motivation; on the role of emotions in problem solving; on which parts of the brain are activated in spatial thought; on the physical maturation of brain components; and on the effects of aging on problem solving, memory, and perception.

One observation seemed to stand out. Cognitive chess research punctured the long-standing myth of the chess prodigy, the born genius—and in doing so, it contributed to one of the great ongoing discussions of our time: *How great minds are formed.* "One of the important points that chess research has made since its inception," concludes Charness, "is that chess experts are made, not born."

We've all heard the story in one version or another: A young child wanders into view of some chess play in progress, watches silently through a few games, and then asks or is invited to play. It's all in good fun, the adults happy to take a break from mind-stretching play and to encourage the child's tiptoe into the world of grownup games. Then the puppy-dog glances and condescending quips suddenly vanish as the child neophyte effortlessly checkmates the adult. Eyes widen. *What the——? That must have been a lark.* The board is quickly reset to the starting position, and the child repeats the feat. The parents, not even aware that their child knew the rules of chess, are stunned. Their darling but otherwise unremarkable child apparently has some sort of extraordinary talent. Their child is *gifted.*

Indeed, something special is going on, but not quite what meets the eye. Like related myths about musical prodigies, math prodigies, and seemingly inborn athletic talents like Tiger Woods or Lance Armstrong, the chess genius myth has been around for ages. It is a common feature in biographies of chess legends like François-André Philidor, Paul Morphy, Bobby Fischer, Garry Kasparov, and Josh Waitzkin, the real-life inspiration for the popular movie *Searching for Bobby Fischer.* As it is popularly understood, these true prodigies are rare and inexplicable—they are, depending on your belief system, either God-given miracles or exquisite accidents of biology. In reality, though, young chess luminaries like Fischer and Waitzkin fit nicely into a much larger spectrum of young chess players—many of whom show promise and keen interest at a very early age and from early on are carefully nurtured, trained into greatness. "He has become a fine player at a very young age," chessville.com columnist Tom Rose writes about Norwegian wunderkind Magnus Carlsen. "But is that because of exceptional innate talent for chess?"

Maybe not! Imagine yourself in young Magnus's place. You play in your first tournament aged eight, do well, and get noticed by [a grandmaster] who decides to help teach you. Immediately you believe that you are special, that you have "talent," that you can really shine. This encourages you to work very hard at this game that gets you such agreeable attention. . . . [M]ore tournament success and more media attention [encourage] you to work even harder. At first you work at it for 2 or 3 hours a day. By the time you are ten years old it is more like 4 or 5 hours a day. . . . With that kind of early start and support, wouldn't almost any of us have been a much better player than we are now?

As Rose suggests—and as studies prove—the phenomenon is much less miraculous and much more interesting than commonly portrayed. There's no question that intelligence and other aptitudes are partly inherited, and that these aptitudes can include specific skills like abstract thinking and perhaps even traits like ambition. But looking closely at genius-level achievement, psychologists have also established that there is an overwhelming correlation between mentoring and practice. The available evidence suggests that nurturing factors can give children an extraordinarily strong incentive to develop certain skills quickly and deeply. "Evidence for the contribution of talent over and above practice has proved extremely elusive," writes University College of London psychology professor David R. Shanks. In contrast, he says, "evidence is now emerging that exceptional performance in memory, chess, music, sports and other arenas can be fully accounted for on the basis of an age-old adage: practice makes perfect."

Shanks cites a number of studies that all point in the same direction. In one study, researchers used anonymous surveys to categorize classical music students into one of three different groups according to skill level: (1) superb, (2) highly proficient, and (3) adequate. Then they asked the students how much they had practiced in the past and how much they currently practiced. The responses were remarkably consistent and showed a high correlation with skill level. Cumulatively, the very best players had each practiced roughly ten thousand hours in their lifetimes. The next-best group had each practiced about eight thousand hours; the least proficient group hovered around five thousand hours of cumulative practice. Similar numbers have turned up in studies on chess masters, athletes, writers, and scientists.

None of this means, of course, that these achievers aren't extraordinary. Quite the contrary. The likelihood that so-called gifted players actually acquire much of their gift on their own adds, rather than subtracts, from the marvel. Bobby Fischer, perhaps the most famous chess prodigy of all time, was far from a chess genius out of the box. After toying with the game for a year, he attended a simultaneous display in 1951, at age seven, and lost very quickly to an expert player. Afterward, Fischer joined a club and studied with ferocity. Six years and thousands of chess hours later, he had a spectacular "breakthrough" at age thirteen and was pronounced a boy wonder.

Perhaps the best-known example of mentored genius comes from Budapest, Hungary. There, in the late 1960s, psychologist Laszlo Polgar embarked on an unusual experiment in order to prove that any healthy baby can be nurtured into a genius: he publicly declared that he would do this with his own children, who were not yet born. He and his wife forged a plan to school their children at home and focus them intensely on a few favorite disciplines—among them chess. From a very early age, the three Polgar daughters, Zsuzsa, Zsófia, and Judit, studied chess for an average of eight to ten hours every day—perhaps a total of some 20,000 hours from age eight to eighteen.

Lo and behold, they all became chess "geniuses." In 1991, at age twenty-one, Zsuzsa (who later Westernized her name to Susan) became the first woman in history to earn a grandmaster title through qualifying tournaments. The second child, Zsófia, also became a world-class player. Judit, the youngest, became at age fifteen the youngest grandmaster in history (a record previously held by Bobby Fischer), and was considered a strong candidate to eventually become world chess champion. "I remember late one night when Susan was analysing with a trainer, a strong IM [International Master]," recalls computer chess guru Frederic Friedel, a close friend of the Polgar family who visited them often at their home in Budapest. "They reached an endgame and could not figure out how to play it. 'There is some trick here,' said the IM. So they woke up Judit and carried the girl into the training room. Judit, still half asleep, showed them the win and was put back into her bed."

Whether one is seeking the smartest chess move or trying to unlock an age-old scientific riddle, very often the most intelligent move a person can make is to acknowledge ignorance and seek assistance. What people casually refer to as "talent" turns out to be among the most complex subjects known to humankind. Scientists in the twenty-first century are still struggling to understand it. They have already learned enough to know that superb ability in chess or any other realm cannot be ascribed to some simple quirk of biology. Hopefully, with the help of a wide variety of tools, we will soon come to a reasonably coherent answer, and we will spread that answer far and wide in hopes of creating a better and more able world.

THE IMMORTAL GAME

Moves 10 and 11

SO MUCH OF "TALENT," of course, is in the ambition to succeed. It didn't take me very long, after I started playing chess again in midlife, to realize that I wouldn't go very far. Among other obstacles, I simply didn't want it badly enough.

I knew the difference. Early on in life, I was something of a wonder at the violin. At the earliest possible age I was awarded prestigious "superior" ratings for three consecutive years in national competition, and thus earned a prestigious solo performance spot in an honors concert. To a stranger listening to me play in those years, or looking at my gilded and framed certificates, my musicality might have appeared to be an unambiguous "talent"—until one learned the backstory: how, when I first took up the instrument in fourth grade, I practiced it with a ferocious intensity—easily eclipsing every other student in the school and setting a new practice record for my suburban school system. Where exactly I derived this compulsion to get up early in the morning and practice ninety ear-screeching minutes—while my poor father tried to eat breakfast and read the newspaper in peace—I don't know. I just wanted to do well at it, and that compulsion was self-reinforcing. My parents were naturally encouraging, and my music teacher Mrs. Schneider was ecstatic. She sat me at the front of the orchestra and treated me as one of her favorites for the next five years of our working together. She treated me like a young genius.

I have since fallen off, way off, and am confident that a violin in my hand today could easily be construed as a dangerous weapon. What happened? I stopped wanting it.

Today, I am lucky enough to be acquainted with a number of extraordinary achievers in various fields. From them, I rarely get the impression that genius is something they were born with and occasionally watered. Rather, these are people who have found something they wanted to do very well, and subsequently spent thousands upon thousands of hours getting good. I had nothing like the necessary drive to achieve such excellence in chess. True, I probably also didn't have nearly enough natural spatial aptitude. But the more important factor by far was lack of ambition. Recognizing that, my reengagement with the game eventually deflated; as my friend Kurt gradually became a reasonably serious competitor, playing chess most weekends in his local park, I slipped in the other direction, playing less and less. We still talked a lot about the game; but we played infrequently. It wasn't so much that I minded losing; I just got tired of my own mediocrity, and realized that I preferred to stay up nights trying to write a better book about chess than studying to be a better player. For whatever reason, my drive was to understand the relentless drive of others to play masterful chess.

At the competitive level, each player brings his or her own humanity to the table. Lionel Kieseritzky was an unpleasant sort of fellow— irritable, obtuse, and with a sharp tongue. Anderssen, by contrast, was a player's player. He had no apparent interests outside of chess, and was well liked by all who knew him—"honest and honourable to the core," remarked his frequent adversary Wilhelm Steinitz.

Both were also true fighters—even in casual play. Move 10 from Adolf Anderssen and Lionel Kieseritzky's casual game at the Grand Divan found Anderssen's Bishop under attack. As a response, he didn't exactly ignore the threat, but instead introduced his own charismatic counterthreat: moving his g Pawn up two squares, giving further protection to his Knight and threatening Kieseritzky's Black Knight.

10. g4
(White Pawn to g4)

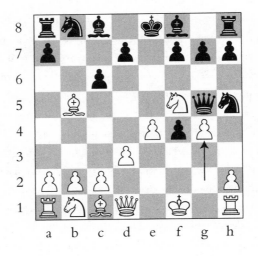

It was a "casual" game, with no stakes (aside from ego and reputation), but that couldn't keep the two players away from tripping into
middlegame's high-voltage zone: a multilayered dynamic of threats
and counterthreats that is not easy to defuse and can at any time blow
up in either player's face. Such dynamic tension is not a guaranteed
component of middlegame, but it is extremely common, and the lat-
tice of active threats can quickly escalate to impossible-to-follow
complexity. What emerges is the board-game version of that ever-
repeated movie scene where the cop sneaks up on the thug, aims his
gun, and says "freeze"—only to find that a moment later, hidden accomplices point their guns at the cop and say, "No—you freeze," at
which point more cops come out from hiding and point their guns
at the new accomplices, and so on. With dozens of weapons cocked
and aimed in every direction, no one knows whether to shoot first
or try to de-escalate.

Chess's middlegame offers the same conundrum—having to choose
whether to continue to escalate threats or start answering them. The

very best players know from experience, intuition, and calculation how a particular multiple-threat board arrangement is best acted on. But in the most complex circumstances, it is not something that any individual could actually articulate.

10. . . . Nf6
(Black Knight to f6)

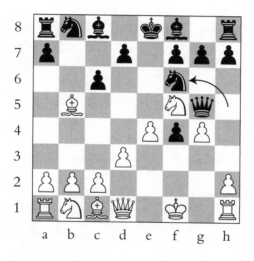

In his move 10, Kieseritzky escaped Anderssen's Pawn threat, while introducing a threat to that same Pawn. Now Anderssen would have to decide whether to protect that Pawn or save his Bishop on b5.

(Here, incidentally, is how the same board position was published in Kieseritzky's journal *La Régence* in July 1851, one month after the Immortal Game took place. Note that the Bishops are represented by Fools—*fous:*)

Now Anderssen did something downright creepy. He moved his Kingside Rook over one square to g1, establishing more support for his Pawn at g4.

11. Rg1
(White Rook to g1)

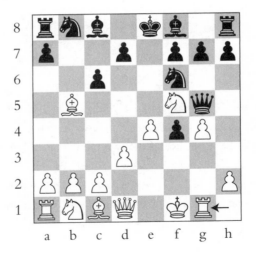

Wanting the Rook in that position made good sense and was not surprising. What was shocking about this move was what Anderssen hadn't done—namely, save his Bishop on b5. He let it go for no particular reason other than to further develop his other pieces. It was a sign of utter confidence, a signal that Anderssen had wrested control away from infinity and truly knew where this game was headed.

Was he bluffing his confidence, or did he actually know what he was doing? It was impossible to tell. But a surprise Bishop sacrifice would unnerve virtually any player. It was the kind of Romantic bravado that endeared Anderssen to chess players all over the world, and that would ultimately bring him chess immortality.

11. ... cxb5
(Black Pawn takes Bishop at b5)

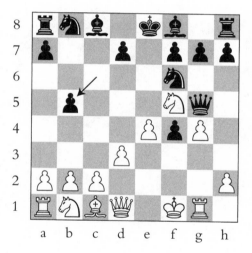

Kieseritzky accepted Anderssen's sacrifice, capturing the Bishop and sticking with his original plan, even if Anderssen seemed to be attempting to undermine it.

8. "INTO ITS VERTIGINOUS DEPTHS"

Chess and the Shattered Mind

"CHESS-PLAY IS A GOOD and witty exercise of the mind for some kind of men," offered Oxford University clergyman and librarian Robert Burton in 1621. "But if it proceed from overmuch study, in such a case it may do more harm than good; it is a game too troublesome for some men's brains."

This was no exaggeration. Chess has, throughout the ages, held the reputation for being a double-edged sword—strengthening some minds (in Benjamin Franklin's words) while shackling others (in the parlance of Albert Einstein). A tiny minority of the most brilliant players have even apparently become unwound through their deep immersion in the game. A closer look at the tragedies of this small group reveals fundamental truths about both chess and the mind itself.

In the late 1850s, Paul Morphy, a twenty-year-old law school graduate from New Orleans, emerged from obscurity first to defeat the top-ranked American players and then—miraculously—to do the same in Europe. His sweep of the great European champions was stunning—equivalent to a Saturday morning social tennis player suddenly entering and winning Wimbledon, the French Open, and the U.S. Open. The only leading player Morphy didn't beat was the Englishman Howard

Staunton—and that was because they never played; Staunton inelegantly ducked him for months.

Just as stunning, though, was Morphy's psychological descent. Returning to New Orleans at age twenty-six, he suddenly abandoned competition and all public play. He became reclusive and paranoid, and in his final years could be found walking the streets of the French Quarter, talking to invisible people. He told his mother and sister that enemies were out to get him. He died at age forty-seven, and was later dubbed "the Pride and Sorrow of Chess."

In his chess prime, Morphy seemed to intuit strategic principles of chess like no one else since the great Philidor. "He was the first successful exponent of *positional play*," writes Anthony Saidy in *The March of Chess Ideas*. "Whereas the Romantic players made moves with specific concerns of attack and defense, Morphy as a matter of course made moves based on quite general aims. He developed and sought open lines for his pieces, knowing that the opportunity for attack would naturally appear."

Shortly after Morphy's sudden exit, a young Austrian named Wilhelm Steinitz won the Viennese championship and moved forcefully onto the international chess scene. For about a decade, Steinitz played in the Romantic style of the era, eventually emerging as the greatest tactical player of his day. Then, in 1872, he completely refashioned his approach, following Philidor and Morphy into strategic, "positional" chess—but taking it far deeper with his painstaking, systematic analysis. The Scientific school was born. Steinitz "was not a poet but a thinker," explains Saidy. "He approached the structure and dynamics of the game of chess as a geologist might analyze a stratum of earth." Steinitz was the world's best chess player for twenty years. In contrast to Adolf Anderssen and Samuel Rosenthal, he was no showman. His painstaking approach of trying to gain tiny advantages over time was dull to watch compared to those of the flashy tactical players. But over time, he changed the game profoundly.

He was also apparently changed by it. Throughout his career Steinitz suffered from insomnia and could be extremely morose after a loss. "I have for years," he told a friend, "been the victim of a nervous affection which often entails loss of memory and utterly incapacitated me for mental work." As years went by, he veered into a much more serious state of psychosis. For a time, he was confined to a Moscow asylum. He insisted that he had played chess with God over an invisible telephone wire. (God lost.)

If Morphy and Steinitz were unique in this respect, there would be nothing more to say. But their similar stories of increasing paranoia and delusion fit an unfortunate pattern—and one which has not gone unnoticed. In 1779 the accomplished French physician and philosopher Jacques Barbeau-Dubourg insisted in a letter to his friend Benjamin Franklin that chess "tires the spirit instead of rejuvenating it, [and] shrivels and hardens the soul."

"A nameless excrescence upon life," H. G. Wells wrote of chess in 1898. "It annihilates a man."

Some chess haters will say anything, of course, and the true danger of chess obsession should not be confused with the healthy competitive intensity displayed by millions of people over the centuries. But neither can that small minority be ignored. As the game began to draw a large professional contingent in the nineteenth and early twentieth centuries, a string of chess victims became highly visible. The tally included:

- Polish sensation Gustav Neumann, one of the five best chess players in the world before his mental illness forced him out of competition in 1872.
- Top German competitor Johannes Minckwitz, who threw himself under a train in 1901.
- Polish contender George Rotlewi, who was forced out of the game by "nervous illness" at age twenty-two, in 1911.
- Polish master Akiba Rubinstein, who withdrew from serious chess play in 1932 because his pathological shyness had evolved into full-fledged paranoia; he spent the last thirty years of his life in a mental institution.
- Mexico's first-ever grandmaster Carlos Torre, a serious con-

tender for the world championship who suffered a breakdown while touring the United States in 1926 (at age twenty-two); returning to the Yucatán, he lived the rest of his life in squalor, and never played chess again.

- Latvian Aron Nimzowitsch, one of the twentieth century's greatest chess theoreticians, whose contributions still stand decades later. Never truly incapacitated by mental illness, he nevertheless had eccentricities that veered toward the pathological, including wearing bedclothes to tournament halls, paranoid rants about being served meal portions smaller than others', and a shocking penchant for actively taunting Nazi enforcers.*

- American Raymond Weinstein, who, at age nineteen, finished third behind Bobby Fischer and William Lombardy in the 1960–61 U.S. Championship and who soon thereafter developed severe schizophrenia and was permanently institutionalized on Ward's Island in New York City.

Finally, there is Bobby Fischer, who, like so many of the others, seemed as a young man to be merely eccentric and (entertainingly) aggressive. "I like the moment when I break a man's ego," he once said in a TV interview. In hindsight, he was shattering his own ego; his public career shows a man in steady, chess-fueled psychological decline. After

---

* Two separate incidents at a 1934 Alekhine-Bogolyubov match in Germany drew attention to Nimzowitsch's questionable judgment. "One day when a high officer in a Nazi uniform entered the press room," recalls veteran chess observer Hans Kmoch, "Nimzovich brusquely demanded to see his credentials. When the perplexed officer didn't answer at once, Nimzovich asked him to leave. The other reporters, including myself, were horrified, expecting the Nazi to react violently after receiving such an order from a Jew. But, amazingly, nothing happened. The officer simply left."

During a separate match in Poland, Nimzowitsch attended a luncheon at the home of the notorious Reichminister Hans Frank (later dubbed the Butcher of

winning the world championship in 1972, he withdrew from competition, refused to defend his title (eventually forfeiting it), and began to publicly rant against "Jews, secret Jews, [and] CIA rats who work for the Jews." Fischer, whose mother is Jewish, depicted the Holocaust as "a money-making invention," and accused the Jews of drinking Christian blood and peddling junk food to the world. In 1992 he became a fugitive from American justice after playing a lucrative, high-profile chess match in Yugoslavia in violation of U.S. economic sanctions. He called the United States a "brutal, evil dictatorship," and moved to Asia. Shortly after the September 11, 2001, attacks on America, Fischer *celebrated*. "This is all wonderful news," he told Philippine radio. "I applaud the act. . . . I want to see the U.S. wiped out."

It is impossible, of course, to definitively diagnose Fischer or any other individual based on sketchy glimpses of public behavior. But it is equally impossible to ignore or deny the pattern: a significant number of the world's most accomplished chess masters have succumbed over time to delusional paranoia, violent feelings of persecution, and severe detachment from the real world—a combination that psychologists recognize as falling neatly into the category of schizophrenia.

> *Schizophrenia*—A psychotic disorder or disorders marked by some or all of these symptoms: delusions, hallucinations, disorganized and incoherent speech, severe emotional abnormalities, and withdrawal into an inner world.

Vladimir Nabokov was fascinated by chess's dark side. The Russian-born novelist and poet was deeply enmeshed in chess throughout his

---

Poland and eventually hanged at Nuremberg). "At the luncheon," recalled Kmoch, "he [Nimzowitsch] demonstrated his usual persecution mania by complaining first about a dirty plate and then about a dirty knife. The Reichminister, seated directly opposite him, pretended not to hear." Nimzowitsch also goaded the Reichminister with boasts of his diplomatic protection—probably not the smartest tactical decision by a Jew in the presence of a powerful, merciless Nazi.

life—its aesthetics, its dynamic tension, its two-dimensionality, and its often profound effect on the human mind. He was passionate about constructing chess problems, and the game was thought to have deeply influenced his structural approach to writing. "Most of his novels," offers Nabokov scholar Anna Dergatcheva, "are recognizably constructed in a way a chess player would design his world: multi-leveled structure, tricking the recipient with unexpected moves and elegant solutions of plot development."

His 1930 novel *The Luzhin Defense*, which explicitly revolves around the game, tracks the tortured mind of a sullen boy who grows up to be a chess grandmaster. Traumatic family events in his childhood encourage young Aleksandr Ivanovich Luzhin to retreat into the safer, two-dimensional world of the chessboard. There he finds great competitive success and some primitive emotional security, but no solace. His life-long struggle for security inside geometric patterns comes to a climax in a chess tournament in Berlin, for which Luzhin has prepared an elaborate defense against his opponent's signature opening. But his opponent shocks Luzhin by not using the special opening. Luzhin's preparation proves a wasteful irrelevance, and he goes into psychological free fall. He stumbles through part of the big game and then, upon a scheduled adjournment, suffers a breakdown.

> He found himself in a smoky establishment where noisy phantoms were sitting. An attack was developing in every corner—and pushing aside tables, a bucket with a gold-necked glass Pawn sticking out of it and a drum that was being beaten by an arched, thick-maned chess Knight. . . . "Go home," [someone] whispered. . . . Luzhin smiled. "Home," he said softly. "So that's the key to the combination."

Luzhin later ends his own life by jumping out of a bathroom window. The novel is oppressively dark, and Luzhin's virtual entrapment in two-dimensional chess space feels almost like a cartoon—until one realizes that it is based in part on yet another real-life chess master: the

German Count Curt von Bardeleben, who jumped out of a window to his death in 1924.

The same year *Luzhin* was published, in 1930, Sigmund Freud's biographer and protégé Ernest Jones offered an ambitious, provocative, and classically Freudian theory regarding what lay behind chess's intensity and peril. "It is plain," Jones wrote, "that the unconscious motive activating [chess] players is not the mere love of pugnacity characteristic of all competitive games, but the grimmer one of father murder."* Thus, Jones unhesitatingly perceived a connection between chess and what Freud called the Oedipus complex—young boys' jealous hostility toward their fathers and sexual attraction to their mothers. According to Freud, successful resolution of these early impulses is critical to adult mental health; an unresolved Oedipal dynamic will guarantee that these impulses continue, resulting in adult neurosis.

Jones judged chess an irresistible outlet for Oedipal neurotics, in that the ultimate object of the game is to kill, or at least disable, the King—an obvious stand-in for the father. And what near-omnipotent figure aids in conquering the King/Father? "It will not surprise the psychoanalyst," Jones wrote, "when he learns . . . that in attacking the father the most potent assistance is afforded by the mother (= Queen)."

The unresolved neurotic, argued Jones, is drawn to chess's violent family conflict and subsequently becomes boxed in by the game's dynamic tension. "The exquisite purity and exactness of the right moves," he said, ". . . [and] sense of overwhelming mastery on the one side matches that of inescapable helplessness on the other. It is doubtless this anal-sadistic feature that makes the game so well adapted to gratify at the same time both the homosexual and the antagonistic aspects of the father-son contest."

---

* While Freud himself apparently never considered the impact of chess on the human psyche, he did pointedly use chess as a metaphor for psychoanalysis. In each, he suggested, one can easily study the basics in a book, but "the gap left in the instructions can only be filled in by the zealous study of games fought out by master hands."

Other dedicated Freudians heartily concurred. In 1931 influential Swiss psychologist Oskar Pfister called chess a "compulsion-neurotic re-action." In 1937 Isador Coriat, the prominent American disciple of Freud, wrote: "The sole object of the game for these individuals was to render the King (the father) helpless through checkmate, that is, castrate him. The winning of the game produced a feeling of intense pleasure, as a checkmate was unconsciously equated as a castration revenge." In 1956 Reuben Fine's dual experience as chess master and psychoanalyst led him to essentially the same notion. The game, he said, "certainly touches upon the conflicts surrounding aggression, homosexuality, masturbation and narcissism. . . . [The King] stands for the boy's penis in the phallic stage, and hence rearouses the castration anxiety characteristic of that period."

(Take deep breath. Pour small glass of Scotch. Enjoy brief comic interlude.)

From *Seinfeld*

(George is playing chess with girlfriend.)

George: Well, you got no place to go. I'll tell you what your problem is: You brought your Queen out too fast. What do you think? She's one of these feminists looking to get out of the house? No, the Queen is old fashioned. Likes to stay home. Cook. Take care of her man. Make sure he feels good.

Liz: Checkmate.

George: I don't think we should see each other anymore.

(Next scene.)

Jerry: And you broke up with her because she beat you at chess? That's pretty sick.

George: I don't see how I could perform sexually in a situation after something like that. I was completely emasculated.

The Freudians, in their misguided fervor and impressive self-regard, established at least one important truth: chess taps into primal forces far beyond our immediate control. Clearly, something profound, thrilling, and even somewhat terrifying takes place on its mental stage. And the game's close association with a particular variety of mental illness suggests that something potentially destructive may lurk beneath the surface for some players.

Most players distance themselves from the topic altogether. But several have bravely faced up to it, offering credible theories for the trouble. "As organizers and players," says the University of Chicago's Tim Redman, "we must admit that at times some very real character disturbances are manifested by our fellow players. . . . After all, what is a chess tournament? A chess tournament is, by definition, an activity in which you spend many hours each day, using your best intellectual and imaginative abilities to figure out how the other player is out to get you. [It is a] constant exercise of [the] 'paranoid faculty.' "

Writer, psychiatrist, and serious chess player Charles Krauthammer attributes the trouble not to latent Oedipal impulses or paranoia but rather to chess's celebrated abstraction. The same quality that makes the game such a useful thinking tool can also completely subvert thought, he suggests, if pushed to its near-infinite edge. The danger lies in what Krauthammer calls vertigo, the cognitive disarray one encounters when facing limitless depths, physical or virtual.

Not many chess players come close. "The *amateur* sees pieces and movement," writes Krauthammer. "The *expert*, additionally, sees sixty-four squares with holes and lines and spheres of influence. The *genius* apprehends a unified field within which space and force and mass are interacting valences—a Bishop tears the board in half and a Pawn bends the space around it the way mass can reshape space in the Einsteinian universe."

A third plausible route to chess madness is suggested by Austrian writer Stefan Zweig in his short story "The Royal Game." Zweig writes of a prisoner held in solitary confinement who has access to only one book—a chess guide with analysis of 150 games. He teaches himself how to play, studies each of the games inside out, and then—much to his later regret—begins to play chess against himself in his own head. "It is an absurdity in logic to play against oneself," he later concludes. "The fundamental attraction of chess lies, after all, in the fact that its strategy develops . . . in two different brains, that in this mental battle Black, ignorant of White's immediate maneuvers, seeks constantly to guess and thwart them, while White, for his part, strives to penetrate Black's secret purposes and to discern and parry them. If one person tries to be both Black and White you have the preposterous situation that one and the same brain at once knows something and yet does not know it; that, functioning as White's partner, it can instantly obey a command to forget what, a moment earlier as Black's partner, it desired and plotted. Such a cerebral duality really implies a complete cleavage of the conscious, a lighting up or dimming of the brain function at pleasure as with a switch."

It is dizzying to even consider, but it does comport with the intense training of some obsessive players who find themselves constantly playing chess games inside their heads. The consequence of this unwinnable inner conflict is what Zweig calls "a self-produced schizophrenia."* While such a condition, if possible, is obviously rare and probably only a danger to the very deepest chess thinkers, it also raises reasonable concern about what deep chess thinking does to the larger population of merely expert players. "In a long match," world champion Boris Spassky once remarked, "a player goes very deep into himself, like a diver. Then very fast he comes up. Every time, win or lose, I am so depressed. I want to die."

Such warnings are not to be taken lightly, and it behooves every chess parent, chess organizer, and chess instructor to be mindful of the game's destructive power—to work on tapping into chess's positive Benjamin Franklin forces while avoiding its corrosive Bobby Fischer forces.

---

* Most cases of schizophrenia have a strong genetic component, but even among that population, the disease is thought to be often precipitated by environmental stress or emotional trauma. Other instances of schizophrenia may well be caused *entirely* by outside stress, with no genetic predisposition at all.

THE IMMORTAL GAME

Moves 12–16

CHESS IS NOT ONLY a game of the mind, but also very much a mind game. Playing games against strangers on the Internet, I would frequently encounter remarks from opponents intended to intimidate me, or at least rattle me a little. If I took more than a few seconds to consider a move, I might get a text message of "You're SLOW!" Barbs like this didn't necessarily make me move sooner, but they certainly affected the quality of my concentration. Even when playing against old friends, there were occasional taunts and distractions—in both directions. It is an unavoidable part of the game.

Such off-the-board techniques go back as far as anyone cares to look. In his treatise published in 1497, the leading Spanish player Lucena revealed a few already well-known tricks:

- During day games, be sure to situate your opponent so that he/she faces the shining sun.
- At night, place a candle by your opponent's right hand. (Most players move the pieces with their right hand; in a dark room, moving the hand between the candle and the eye draws much attention away from the board.)
- It is best if your opponent eats and drinks well. But for you, only a light meal and *no wine*.

Five hundred years later, most techniques of distraction, intimidation, and coercion are no less mundane, ranging from provocative clothing to noisy drink twizzling or slurping to expertly timed grunts and groans. Walking away from the board between moves can give off an air of overwhelming confidence that opponents find unnerving. Pretending that a clever trap is actually an unsure or mistaken move might help lure your opponent more easily into the desired position.

A thousand other less crude and often less conscious maneuvers can also sway the thinking and the resilience of an opponent. No one can ignore the psychological and physical dimensions of this very human game. What is ostensibly a contest of calculation and geometric cleverness turns out to be just as much about morale, stamina, charisma, and raw desire to win. Some players have less a motivation to claim victory than a powerful desire to see the other guy lose. "I like to make them squirm," Bobby Fischer has said, articulating the motivation of the most severely competitive type of player. Few share Fischer's bloodlust, but every player unavoidably brings the force of his or her own character to the chess table. Even the meekest, most scholarly contestant must contend not only with thirty-two inanimate pieces, but also with the intangible and often unpredictable "human element."

Needless to say, the chess game between Anderssen and Kieseritzky included its psychological elements. For two highly sophisticated players, each move may have potentially complicated motives: Does he want me to think he's doing this? Does he want me to react in that way?

Anderssen, having sacrificed his Bishop on b5, now continued his offensive march on the Kingside. Moving up his h Pawn—on the far right edge of the board—he developed a Pawn *and* directly attacked the Black Queen.

12. h4
(White Pawn to h4)

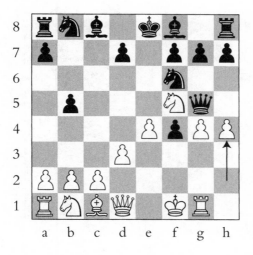

This was not a move that Kieseritzky likely saw coming. He would now lose another tempo in further Queen retreat.

12. . . . Qg6
(Black Queen to g6)

This retreat was triply bad for Black. First, in a game where a single move can produce a mile of significance, a retreating move that has no tactical or strategic value is worse than a waste. It's like coming to a sudden stop on a racetrack while all of the other runners race on.

Second, this particular retreat didn't even move Black's Queen to safety. After the move, she was still in grave danger of being boxed in.

Third, Anderssen was carrying out a rather dastardly plan in which his long-term goals meshed nicely with his tactical threats against Kieseritzky's Queen.

His squeeze continued:

13. h5

(White Pawn to h5)

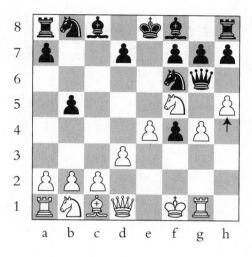

Anderssen moved his h Pawn up yet one more square, again developing a Pawn and again attacking the Black Queen.

13. . . . Qg5
(Black Queen to g5)

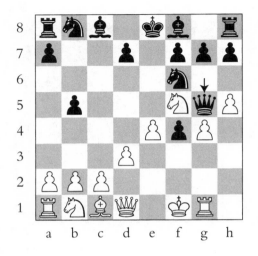

Black's Queen was now forced into the only available safe square. Things have sunk pretty low when a player has not only no choice of which piece to move but also no choice about which square to move it to.

14. Qf3
(White Queen to f3)

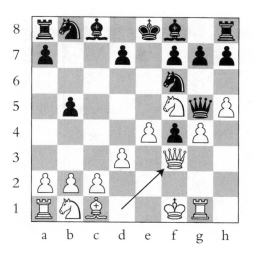

Anderssen continued to apply pressure to Kieseritzky's Queen, and also advanced his own position in a way not yet entirely transparent.

14. . . . Ng8
(Black Knight returns to g8)

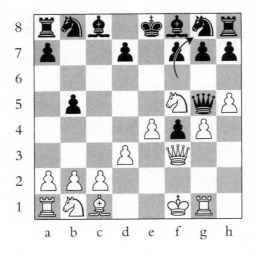

Another full-on retreat for Black (and a loss of a tempo), in this case moving the Knight to free up space for the retreating Queen. This was a new low for Black: having to waste an entire move in middlegame to a retreat back to a starting square. Few pieces had been exchanged, and Black was still a piece ahead, so it would have been silly to say that all was lost. But momentum seemed to be overwhelmingly on the side of White—even if it was still impossible to discern his precise plan.

15. B×f4

(White Bishop takes Pawn on f4)

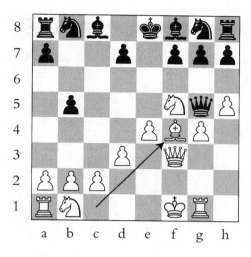

Anderssen then advanced his Bishop, capturing the Black Pawn at f4 and further pressing his attack on Kieseritzky's Queen.

15. . . . Qf6
(Black Queen to f6)

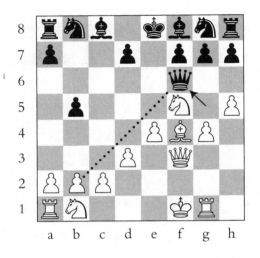

Kieseritzky retreated to f6, and behold the change in momentum. One of the magical qualities of chess is its potential for a lightning-quick reversal of fortune. The complexity of the game often hides traps and opportunities so well that neither player is aware of the new paradigm until it stares at them from the board.

Suddenly, with the Black Queen moving to an adjacent square, an enormous opportunity had opened up. The Queen, now safe, menacingly threatened Anderssen's b2 Pawn and his Queen's Rook. Had Anderssen wasted a crushing attack on the Black Queen and inadvertently walked himself into a highly vulnerable position?

16. Nc3
(White Knight to c3)

Anderssen appeared to be concerned enough about the Queen threat that he developed his Knight as a block against the Queen—or so it would seem. (At this point, Anderssen was actually playing a very different game in his mind from what observers could see on the board.)

16. . . . Bc5
(Black Bishop to c5)

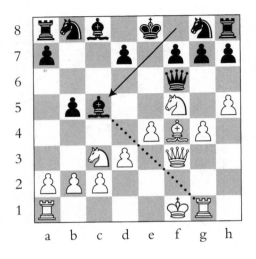

Now it was Kieseritzky who was on the offensive, advancing his Bishop so that it directly attacked Anderssen's King's Rook, and also cutting off two of five retreat squares potentially available to the White King.

How would Anderssen answer this new threat?

9. A VICTORIOUS SYNTHESIS

Chess and Totalitarianism in the Twentieth Century

IN THE TWENTIETH CENTURY chess became a symbol of nationalistic pride for totalitarian regimes seeking to prove their moral and intellectual superiority.

The Nazis were fascinated with chess as a game of war, discipline, and purity. In the late 1930s they made a propaganda film in the chess-loving town of Ströbeck, in eastern Germany, showing off the chess-playing schoolchildren as ideal Aryan citizens.* A Nazified version of chess called *Tak Tik* (Tactics) replaced the traditional pieces with modern war implements—air force, soldiers, bombs, etc.

In 1941 the Germans scored a stunning propaganda coup, persuading the world chess champion Alexander Alekhine, a Russian by birth, to embrace the Nazi ideology and very publicly adapt it to chess. Chess play, according to Alekhine, was yet another window into the inherent moral and intellectual depravity of Jews. Jews played cowardly, empty chess, he argued, in contrast to the obviously superior Aryan courageousness. Indeed, Jews had nearly ruined the game. Under so much Jewish influence, Alekhine said, most of the first half of the twentieth

---

* Ironically, Ströbeck's school was later named after Germany's most famous chess champion, the Jewish mathematician Emanuel Lasker, who had been forced to flee the country in 1933.

century had been a "period of [chess] decadence" where too many players "relied not in victory but in not losing."

Alekhine's defenders like to point out that he offered up this nonsense under duress. Alexander Alexandrovich Alekhine had been born into an aristocratic Russian family. After slipping in and out of Soviet government favor, including one very close brush with a firing squad, he eventually fled the Soviet Union and settled in France. When the Germans captured France in 1940, Alekhine agreed to write about and play chess on their behalf in order to protect his family's assets. Whatever the motive, Alekhine spewed the worst kind of racist invective. His essay "Aryan Chess and Jewish Chess" blasted Jews—including German Jew and former world champion Emanuel Lasker—as playing inferior, defensive chess. Coming from someone with so much authority in the game, the essay was analogous to "Jewry in Music," the German composer Richard Wagner's anti-Semitic diatribe from the previous century.

"Can we hope," wrote Alekhine, "that after Lasker's death—the second and probably the last world champion of Jewish descent—Aryan chess will finally find its path, after having been led astray by the influence of Jewish defensive thinking?" (Invoking the Lasker name was particularly depraved considering that Lasker's sister would ultimately die in a Nazi concentration camp.)

As with every piece of successful propaganda, there were kernels of reality within Alekhine's claim. First, Jews did have a long and special relationship with the game, and had made a disproportionate impact on it. The connection went back many centuries and was rooted in the very character and culture of Judaism. The Talmud, the central Jewish text of laws and ethics, was built on a culture of curiosity and verbal combativeness, in accordance with the idea that constant, animated discussion and relentless interpretation and reinterpretation of ideas would bring people closer and closer to the truth.* This sense of never-ending

---

* There are persistent claims that chess is mentioned in the Talmud, either as *nard-shir* (sometime before the sixth century C.E.) or as *iskundrée* (third century C.E.). If

argument became a part of the core of Jewish character and drew many Jews to chess, which, in its highest form, also demanded endless examination and interpretation.

Abraham ibn Ezra, the Spanish poet who became one of the great medieval Jewish scholars, championed the game in the twelfth century, writing:

> I will sing a song of battle
> Planned in days long passed and over.
> Men of skill and science set it
> On a plain of eight divisions,
> And designed in squares all chequered.
> Two camps face each one the other,
> And the Kings stand by for battle,
> And 'twixt these two is the fighting.
> Bent on war the face of each is,
> Ever moving or encamping,
> Yet no swords are drawn in warfare,
> For a war of thoughts their war is.

Since then rabbis have incessantly debated the game's virtue, some objecting that it took too much time away from scholarship but most praising chess and encouraging it among youth as a tool to focus the intellect. From century to century the game became increasingly inter-

---

either reference were substantiated as chess, this would make it the earliest known references to the game and would cement indeed the special relationship between chess and the Jews. But the arguments are far from convincing. In the eleventh century the Jewish scholar Rashi interpreted *nardshir* as chess. It is much more likely that the term referred to the backgammon precursor *nard*. More recently, several scholars have made the case that *iskundrée* must be chess, since it is portrayed in the Talmud as distracting ancient scholars from their studies. "This can only mean a game which is serious even in play—it can only be chess!" insists Alexander Kohut. While it is not impossible that Jews from the Talmudic age were acquainted with the game, the evidence is just not there.

166 THE IMMORTAL GAME

woven with Jewish culture. In Germany, it became customary for Jews to play with special silver pieces on the Sabbath, putting aside their weekday wooden pieces. In the nineteenth and twentieth centuries, a number of Jews became dominant players. World champion Wilhelm Steinitz, father of the Scientific school, who changed the game perhaps more than any other single individual and dominated it for decades in the late nineteenth century, was Jewish. His successor, Emanuel Lasker, world champion from 1894 to 1921, was the son of a cantor and the grandson of a rabbi. Lasker's most persistent challenger during his long reign was the German Jew Siegbert Tarrasch. (Tarrasch and Lasker became such bitter rivals that in 1908 Tarrasch publicly declared that he would henceforth only speak three words to Lasker: "check and mate." Alas, he got to speak to his rival only a few times after this declaration. But even without capturing the title, Tarrasch's further clarification and expansion of Steinitz's ideas made him the more influential player in the long run.) The Polish player Akiba Rubinstein, another major contender to Lasker's title, was the product of a yeshiva, a Jewish religious school, as was the Latvian Aron Nimzowitsch—a chess revolutionary who was later credited with inspiring the Hypermodern school of chess theory and reinvigorating play for the twentieth century.

The second kernel of truth that gave Alekhine the space to make his outrageous accusations was that Steinitz and his successors *had* indeed overwhelmed the thrilling Romantic school with a new style of play that was inherently cautious, plodding, and defensive. Compared to the swaggering Romantics, Scientific players were about as dull to watch as the name promised. Steinitz revealed that chess had an inherent logical structure (albeit an ultracomplex one) and that a careful player could prevail by respecting it. Like medical pioneers who took the time to actually count, measure, map out, and name all the bones, muscles, and tendons in the human body, the Scientific players laid chess bare. They proved that even the most far-reaching combinations could be thwarted by cautious positioning. The wise player no longer aimed to captivate an audience's imagination with previously unheard-of combinations, but to induce small weaknesses in the opponent's position and gradually exploit these weaknesses to gain an advantage, eventually achieving a position sufficient for a win. Chess was now less like a parlor trick and more like a mathematical proof.

But it was still more sophisticated than nineteenth-century Romantic play, and Alekhine knew it. After the tide turned against the Germans, Alekhine not only disavowed his six pro-Nazi essays, he also explicitly denied writing them, hoping to erase the permanent stain on his international reputation. Sadly, the truth was irrefutable: after his death in 1946 the original manuscripts were found in Alekhine's own handwriting.

As it turns out, the Nazis' abuse of chess for propaganda purposes was just a warm-up for the real specialists at nationalistic chess: the Soviets.

ON SEPTEMBER 1, 1945, seventeen days after Japan unconditionally surrendered to the United States, effectively ending World War II, a symbolic new war began. With a thousand American spectators looking on inside a ballroom in Manhattan's Henry Hudson Hotel, Mayor Fiorello La Guardia of New York played the ceremonial first move in a radio telegraphy chess match between the United States and the Union of Soviet Socialist Republics. A few minutes later came the reply from Moscow's Central Club of Art Masters, five thousand miles away. This was the first international sports match since the conclusion of the war, and the first ever official team sporting event for the USSR. In due course, the cold war would be waged through proxy armies across every continent, would stretch out over nearly five decades, and would threaten the planet with nuclear annihilation. But for now, in its germinal moments, it was fought between a brainy American businessman and an electrical engineer marshaling the Semi-Slav Defense (1. d4 d5 2. c4 e6 3. Nc3 c6 . . .).

That first game, between U.S. champion Arnold Denker and USSR champion Mikhail Botvinnik, went to the Soviets in a scant twenty-five moves per player, and it was all downhill for the U.S. team from there. Over four days and twenty games, the Soviets obliterated the Americans with a score of 15 ½ to 4 ½ points. Of the ten players on the American team, only two actually won a game. If this high-profile competition was an indicator of each nation's collective intellectual prowess, the United States was in for some rough times ahead.

Most people on both sides, though, realized that the trouncing reflected not raw intellect but the Soviets' far richer chess history and ravenous political ambition with regard to the game. In reality, the outcome of the match was virtually preordained, as the Soviets had long been putting enormous resources toward the goal of an overwhelmingly powerful national chess team. The United States just happened to be the victim of their debut.*

Whatever the Nazis made of chess to further their political agenda, it was nothing compared to the Soviet appropriation of the game. Russia had a special relationship with chess, having imported the game directly from the Persians and the Muslims centuries before, in established trade routes along the Caspian Sea and the lower Volga and Don rivers. It seemed to spread everywhere, and to find a special fit with the Russian temperament—long before it was embraced and popularized by such figures as Pushkin, Tolstoy, Turgenev, and Lenin.†

Deep admiration for the game was practically universal among the Bolshevik revolutionaries (as it had also been a passion of their philosoph-

---

* One pithy illustration of the drastic differential in preparation is the Round One game between the American Samuel Reshevsky and the Soviet Vasily Smyslov. Reshevsky took ninety minutes to make his first twenty-two moves. Smyslov took eight minutes. The Russian team had exhaustively worked out an opening preparation that went that deeply into the game.

† "We should note," writes Russian historian Isaac M. Linder, "that chess has been found not only in excavations of princes' citadels (Grodno, Drutsk, Volkovysk, and Novgorod), but also in excavations around cities (Vitebsk), in semi-dug-out living quarters, and in the courtyards of craftsmen and other simple people (Vyshgorod, Nikolo-Lenivets, Minsk)."

ical hero, Karl Marx).* Vladimir Illych Lenin was a serious player who "grew angry when he lost, even sulking rather childishly," recalled the writer Maxim Gorky. (He also leaned on chess for its metaphorical power, as in 1917 when he referred to the interim Russian prime minister Alexander Kerensky as a pawn shifted around by imperialist forces.) Leon Trotsky was also serious about chess, playing often in Vienna and Paris before the Revolution. Not long after the 1917 takeover, Nikolay Krylenko, Lenin's supreme commander of the Soviet Army, took on chess as a personal project. Seeing it as "a scientific weapon in the battle on the cultural front," he enlisted strong government support for the game, including financial assistance for its most promising players. He also organized prominent international tournaments. "Take chess to the workers," was one of the early slogans of Krylenko's chess movement.

"The Bolsheviks' motives for promoting chess were both ideological and political," explains British grandmaster Daniel King. "They hoped that this logical and rational game might wean the masses away from belief in the Russian Orthodox church; but they also wanted to prove the intellectual superiority of the Soviet people over the capitalist nations. Put simply, it was a part of world domination.

"With chess," King continues, "they hit upon a winner: equipment was cheap to produce; tournaments relatively easy to organise; and they were already building on an existing tradition. Soon there were chess clubs in factories, on farms, in the army. . . . This vast social experiment quickly bore fruit."

In the 1920s the Bolsheviks turned the popular but ragtag nature of public chess play into one of the self-identifying marks of emerging Soviet culture. By 1929, 150,000 serious amateur players were regis-

---

* "Marx adored chess," writes Daniel Johnson, "and—much to his wife Jenny's exasperation—would disappear with his fellow émigrés for days at a time on chess binges. Despite devoting much time to chess, he never rose above mediocrity." One story has Marx so agitated about a late-night chess loss to a friend that he stalked over to his opponent's house early the next morning to demand a rematch.

tered with the state chess program. That number swelled to 500,000 by 1934—which meant, by the estimate of American grandmaster and chess author Andy Soltis, that "perhaps half the world's chessplayers were citizens of the USSR." The growth was obvious in both quantity and quality, with a whole suite of world-class players quickly coming into view.

To no one's surprise, the Soviets put their own philosophical and stylistic imprint on chess play. Not all of their great players played exactly the same, of course, but there was a distinctive Soviet approach that put a high degree of emphasis on pregame preparation and on gaining the initiative, even at the expense of weak Pawn structures.

After a few setbacks—including the defections of two champions, Alexander Alekhine and Yefim Bogolyubov, and an embarrassingly strong showing by Western players at the 1925 tournament in Moscow—the Soviet program started to gain steam in the late 1920s and early '30s. The greater their individual achievements, of course, the more Soviet players were required to reinforce their allegiance and collective goals. "During the 1930s," write Larry Parr and Lev Alburt, coauthors of *Secrets of the Russian Chess Masters*, "successful Soviet grandmasters spent much of their time dispatching telegrams to the 'Dear beloved teacher and leader' who made their various victories possible. 'I sensed behind me the support of my whole country,' wrote one grandmaster, 'the care of our government and our party and above all that daily care which you, our great leader, have taken and still take.'"

That "great leader," Joseph Stalin, took a personal interest in chess. Not a strong chess player in reality, Stalin was nevertheless transformed into a chess virtuoso in public: his aides publicized at least one fake game, a thirty-seven-move contest from 1926 in which Stalin allegedly defeated the ruthless party functionary Nikolay Yezhov (later chief of the secret police and director of the Great Purge). Commentaries accompanying the fabricated game praised Stalin for his strategic vision.

Chess was a good philosophical fit for the Soviet empire. Army chief Nikolay Krylenko called it "a dialectical game illustrating . . . Marxist modes of thought." This piece of Soviet propaganda did contain some truth. "Dialectic," as tendered by Hegel and then Marx in the nineteenth century, refers to a back-and-forth volley of opposing truths or assertions, resulting in a more complete understanding—a "synthesis." Marxist ideology was built on the idea that Communism is the natural, inevitable synthesis of previous political systems.

Chess, with its move/countermove dynamic, is inherently dialectical, resonating with a tension that builds and builds as the game proceeds. Each move is its own bold assertion. Black counters White, which then counters Black, which then counters White. Individual moves are, in turn, a part of each side's larger strategic assertions which evolve and steadily counter one another: White protects his Kingside; Black attacks the Queenside; White "fianchettos" his King's Bishop (moves it to the central g2–a8 diagonal); Black reinforces his Pawn center.

Move by move, combination by combination, the game evolves and the implications of the opposing pieces are increasingly better understood. A larger truth—Hegel's synthesis—evolves out of the clash of opposing interests. "Following every move," write Larry Parr and Lev Alburt, "a new situation arises. Call it a *thesis*. The requirement is to find the correct *antithesis* so as to create a victorious *synthesis*. . . . Dialectical struggle. Negation of negation. That's chess."

Unfortunately, the Soviets not only reveled in chess's ideological purity. They also contaminated the game and its players. Observers called the national team the "Soviet chess machine," in part because it was a juggernaut that made its own rules. "In 1946," recalls American master Arnold Denker, "I had an adjourned game with Mikhail Botvinnik in which I was ahead. During the break I saw Botvinnik eating dinner and relaxing. I didn't have dinner. I went to my room and studied. When the game resumed, Botvinnik remarkably found the only move to draw the game. I said, 'How is that possible?' Someone told me, 'Listen, young man, all of these people were analysing for him while he was having his dinner.' I was naive in those days."

Another useful Soviet tactic was to prearrange the outcome of games between Soviet players in the early rounds of international tournaments, giving the winning players a free pass to the next round. In the all-exhausting environment of a world-class tournament, helping a player easily pass through several rounds is like driving a climber most of the way up Mt. Everest. The end is still monumentally difficult, but an advantage will go to the skilled player who hasn't already had to expend valuable energy in earlier competition.

In 1962 an ambitious young American player named Bobby Fischer publicly accused the Soviets of just such maneuvers in a major tournament on the Caribbean island of Curaçao. "I'll never play in one of those rigged tournaments again," Fischer declared after losing to the major Soviet contender Tigran Petrosian. "[The Soviets] clobber us easy in team play. But man to man, I'd take Petrosian on any time."

Fischer, already a world-class player, was also known as a hothead, and his comments were taken by many as evidence of his being a sore loser. But it later became clear that Fischer's charges were dead on. "There were some agreed draws at Curaçao," admitted the Soviet grandmaster Nikolai Krogius after he moved to the United States.

Amazingly, Fischer went on to become a one-man counterweight to the Soviet chess juggernaut. Raised in Brooklyn, he had burst onto the scene in 1956, at age thirteen, when he became the youngest player ever to win the U.S. Junior Championship. "[It] wasn't simply that a gawky 13-year-old kid in blue jeans was suddenly winning tournaments," journalist Rene Chun writes in the *Atlantic Monthly*. "It was the way he was winning. He didn't just beat people—he humiliated them." Two years later, at age fifteen, he became the youngest-ever grandmaster.*

★ "Grandmaster," the most exalted title in chess, is a lifetime designation conferred on its best players by the world chess organization, the Fédération Internationale des Échecs (also known as FIDE), since 1950. One can earn the title in several different ways, the most common being the triumph over other grandmasters in a minimum of three official tournaments. In 1950, there were twenty-seven officially recognized grandmasters; in 2005, there were about 1,100.

The more precise method for rating top players was the Élo system, developed in 1964 by the Hungarian-born American physics professor Árpád Élo. Élo rat-

Through the late 1950s and early 1960s, Fischer continued to play re-markable chess and to draw wide public admiration for his abilities. After a tournament in Yugoslavia in 1970, he was able to recall instantly every move from each of his twenty-two games—totaling more than a thousand.

He also drew attention to his eccentric behavior. A devoted chess player from a young age, Fischer had never developed any social skills or knowledge (or curiosity) outside of chess. "If you were out to din-ner with Bobby in the Sixties, he wouldn't be able to follow the con-versation," recalled an old friend. "He would have his little pocket set out and he'd play chess at the table. He had a one-dimensional outlook on life." He devoted his every waking hour to the game, rotating be-tween stations in his apartment to play game after game against himself. (One cannot help but recall Stefan Zweig's warning of a subsequent "complete cleavage of the conscious [mind].")

In September 1971, Fischer defeated his archrival, former world champion Tigran Petrosian, thus winning the right to directly challenge the reigning champion, the Russian Boris Spassky. For the first time since World War II, an American would have a shot at the top chess ti-tle. This "Match of the Century" immediately took on colossal signifi-cance. As most of the planet was by now entrenched in cold war politics, a head-to-head Soviet–American contest of wits couldn't help but symbolize the underlying clash of political ideologies, economic sys-

---

ings were rooted in a statistically based mathematical formula that gives a running game-to-game score to all competitive chess players, as if each player is playing in one long tournament throughout his or her entire career. Every player's score is adjusted after each official game against another rated player. The amount of the adjustment is determined by the rating of the player's opponent, along with the totality of prior wins and losses. A specific rating does not guarantee but usually closely corresponds to a FIDE title. Most players with a rating of 2500 or higher, for example, are grandmasters. Most players rated between 2400 and 2499 have the second-highest title, "international master."

When Élo first debuted his rating system in 1964, two players shared the high-est rating of 2690, world champion Tigran Petrosian and Bobby Fischer.

tems, and fundamental philosophic differences regarding property, loyalty, and freedom. Like the game itself, the Spassky–Fischer chess championship had no direct relevance to any real-world matter. And yet it seemed to stand for almost everything.

The opening ceremony was set for July 1, 1972, in Reykjavik, Iceland—politically neutral territory. But on that day Fischer was still home in New York issuing demands for more money and control. A British businessman stepped forward to double the prize purse to $250,000. All seemed resolved, but Fischer quickly came up with new peeves, new reasons to stay home. At one point, Henry Kissinger, President Nixon's secretary of state, reportedly phoned Fischer and urged him to go ahead with the match. ("I told Fischer to get his butt over to Iceland," Kissinger recalled. It is, however, still a matter of dispute whether Fischer actually took Kissinger's call.)

Finally, Fischer did fly to Reykjavik. On July 11, in front of TV cameras and a live audience in the Laugardalshoell Sports Exhibition Palace, the match began. Game 1 opened with a Queen's Gambit. On the twenty-ninth move, Spassky, playing White, lured Fischer into capturing a "poisoned Pawn"—a trick in which the Pawn is sacrificed in order to trap the capturing piece; Fischer's Bishop was cornered and he eventually resigned. Analysts were floored by Fischer's defensive blunder. Many had considered his prematch antics part of a careful strategy to gain the psychological upper hand; but from the looks of things in Game 1, Fischer seemed to have psyched *himself* out.

Things got even worse for him in Game 2. Fischer demanded that the TV cameras be removed before the game, and there was a lengthy standoff over the issue. Eventually, the cameras were taken out, but not before the referee had started the official game clock. Fischer demanded that the clock be reset to zero. When it was not, he refused to play, and the game was eventually forfeited to Spassky without a single Fischer move. In a blink, Spassky was leading the world championship match two games to none. The United States seemed headed straight for another chess humiliation.

Fischer was undeniably superb at chess and had proven his greatness over and over again. But could he actually beat Spassky? He never had before. Of the five games the two had played together in previous tournaments, Spassky had won three and they had drawn the other two. Spassky was world champion for a reason. In a nation crammed with dynamic, cunning, fierce players, he stood out for his ruthless pragmatism. He was so highly adaptable that he could resist and work around fierce tacticians like Mikhail Tal but also poke holes in the painstaking caution of Tigran Petrosian. On top of this, Spassky had a particular systemic advantage over Fischer: a team of thirty-five grandmaster assistants standing by to suggest special anti-Fischer moves, analyze every ongoing position, and feed Spassky intelligence during breaks. By contrast, Fischer had one grandmaster assistant, the American William Lombardy, whom he was reluctant to use. Fischer liked to keep all the play inside his own head.

In this way, each player signified his home nation's creed. Spassky and his team stood for the socialist ideal, all working together to seize collective glory. Thirty-six grandmasters versus two was not exactly the most honorable way to win a chess game, but a win was a win, and proving superiority any way possible was a central goal of the Soviet regime.

Fischer's bravado, by contrast, was seen as quintessentially American. He was unwilling to compromise his individuality. He was a loner, a renegade, an entrepreneur. Americans fell in love with their Brooklyn chess maverick, and as he rose to the championship, chess itself became popular in the United States as never before.* PBS's broadcast of the Fischer–Spassky contest—"there just isn't enough televised chess," David Letterman would later joke—became the highest-rated PBS show to date.

After the fiascoes of Game 1 and Game 2, many expected that the temperamental Fischer would simply pack up and fly home. Instead, after a three-day break, he turned a corner: he won Game 3, drew Game 4,

---

* Ironically, just as Fischer became an American hero, he and his mother came under FBI suspicion of being Soviet agents.

won Game 5—evening the score—and then won Game 6 in spectacular fashion. "[When] he won Game 6, which was the best game of the match," recalled Larry Evans, coauthor of the definitive chess-analysis book on the match, "Spassky stood on stage applauding him with the audience. It was an amazing moment. This never happened before. I had never seen a player lose and then start applauding his opponent."

Fischer's momentum continued. He drew Game 7, won Game 8, drew Game 9, and won Game 10. Now all of a sudden it was Spassky who couldn't win a game off Fischer, prompting the Soviets to accuse the Americans of using chemicals or electronic devices to interfere with Spassky's thoughts. (Spassky, to this day, will not discount this possibility.) The stage was swept for electronics, the chairs tested and x-rayed, the air analyzed. No mind-zapping devices were found. Fischer was just playing breathtaking chess. "Fischer played into the match, and learned how to beat Spassky," said Fischer biographer Frank Brady. "Each game he got better." He was also doing what he publicly had said he most relished: he was breaking Spassky's ego; he was watching Spassky squirm.

Of the next ten games, eight were drawn, but the momentum never left Fischer's side of the table. At such a stratospheric level of chess play, it's reasonably easy for one side to force a draw—and that's what an exhausted Spassky often resorted to as the games wound on. (Fischer, with the lead, may have been complicit in this strategy, knowing that victory would soon be his.) Psychologically, Spassky was already beaten. Finally, after nearly two months of grueling competition and endless mind games, Fischer wore Spassky down, forcing his resignation in Game 21 and winning the world championship.

Fischer was an American hero. He had predicted he would become champion of the world, and he did. He had boasted he would single-handedly break the Russian machine, and he did. All of his quirks could be forgiven, even cherished, as a part of his rugged American spirit. He came back to televised celebrations, lucrative endorsement offers, interviews with Dick Cavett and Bob Hope, and a country that suddenly seemed to genuinely care about chess.

Then he dropped out. He turned down the millions of endorsement dollars, turned away from the media, and even turned away from chess itself. The man who had said playing chess was all he ever wanted to do with his life ceased playing publicly. After once suggesting that his world championship reign would be the most accessible in history, giving ordinary players a crack at his title on a monthly basis, he in fact refused to defend his title against anyone—including the legitimate challenger Anatoly Karpov in 1975. In the face of Fischer's total refusal, his title was stripped that year and awarded to Karpov.

However awkwardly, the Soviets had their title back. In chess, as in life, a win is a win.

THE IMMORTAL GAME

Moves 17-19

NOW THE CASUAL GAME between Anderssen and Kieseritzky was transformed. Anderssen, whose g1 Rook was under attack from Kieseritzky's c5 Bishop, did a shocking and unsettling thing: he ignored it, instead launching a series of moves that turned an insignificant practice game into something immortal.

17. Nd5
(White Knight to d5)

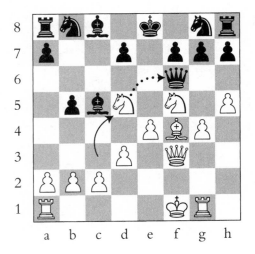

In moving his Knight further up the board, Anderssen not only ignored the threat to his King's Rook, he also reexposed his Queenside. In fact, by attacking the Black Queen (dashed line), he forced the Queen to move somewhere—essentially inviting Kieseritzky to take the b2 Pawn and attack his other Rook.

This was unusual and intriguing, to say the least. Rooks are widely considered to be the second-most-powerful pieces on the board, behind the Queen. A player like Anderssen doesn't accidentally expose two Rooks. What was going on?

17. . . . Q×b2
(Black Queen captures Pawn at b2)

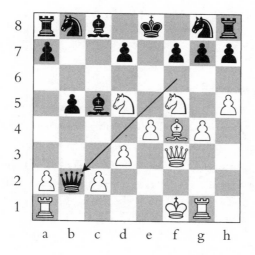

Suspicious but not yet aware how an opportunity to go after two Rooks could put him in jeopardy, Kieseritzky took the bait. He captured a Pawn with his Queen and threatened Anderssen's a1 Rook.

18. Bd6

(White Bishop to d6)

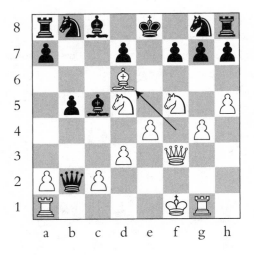

Anderssen's reaction? Again, he ignored the colossal threat. As if not even seeing both of his Rooks in jeopardy, Anderssen now moved his Bishop two spaces—nominally threatening Kieseritzky's Bishop but, again, essentially inviting him to use that Bishop to capture the King's Rook. If Kieseritzky didn't know better, this kind of play could be mistaken for that of a bumbler who was barely even aware of how the pieces moved.

18. . . . B×g1

(Black Bishop captures Rook on g1)

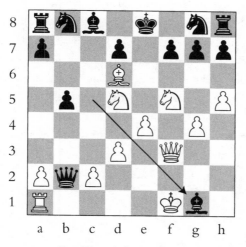

Seizing the opportunity, Kieseritzky captured Anderssen's g1 Rook. How would Anderssen respond? Save the other Rook? Capture the Bishop?

19. e5

(White Pawn to e5)

Another stunning move by Anderssen, who was now not only neglecting to take Kieseritzky's Bishop in return for his lost Rook *and*
sacrificing his second Rook in as many moves, but was also openly
inviting a check in the process. The biggest risk of all was that
Anderssen would soon be put on the defensive, never again to regain
the offensive. He was making what could very well have been his last
offensive move of the game. At this point, Kieseritzky could be forgiven for wondering if an exhausted Anderssen was throwing the
game.

In hindsight, this tiny Pawn move was regarded as pure genius by
analysts because of how White managed to seal off the Black Queen
from a diagonal retreat in defense of her King.

19. . . . Q×a1+
(Black Queen captures Rook on a1; puts White in check)

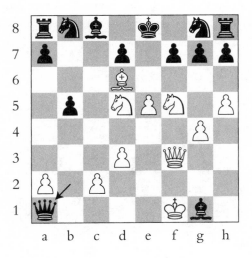

Kieseritzky now took Anderssen's second Rook and put him in
check. On the surface, it seemed like a devastating move, and not one
that a sensible opponent would openly invite. But a closer look reveals that this particular check didn't pack a lot of punch. It did in-

deed put Anderssen on the defensive, but Kieseritzky's follow-up move wasn't obvious. With five of his major pieces still stuck on his back rank (i.e., undeveloped), he didn't have sufficient firepower to deliver a crushing blow.

By contrast, Anderssen had aggressively developed several pieces and Pawns. He'd sacrificed a couple of limbs to get there, but his attack position was admirable. If he could regain the offensive—a big if—he looked to be in a strong position to finish Kieseritzky off.

| BEAUTIFUL PROBLEMS

Chess and Modernity

AT THE TAIL END of his career, Marcel Duchamp was frequently asked why chess had become such an important part of his life. "I always loved complexity," he said. "With chess one creates beautiful problems."

That sentiment—*beautiful problems*—could serve as a motto for twentieth-century artists and intellectuals, all of whom had to extract truth and beauty from complexity in one way or another. Even as nations exploited chess for political gain, the ancient game lost no significance as a thought tool. A stream of modern artists, scholars, and scientists leaned on the game to work through problems of their age. "As metaphor, model and allegory, chess performs powerful cultural work," offered Pennsylvania State University social theorist Martin Rosenberg. The world had changed substantially since A.D. 600, but chess still somehow had that fundamental ability to explain the unexplainable, make visible the abstract, and extract simple truths from complex worlds.

This was not the intellectually cohesive world of John Locke and Benjamin Franklin, where all available knowledge could still fit into a single library building and where adventurous thinkers could simultaneously engage in medicine, engineering, philosophy, and diplomacy. The twentieth century saw knowledge explode and all thought become hyperspecialized, with each specialty employing its own idiomatic terminology and belief system. Naturally, every discipline needed its own particular metaphors to help convey meaning. What's striking about chess in this era is that it transcended the many narrow corridors of language and thought, finding equal utility in the behavioral labs of cognitive science (already discussed in Chapter 7), the silicon forests of artificial intelligence (to be discussed in Chapter 11), the notebooks of novelists, the whiteboards of physicists, the logical matrices of philosophers, and on and on. Three quick examples will demonstrate the game's modern breadth:

- Austrian-born British philosopher Ludwig Wittgenstein, regarded by many as the most important philosopher of the twentieth century, was utterly fascinated by chess, referring to the game nearly two hundred times in his writings. As a contained entity with simple, fixed rules and near-limitless possibility, chess served as a model through which he could study other abstract systems such as mathematics and language. Chess was his logic and systems abacus, always at the ready to work out a particular thought problem.

- The legendary American physicist and physics teacher Richard Feynman relied heavily on chess in his lectures at the California Institute of Technology (later published in the 1994 book *Six Easy Pieces: Essentials of Physics Explained by Its Most Brilliant Teacher*) to help decode the scientific process for his students. Walking through detailed references to the game, Feynman conveyed the process of both devising and testing hypotheses.

- Italo Calvino, the whimsical and postmodern Italian author of *Cosmicomics, If on a Winter's Night a Traveler*, and other influential fictions, was impressed by chess's ability to transform limitless data into a simple impression. In his novel *Invisible Cities*, the vast empire of the aging Mongol warrior Kublai Khan has grown beyond his ability to govern and even beyond his comprehension. He sees his holdings only as "an endless, formless ruin." Enter the young Venetian explorer Marco Polo, who surveys dozens of the Khan's cities and reports in great detail back to him. When Polo relays his experience by shifting around symbolic objects on a large checkered tile floor, Kublai Khan becomes convinced chess is all they need to communicate. "Kublai was a keen chess player. . . . He thought: 'If each city is like a game of chess, the day when I have learned the rules, I shall finally possess my empire, even if I shall never succeed in knowing all the cities it contains.'" As with Wittgenstein and Feynman, chess for Calvino was a window into grasping complex systems. For anyone interested in language or mathematics or geography, what really mattered wasn't the catalogue of individual words or numbers or alleyways so much as the system that bound them together. Rules, governed by logic, were the key to understanding and administering complex worlds.

Chess in the twentieth century was so pervasive, in fact, that it became a central part of the study of metaphor itself. In his essay "Chess Rhizome: Mapping Metaphor Theory in Hypertext," Penn State professor Martin Rosenberg attempts to decode what he calls "the interdisciplinary dimensions of metaphor." He also poses perhaps the most pressing question about its power: Does metaphor work by bringing language close to reality or by effectively—seductively—shaping reality? If the latter, the use of metaphor needs to be taken extremely seriously; its choice and precise deployment can shape cultures and nurture or destroy lives. This idea also suggests that even the best and most agreeable metaphors should be treated skeptically, monitored for cognitive trickery, and regularly reexamined in hindsight to ensure that their consequences are desired and beneficial.

SOME IN the twentieth century applied chess to difficult thought problems, and others were drawn to its aesthetics. Marcel Duchamp's resonant phrase *beautiful problems* referred, of course, not to the physical beauty of the board or its pieces, but to the dynamic struggle of the game and its unpredictable outcomes. Chess was, to most serious players and observers, a highly ritualized aesthetic event. "All chess-players are artists," Duchamp declared in 1952. Not surprisingly, an awful lot of serious artists were fascinated by the game.

For a brief time in the 1920s, chess and its dynamic energy had seemed imperiled. Over several decades, Wilhelm Steinitz's Scientific revolution had generated such intensive analysis that many feared the game was nearing some sort of intellectual end point, its creative possibilities nearly exhausted. Cuban sensation José Raul Capablanca, world champion from 1921 to 1927, publicly expressed this sentiment.

To the rescue came the third great style of chess play, after the Romantic school and the Scientific school: the Hypermodern school, a paradigm-shattering gift to chess from Aron Nimzowitsch, Richard Reti, and other players in the 1920s and '30s. In a sharp turn away from over four centuries of master-level play, the Hypermodernists sought (among other things) not to "overburden" the center of the board with Pawns early in the game. Instead, they first developed their Knights and Bishops to put pressure on the center, operating from the flanks. (Eventually a Hypermodern player might attack an opponent's center-board Pawns after those Pawns had become overextended or vulnerable in some other way.) Even more than this one radical idea, the Hypermodernists rejected the Scientific school's proposition that only one set of principles could be applied to the game. In doing so, they reaffirmed chess's limitlessness. The lesson of the Hypermodern revolution was that anything was still possible, that discovery of the game had only just begun.

Since the Hypermodern pioneers were Jewish, Nazi collaborator Alexander Alekhine later railed against the new style as "fear to struggle, doubts about one's own spiritual force, a sad picture of intellectual self-destruction." The truth, as Alekhine knew better than most, was precisely the opposite: Hypermodernism was not about fear, but about the love of intellectual adventure. It was, in fact, archetypal modernism— the spirit of breaking decisively with past styles in order to make a new aesthetic contribution to the world. Thus it was closely connected to the early twentieth-century intellectual ferment that spawned the fiction of Joyce, Proust, and Kafka, the theater of Brecht and Pirandello, the fabulist tales of Jorge Luis Borges, the slapstick of Charlie Chaplin and the Marx Brothers, the experimental music of John Cage, and the conceptual art of Marcel Duchamp. These intellectual-aesthetic warriors and many others were part of an existential reach for something new and great; they willingly, even eagerly, tore down old conventions to get where they needed to be. As different as their works were from one another, there was a seamless spiritual connection running between them. Not surprisingly, many of these avant-gardists were also dedicated chess players, and several incorporated the game into their work.

Duchamp led the way. Having enjoyed chess since childhood, his passion for it escalated in his twenties until it apparently began to eclipse his interest in producing art. If his peers thought this intense phase would quickly pass, they miscalculated. In 1921 Duchamp informed the painter Francis Picabia that he wanted to be a professional chess player and started on an intensive course of training and competition. In the early 1930s he played for the French national chess team, which was then led by world champion Alexander Alekhine. (Records still exist of an Alekhine–Duchamp game during an Alekhine simultaneous display, which Duchamp won.)

Duchamp did not, of course, stop being an artist. Chess did not so much overshadow Duchamp's aesthetic as merge with it, according to his biographer Calvin Tomkins. What to the outside world looked like Duchamp leaving his art behind was, in his own mind, a logical extension of where he had been heading all along. "Chess was much more than a retreat or a refuge," writes Tomkins. "It was a near-perfect expression of the Cartesian side of his nature. . . . Duchamp's working methods were marked by an almost mathematical precision, and one of the things he loved about chess was that its most brilliant innovations took place within a framework of strict and unbendable rules."

Duchamp, in other words, was in love with logic and its consequences. His cheerful curiosity seemed to compel him to see beauty not just in colors and shapes but also in the very components of thought. "Chess is a marvelous piece of Cartesianism," he told Tomkins, "and so imaginative that it doesn't even look Cartesian at first. The beautiful combinations that chess players invent—you don't see them coming, but afterward there is no mystery—it's just pure logical conclusion."

In the 1930s Duchamp struck up a friendship and chess camaraderie with the writer Samuel Beckett. They met through Duchamp's close companion Mary Reynolds, a surrealist artist. Beckett had also been a lifelong addict of the game, playing on the chess team at Dublin's Trinity College and often incorporating it into his work. "Assumption," his first published short story, contained allusions to chess. As a player, Beckett had closely followed the chess column that Duchamp was writing at the time for the Paris daily newspaper *Ce Soir*.

The two were not evenly matched. Duchamp was one of the best players in France, and no doubt swept Beckett off the board in most of their encounters. But still they enjoyed each other's company, and continued to play. The two came together again in the summer of 1940, converging on the Atlantic coastal town of Arcachon, southwest of Bordeaux, as they fled the Nazi onslaught. All summer they played lengthy chess games together in a seafront café. While their conversations were not recorded, we can imagine that they discussed their mutual interest in chess's dialectic between total freedom and complete constriction, between choice and futility. Beckett, one of the most pessimistic writers of the century, was fascinated by the futility of human action and by human interdependence, among other matters. He also consistently worked to undermine every possible aspect of conventional narrative, and once remarked that the ideal chess game for him would end with the pieces back in their starting positions.

Endgame, the distinct and stark final phase of chess, particularly fascinated both Duchamp and Beckett. In the classic endgame scenario, only a handful of pieces are left on the board—often just a King and one or two other pieces on each side—and the thrilling, maddening complexity of middlegame has been supplanted by a barren geometric landscape where one simple blunder can easily cost either player the game. For some, endgame play is intuitive, for others, it must be studied intensively; many lopsided chess positions have been quickly reversed by crafty endgame players.

In 1932 Duchamp published his only chess book, the elegiacally titled *Opposition and Sister Squares Are Reconciled*, which focused on one particular endgame scenario. In a domain where thousands of books are written about specific openings and very specific strategies, *Opposition* holds, even today, the strange distinction of being perhaps the most obscure chess book ever published. The book had a limited printing—which made sense, since its subject matter was limited to a particular board position that was very, very rare. "[It] would interest no chess player," Duchamp bluntly remarked. "Even the chess champions don't read the book, since the problem it poses only comes up once in a lifetime. They're end-game problems of possible games but so rare as to be nearly Utopian."

The book was obviously more of a thought experiment than a chess guide, and perhaps its most profound effect had nothing to do with the game. Nearly two decades after his series of chess games with Duchamp, Beckett published his second play, *Endgame*, which was inspired in part by Duchamp's endgame chess book. Aside from its title, Beckett's play does not explicitly refer to chess, but alludes strongly to the feeling of pointlessness often experienced by a chess player in the final moves. The protagonists are a master and his servant who seem existentially bound to one another, to the lifeless life they live together in their cramped seaside home. Hamm, the master, Beckett later explained, is "a King in a chess-game lost from the start. From the start he knows he is making loud senseless moves." The hopelessness of the play marked other gloomy Beckett works, including *Waiting for Godot*. Beckett's entire literary career, in fact, is nicely summed up by his proposed ideal chess game—the chess pieces may move around for a while in futility, but in the end are back in their starting positions.

Beckett's celebration of futility nicely contrasts with the optimistic energy of Duchamp, one of whose mottos was "yes and chess." Each artist and intellectual, of course, has his or her own particular temperament. Chess has proven to be a pliable enough tool to help deliver a variety of aesthetic statements. Duchamp's optimism and Beckett's pessimism make elegant bookends on a very wide shelf of beautiful problems.

THE IMMORTAL GAME

Moves 20 and 21

ANDERSSEN WAS AGAIN UNDER attack, and needed to escape check immediately—the ultimate in tempo-losing positions. He had only two choices: moving his King to e2 or moving it to g2.

20. Ke2
(White King to e2)

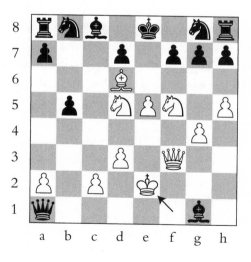

He chose e2.

20. . . . Na6
(Black Knight to a6)

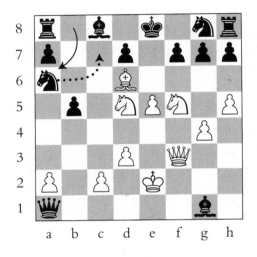

Kieseritzky, unable to find the perfect offensive move to keep Anderssen off balance, instead fell back to defense, developing his Knight to threaten any piece that moved onto the c7 square. Having lost his own momentum, he knew that Anderssen was about to mount a strong attack.

21. N×g7+

(White Knight captures Pawn on g7; check)

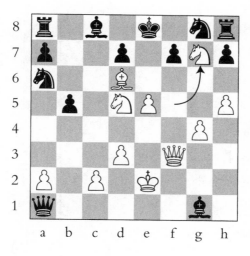

Anderssen now began his final assault, putting the Black King in check with his Knight on g7. (He had previously made this square safe by moving his e Pawn to e5, blocking the Queen from a diagonal rescue mission.) A close observer could see that Anderssen was in good attack position, even without his two Rooks. In fact, it was the Rook sacrifices that enabled him to so quickly put such a tight squeeze on the Black King.

21. . . . Kd8

(Black King to d8)

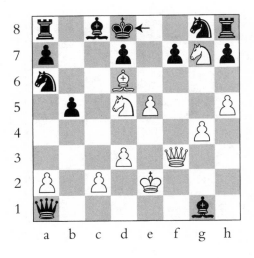

Kieseritzky escaped check with his only possible move, feeling the vice squeezing tight on his precious King. But how would Anderssen press his attack?

III.
ENDGAME

(Where We Are Going)

"WE ARE SHARING OUR WORLD WITH ANOTHER SPECIES, ONE THAT GETS SMARTER AND MORE INDEPENDENT EVERY YEAR"

Chess and the New Machine Intelligence

HAL: *Bishop takes Knight's Pawn.*
FRANK: *Lovely move . . . Rook to King one.*
HAL: *I'm sorry, Frank, I think you missed it. Queen to Bishop three, Bishop takes Queen, Knight takes Bishop, mate.*
FRANK: *Yeah, looks like you're right. I resign.*
HAL: *Thank you for a very enjoyable game.*

—*2001: A Space Odyssey*

JANUARY 2003. UP ONSTAGE, microphone in hand, former world champion Garry Kasparov was effervescent. He'd just trounced an opponent that, until this day, had not lost to a single person in two years, a player that was beginning to seem invincible—a player that never, ever worries.

This was a new sort of chess match. Only one of the contestants could sweat; only one required sleep or food. Towering over Manhattan's Central Park, on the twelfth floor of the well-appointed New York Athletic Club, Kasparov was taking on the world computer chess champion, a ruthlessly efficient Israeli software program known as Deep Junior. After months of exhaustive preparation, he had just won the first of six scheduled games in a scant twenty-seven moves. He was ecstatic, not just for his victory, but also for how easily it was accomplished. Though he was careful not to suggest it himself, this rout obviously augured well for the rest of the match. "Computers still have plenty of weaknesses," a visibly relieved Kasparov told a large crowd of grandmasters, club players, and schoolkids in his rich Azerbaijani-accented English after the game.

Although these two champions had never played an official game together, it was publicly a kind of rematch for Kasparov, who in 1997 became the first world champion ever to be beaten by a chess machine—the customized IBM supercomputer known as Deep Blue. That loss was a humiliation for Kasparov, who later charged that the rules (which he had agreed to) were unfair, and that Deep Blue's chess-expert operators cheated by giving their machine some human help during the match. ("I do not want to go into legal details," he said. "I do not want to waste money for the lawyers.")* Now, six years later, came his opportunity to replay history. This contest, recognized as the first official "man-versus-machine" match by the World Chess Federation (also known by its French acronym, FIDE), was Kasparov's chance not only to revitalize his image but also to cleanse the past. This was, he declared, the first "purely scientific match, because we had fair conditions for both the human player and for the machine." He wanted

---

* Kasparov demanded a rematch, which IBM rebuffed, preferring to bask in its victory. Deep Blue was permanently dismantled shortly afterward. Ever since, Kasparov has many times aimed to undermine the credibility of the Deep Blue team and the validity of the 1997 match. He spent much of a 1999 speech raising suspicions, concluding with a rhetorical flourish: "The reason I am telling you the story is not to wake up some old ghosts or to tell how badly IBM behaved. But I think that IBM committed a sort of crime against science, because by claiming the victory in the man-versus-machine contest, which was not accomplished, IBM dissuaded other companies from entering the competition."

history to regard the Deep Blue match as so badly tainted that it could not be taken seriously.

In fact, the Deep Blue win in 1997 was fair and unambiguous. It was also a historic achievement, the culmination of a fifty-year odyssey whose implications went far beyond chess. Since the mid-1940s, scientists had aimed to create a thinking machine, an apparatus that could compete with or even surpass the human brain in logical operations, pattern recognition, problem solving, and even language. Chess was found to be a useful testing ground because of its combination of simple rules and mind-bending complexity. Playing chess was also a goal whose progress could be easily measured: a chess machine could compete against expert players and be ranked according to its wins and losses. Chess was a founding and enduring experimental model for what came to be known as artificial intelligence, or AI.

For many decades, chess computers fell woefully (laughably) short of their designers' ambitions. Then in the 1980s, as computing made important strides, chess engines finally began to sharpen. In the early 1990s, the Carnegie Mellon–trained engineer Feng-Hsiung Hsu emerged with a spare-parts machine called Deep Thought that dominated other machines and even seemed competitive with humans. After taking on IBM sponsorship, Hsu's newly named Deep Blue played its first match with world champion Kasparov in 1996, losing decisively. With further tinkering, though, it quickly became even stronger, and a year later it won a close rematch.

The victory was a profound and chilling moment whose importance was immediately and intuitively understood around the world: technology was now moving into an ominous new realm. It was one thing to build machines that could move earth or fly over the ocean or even recognize a face. Deep Blue's victory over Kasparov signaled that we were now making machines that could conceivably compete with us. "We are sharing our world with another species," *Newsweek*'s Steven Levy would later write, "one that gets smarter and more independent every year."

This 2003 rematch of sorts seemed to be yet another important milestone. The world was watching to see if we were yet one more step closer to "Hal," the highly intelligent and manipulative computer from Stanley Kubrick and Arthur C. Clarke's film, *2001: A Space Odyssey*. Reporters from the *New York Times* to *Pravda* to *Libya Online* were following it game by game. ESPN would be broadcasting the finale—the first live national and international TV coverage of chess since the 1972 Fischer–Spassky match in Reykjavik.

So how did Kasparov pull off such a spectacular win in the first game? "One of the ways to win [against computers] is to find a hole in the opening preparation," he explained afterward. By mutual agreement, Kasparov and his seconds possessed a copy of the Deep Junior program for six months prior to the match, and they had been relentlessly competing against it ever since, probing it for weaknesses, trying out innumerable different combinations to learn how it "thought." They also relied on other computers to help them beat this computer: sophisticated new databases like ChessBase, which contained over two million chess games played over the last five hundred years; and spectacular analysis software such as Fritz, which could analyze millions of positions per second and rank them for human consideration. With these advanced tools in place, the pile of collective knowledge increased game by game; players of Kasparov's (and Deep Junior's) caliber appeared, game by game, to be doing the unthinkable—*mastering* chess.

But they weren't there yet. Even with the enormous electronic database at hand, there were still plenty of new tricks to be discovered. In preparation for Game 1, the Kasparov team unearthed a little-used combination that knocked Deep Junior off balance. It was a surprise Pawn sacrifice on Kasparov's seventh move. After a fairly conventional opening where the Pawns and Knights jockeyed for control over the center board, Kasparov suddenly thrust out his King's Knight Pawn two spaces to the g4 square, weakening his Kingside.

GARRY KASPAROV VS. DEEP JUNIOR
JANUARY 26, 2003
NEW YORK
GAME I

7. g4
(White Pawn to g4)

This was a terrific gamble and could have backfired. "In order to expose [the computer's weak spot]," said Kasparov after the game, "you have to have a lot of courage. All morning I was saying, 'Should I play g4 or should I not play g4?'" The strength—and weakness—of this move was in its unpredictability and counterintuitiveness. It left his entire position surprisingly vulnerable on both the Kingside *and* the Queenside. (Notice how disconnected the White Pawns are across the entire board; disconnected Pawns cannot defend one another.) But that was also precisely the advantage of the move as well. From his practice experience with the Deep Junior program, Kasparov knew that this unusual move, 7. g4, was not included in Junior's openings database (its "opening book"), and would thus force the computer to start thinking on its own earlier than expected. Every computer has to come "out of book" at some point during the opening. Kasparov knew that it was advantageous to trigger this early, and in an unexpected way.

The most striking thing about this and other Kasparov decisions in Game 1 was that they were both tactical (short-term) *and* strategic (long-term). Until recently, human masters had successfully thwarted even the best computer programs by carefully avoiding short-term tactical skirmishes. Modern computers' ability to calculate at blinding speeds made them tactical masters, but strategic advantage still lay with expert human players who could think through long-term strategies in a way that had more to do with spatial perception and planning than mathematics. Whole-game strategies in chess were ideas, not calculable equations. One of the things chess computers still could not do was to grasp an idea.

Against Deep Junior, Kasparov was signaling something new. He was not employing classic anticomputer chess. Rather, he played it as he would play another human grandmaster. It was the highest compliment he could pay to Junior's programmers: they had developed a machine with true strategic ability. They had developed a machine that appeared to be thinking.

This was not much consolation in the immediate wake of such a powerful defeat of the computer program. Kasparov's performance left many experts in the observation hall wondering aloud whether he would not merely win the match but crush Deep Junior and humiliate its creators. Perhaps the fearsome computers weren't as advanced as many had thought. Perhaps human players possessed the ability to adapt and improve even more quickly than machines.

Amir Ban and Shay Bushinsky, the Israeli creators of Deep Junior, were fearing the exact same thing. As Kasparov departed for his New York victory dinner, the vanquished programmers shuffled onto the stage looking pale and somewhat embarrassed. They had expected much more of a fight from their baby. "If Kasparov does this to Junior every game, then we don't deserve to be here," Ban admitted. He shook a few hands and quietly headed down to Fifty-eighth Street to smoke a cigarette.

GARRY KIMOVICH KASPAROV was born in 1963 in the ancient port city of Baku, Azerbaijan, on the western edge of the Caspian Sea. In the ninth century chess migrated directly through Baku on its way from Baghdad to Kiev. The game came to be known in the region as *shahmaty,* after the Persian term *shah-mat,* which later evolved into the English *checkmate*—*shah* (the King) *mat* (is defeated). The eleventh-century Azerbaijani poet Khagani wrote that "time checkmates shahs like elephants gone far astray" and made a reference to "Ne'eman, the great master of chess." Over time, chess in Baku became like ice fishing in Norway, an indelible part of the culture stretching back more generations than anyone could count.

When Kasparov was six, he shocked his family by solving a difficult endgame puzzle from the newspaper. "Since Garry knows how the game ends," his father remarked, "we ought to teach him how it begins." Sixteen years and many thousands of training hours later, Kasparov became the youngest-ever world chess champion at twenty-two. His greatness was also enduring. Kasparov held the world championship from 1985 to 2000, and even after losing the title he retained the highest ranking in the world. Perhaps more significantly, as he neared middle age at the dawn of the twenty-first century, Kasparov was one of the few human beings left who could effectively compete with the top chess computers.

Now, in Game 2 of the 2003 match, he had the unenviable task of proving he could beat Junior again—and this time as Black, which always has the inherent disadvantage of moving second. But Kasparov did not come to the table to fight for a draw. From the start, he surprised expert onlookers with another aggressive game, an unorthodox version of one of his specialties, the Sicilian Defense. Just as in the first game, he boldly took on the computer in tactical play. And he seemed in command for much of the game. Now there was no doubt about it: tactical play—trying to achieve short-term gain—was clearly an emerging theme in this match. In recent years, it had become axiomatic: *Humans cannot win tactical battles against computers.* A squishy and vulnerable human brain cannot compete move by move with a computer that analyzes millions of moves per second. In New York, Kasparov was challenging this widely held belief, and in Game 2 he again took on Deep Junior both strategically and tactically. Specifically in this game, explained commentator John Fernandez, "Kasparov's wrinkle was to employ a rare development of his dark-squared Bishop on the square a7, where it controls many squares in the heart of Deep Junior's position from the protective bunker of the corner of the board."

DEEP JUNIOR VS. GARRY KASPAROV
JANUARY 28, 2003
NEW YORK
GAME 2

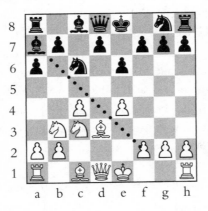

Commentators noted that Kasparov had successfully played this exact Bishop move in a recent exhibition match. It worked this time too, for a while. But then on move 25 he was outfoxed. Deep Junior offered Kasparov the chance to check with his Queen. Kasparov had been planning another move, but the check was too tempting to pass up. At the least, he couldn't see how taking the check could do any harm.

"It was a human move," he said later. "You see a check like that and you simply play it. But I immediately realized that I had let [Junior] off the hook."

The game ended in a draw—all in all, not a bad deal for Kasparov, who as Black had avoided a loss. The ambassador for human intelligence was still doing humans proud, still winning the match against an inexhaustible and savvy machine. At the same time, Deep Junior was surprising the experts with its *humanity*. "Its play has been almost completely indistinguishable from that of a human master . . . it hasn't made any obvious computer-like moves," commented popular American chess columnist Mig Greengard.

"Deep Junior," he declared, "has so far passed the chess Turing Test."

IN THE WORLD of computer professionals, Greengard's remark was equivalent to declaring that someone had just landed on Mars. Passing the Turing test was an extraordinary feat of engineering. It meant that machines were now crossing the threshold into the realm of human intelligence—or at least the appearance of intelligence.

Trained as a mathematical logician in the 1930s, British computer pioneer Alan Turing was recruited by British Intelligence in World War II. At the Bletchley Park military intelligence campus north of London, he led a team that cracked the vexing Enigma encryption code used by German U-boats. (Field Marshal "Monty" Montgomery thanked Turing's squad for letting him "know what the Jerries are having for breakfast.") They also helped the Allies create uncrackable encryptions of their own so that commanders and leaders, including Roosevelt and Churchill, could talk to one another in confidence.

After the war, Turing introduced concepts necessary for the invention of digital computing. Among other things, explains Andrew Hodges in his biography *Alan Turing: The Enigma*, Turing contributed "the crucial twentieth-century insight that symbols representing instructions are no different in kind from symbols representing numbers." That meant that computers could potentially do much more than calculate—they could also take on a wide variety of other tasks involving the manipulation of data, patterns, and even decision making. Building on that and other Turing insights, the first generation of primitive computers (including the famous ENIAC and UNIVAC machines) was built in the late 1940s and early 1950s. The early history of computing is nearly impossible to imagine without him.

His legendary Turing test came in response to the giant question that he posed in a 1950 article for the journal *Mind*: "Can machines think?" After considering the technological, cognitive, philosophical, and theological implications of that question, Turing argued that yes, a true thinking machine could eventually be built—and he expressed confidence that one day it would happen.

But how to tell? How could anyone properly determine if a machine was engaged in humanlike thought? Turing concluded that there would never be a satisfactory objective standard. Instead, he proposed, it was ultimately a matter of human perception. If, in response to human questions, a computer could consistently provide answers indistinguishable from human answers—answers that would fool a human on the other side of a curtain—then that machine would ipso facto be demonstrating thought. The Turing test was born.

In chess, the equivalent question was whether a computer player might someday fool people into thinking it was a human player. Any computer could be programmed to respond to certain moves with other moves, or to value certain pieces above other pieces. But could humanlike play involving intuition, creativity, risk taking, and opponent psychology ever be convincingly mimicked by a machine?

Alan Turing loved chess and played all the time, though he wasn't nearly as adept on the chessboard as he was on the chalkboard. At Bletchley Park he was fortunate to be surrounded by accomplished players, and the chess pieces were always handy. The onetime British champion Conel Hugh O'Donel Alexander was Turing's deputy. Future British champion Harry Golombek was also on the staff; Golombek's chess superiority over Turing was such that he could overwhelm Turing in a chess game, force Turing's resignation, and then turn the board around to play Turing's pieces against his own original pieces—and win.

Turing and his colleagues played not just for the diversion, but also because chess was such a useful tool. It helped them work through ideas and problems, explore logic and mathematics, and experiment with mechanical instructions. Contrary to what one might have supposed, the busy nexus of chess and mathematics had not diminished as mathematics itself became more nuanced in the modern age. One might expect that highly advanced concepts like cycloids, primary decomposition, and transcendental numbers would render the medieval chessboard an obsolete tool. On the contrary, the game seemed only to become more and more entrenched in classrooms, journals, blackboards, and, eventually, on Web sites. In the late nineteenth century, number theory pioneer Edmund Landau wrote two books on mathematical problems inherent in chess. (More than a century later, the connection would still be vibrant: in 2004 Harvard University offered the course "Chess and Mathematics," whose aim was to "illustrate the interface between chess problems and puzzles on the one hand, and mathematical theory and computation on the other." Chess, it seemed, would never lose relevance, since its vitality was based not on any particular set of ideas, but on its symbolic power.)

For Turing during World War II, chess was also particularly attractive as just about the only part of his intellectual life that was not top secret. Turing and his Bletchley Park colleagues could discuss chess problems anytime and anywhere without compromising their military work. One emerging thread of their discussions was the possibility of building a chess-playing machine, which would allow them to test their ideas about the mechanization of thought. They considered chess an excellent model for such a test. Among other attributes, it was an elegant example of what Princeton mathematics guru John von Neumann (a mentor of Turing) called games of perfect information, meaning that all variables were always known to all players. Nothing about the game was hidden. The same was true of less complex games like checkers, tic-tac-toe, and others—all of these games stood in contrast to poker, for example, where cards are concealed and players can bluff. In his work, von Neumann had established that each game of perfect information has an ideal "pure strategy"—a set of rules that will suit every possible contingency. Theoretically at least, the perfectly designed computer could play the perfect game of chess.

In 1946, as part of an exploration about what computers could potentially do, Turing became perhaps the first person to seriously broach the concept of machine intelligence. Chess was his vehicle for conveying the notion. "Can [a] machine play chess?" he asked, and then offered an answer:

> It could fairly easily be made to play a rather bad game. It would be bad because chess requires intelligence. . . . There are indications however that it is possible to make the machine display intelligence at the risk of its making occasional serious mistakes. By following up this aspect the machine could probably be made to play very good chess.

Today the words fall flat on the page. Sixty years ago, they were revolutionary. The most startling word of all was *intelligence*, which Turing did not use casually. He was not merely talking about the ability to follow complex instructions. "What we want," Turing explained, "is a machine that can learn from experience . . . [the] possibility of letting the machine alter its own instructions." It was a stunning prognostication, and Turing is today revered for his vision. For someone surrounded at the time by machines not much smarter than a light switch to imagine a machine that could someday learn from mistakes and alter its own code was like an eighteenth-century stagecoach driver envisioning a sporty car with a hybrid engine and satellite navigation.

Two years later, in 1948, Turing and his colleague David Champernowne built a computer chess program called "Turochamp." Compared to later such programs, it was extremely primitive. But at the time their program was too complex for the available hardware. Of the few actual computers in existence at that time, none of them was even remotely powerful enough to execute their software. So Turing himself became a machine: in a game against Champernowne, Turing followed the Turochamp instruction code as if he were the computer, making the computations by hand and moving his pieces accordingly. It took Turing about thirty minutes to calculate each move. Not surprisingly, the program lost to the experienced human chess player. But subsequently, it managed to beat Champernowne's wife, a chess novice. Chess computing—and artificial intelligence (AI) itself—had taken its first baby step forward.

VERY EARLY ON, AI pioneers in the United States and Britain hit on a conceptual quandary: should they design machines to actually think like human beings—incorporating experience, recognizing patterns, and formulating and executing plans—or should they play to the more obvious strengths of machines' ability to conduct brute-force mathematical calculations? In his 1947 essay on machine intelligence, Turing had suggested that he would pursue the former—"letting the machine alter its own instructions." But from a practical standpoint, he focused on the latter. Turing's counterparts across the Atlantic, including MIT's Claude Shannon, independently came to the same way of thinking. Like Turing, Shannon was fascinated by chess's potential in the pursuit of what he called "mechanized thinking." But he became convinced that computer chess and other AI pursuits should not be modeled on human thought. Unlike human brains, computers did not have scores of different specialized components that could read information, contextualize it, prioritize it, store it in different forms, recall it in a variety of ways, and then decide on how to apply it; computers, at least as they were understood then, could calculate very quickly, following programmed instructions. This particular strength—and limitation—of computers suggested a different route for AI, a new sort of quasi-intelligence based on mathematical computation.

Chess would be a central proving ground for this new type of intelligence. Theoretically, at least, the game could be fully converted into one long mathematical formula. The board could be represented as a numerical map, pieces weighted according to their relative value, moves and board positions scored according to the numerical gain or loss that each would bring. But the scope of computation was immense—too much for the earliest computers to handle. One of the first was John von Neumann's Maniac I, built in 1956 in Los Alamos, New Mexico, to help refine the American hydrogen bomb arsenal. With 2,400 vacuum tubes, the machine could process a staggering ten thousand instructions per second. It could not, though, handle a full-scale chessboard. Playing a simplified version of chess on a chessboard six squares by six with no Bishops, no castling, and no double-square first Pawn move, Maniac I required twelve minutes to look just two full moves ahead. (With Bishops, it would have needed three hours.) The machine did go on to help design potent nuclear warheads, but as a chess player it was pretty hopeless.

The problem, put simply, was time. Even as programmers devised increasingly elegant equations to represent quasi-intelligent chess decisions, the computers still had to evaluate an overwhelming number of positions in order to play competently. Human experts could get around this problem using intuition to ferret out most of the silly moves and narrow their decision down to a few strong possibilities. But machines couldn't do this. They had to consider all of the choices equally, and to look ahead as many moves as possible to see how each choice would play out. That amount of calculation took a lot of time. With an average of thirty-five or so options per turn, and then thirty-five different subsequent responses for each possible move, and so on, geometric progression quickly made the large number of calculations untenable for even a speedy computer. To look ahead a mere two moves each, the computer would have to evaluate $35 \times 35 \times 35 \times 35 = 1,500,625$ positions. Three full moves required analysis of 1,838,265,625 (nearly two billion) positions. Four moves: 2,251,875,390,625 (over two trillion) positions.

This was not a short-term problem for engineers. Even as computers got faster and faster, they would not come remotely close to truly managing chess's near-infinity. In fact, it seemed safe to predict that no machine would be able to overcome this problem for many centuries, if ever. Computer scientists estimated, for example, that a future computer examining moves five times faster than Deep Blue's supercomputing 200 million positions per second would take an estimated 3.3 billion years to consider all of the possibilities for ten moves by each player.

In Bletchley Park during the war, Turing realized that the single most essential tool for the mathematizing of chess would be a technique developed by his Princeton mentor John von Neumann called minimax. Short for "*minimizing* the expected *maximum* loss," minimax was essentially a method for choosing the least bad move. It came out of the logical recognition that, when competing in a game where one player's success is another player's failure (also called a zero-sum game), Player A will always try to choose the moves that are best for him and worst for Player B. It therefore behooves Player B to identify not his absolute ideal series of moves—since no worthy opponent will allow that course—but rather the moves which will deprive Player A of his best moves. Player B, in fact, wants to move in such a way as to leave Player A with his least best option, his minimum maximum.

The minimax logic applied to any game where all the information was known by every player—chess, checkers, tic-tac-toe, and so on. In practice, it required placing all game decisions onto an enormous "game tree," with a single trunk (the current board position), some primary branches (all of White's next possible moves), a larger number of secondary branches (all of Black's possible responses to each of White's next possible moves), and on and on, eventually ending with an abundance of "leaves" (representing the deepest level being analyzed at the time).

Imagine, for example, that each one of the following tiny squares is a chessboard with an array of pieces. This artificially simple chess game tree represents three possible moves by White, each one of which is followed by three possible moves by Black, each of which is followed by two possible moves by White:

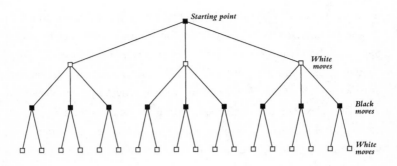

The object is to determine the best of the possible moves by White at the beginning of the tree. Using the minimax procedure, the computer first scores each of the boards on the *last* level of the tree—the leaves. Imagine that, in the following diagram, a computer has examined each of the leaves and has scored each board according the relative advantage for White. The highest numbers represent the better positions for White:

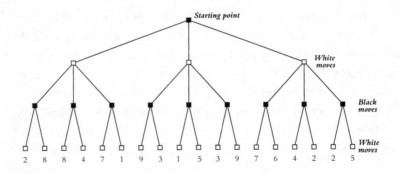

Now, according to minimax logic, the computer assigns scores to branches higher up on the tree—the moves happening earlier. First it determines the best board position from each of the leaf choices, and assigns those values to the next level up.

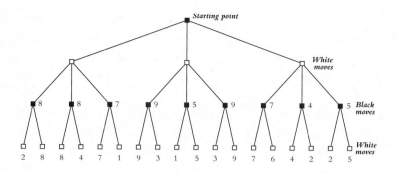

Then the computer considers how Black will move. Black will want the least advantaged position for White—the lowest score. So it moves those low scores up to the top level:

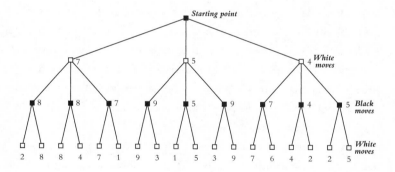

Now White must decide how to move. White will choose the move with the highest score—the board represented by the score of seven.

Needless to say, if chess trees were anywhere near as simple as the demonstration above, they wouldn't be necessary in the first place. Minimax enabled computers to sort through chess trees with millions of branches on the fourth and fifth branch levels, billions on the sixth and seventh levels, and trillions on the eighth level. In tackling such logical complexity, the technique emerged as far more than a computer chess tool. It became a foundation stone of modern game theory, applicable to war gaming, economics, coalition building, and a wide variety of other systems involving two or more competitive parties. It helped jump-start artificial intelligence research, and has since enabled us to look scientifically at human endeavors such as voter participation. Minimax enabled social scientists to mathematize large chunks of public life.

In the nearer term, it also quickly put computer chess programmers in a serious bind. By opening up chess to a nearly endless series of calculations, minimax made chess computing both possible and impossible. The equations could be continually improved to make better and better chess decisions, but it simply took too long for computers to analyze all the possibilities. Then, in 1956, American computer scientist and AI pioneer John McCarthy—he had actually coined the term *artificial intelligence* one year earlier—came up with an ingenious revision of minimax called alpha-beta pruning that allowed a computer to ignore certain leaves on a tree whose evaluations wouldn't make a difference in the final result. Like the minimax concept, the idea wasn't based on any particular insight into chess, but was a simple matter of logic: certain leaf evaluations are irrelevant if other leaf values on that same branch have already taken that particular branch out of contention. A computer instructed not to bother calculating such nonactionable leaves could accomplish its work in much less time.

Alpha-beta pruning was, in a sense, the first true piece of artificial intelligence: an algorithm (a step-by-step procedure for solving a problem) that helped machines logically rule out certain options in a crude analogue to how humans do the same thing through intuition. An expert human player could tell with a quick glance and a split-second subconscious memory sweep which moves could be ignored and which should be prominently considered. Alpha-beta pruning was the computer's way of setting similar priorities.

In 1966, MIT's Richard Greenblatt introduced yet another critical innovation called transposition tables. This technique allowed a computer to cache (temporarily remember) the value of certain chess positions so that when they came up again they wouldn't have to be fully reevaluated. It took advantage of the observation that identical chess positions were often produced by moves in different sequence. These two separate openings, for example, produce exactly the same board position, since they are the same moves in different order:

1. e4 e5 2. f3 c6

1. f3 c6 2. e4 e5

Such duplications of positions are called transpositions. A program that could recognize and remember transpositions could trim the necessary number of calculations. This was the earliest glimpse of what Turing had fantasized as machine learning, since a cached position would enable the computer to remember certain truths as a game progressed—and potentially even from game to game. With this new way for computers to remember game positions, it would henceforth no longer be possible, for example, for a human player to beat a computer exactly the same way twice in a row. (How many players wish they could say as much for themselves?) Computers could essentially remember their mistakes.

None of these improvements in searching and pattern recognition were restricted to chess, of course. But for many years, from the 1970s through the mid-1990s, chess continued to be a choice vehicle for AI research and experimentation. At engineering schools like MIT and Carnegie Mellon, graduate students married software advances with faster and faster processors in a competitive race to build the ultimate chess computer—a machine that could beat the world chess champion. Teams on campuses formed around one chess project or another, with students custom-designing, redesigning, and re-redesigning tiny silicon "chess chips." The progress was slower than many had hoped for, but it was steady. In 1978 the leading machine of the time, known as Chess 4.7, developed by David Slate and Larry Atkin at Northwestern University, forced Scottish master player David Levy into a draw—a first. A few years later, the leading computers started winning the occasional game against expert players, and in 1988 the Carnegie Mellon machine HiTech became the first computer to be ranked as a grandmaster. When Garry Kasparov first played and defeated Deep Blue in 1996, beating the machine with three wins, one loss, and two draws, the world champion reported that he had detected stirrings of genuine thought in the machine. The following year, after some major processor and programming upgrades, Deep Blue defeated Kasparov, with two wins, one loss, and three draws. The result sent a quick chill around the world. Much soul searching began.

Was this the end of chess? The end of us? What did Deep Blue's victory mean?

Some were quick to point out that the stunning achievement was limited to a mere board game. Deep Blue didn't know to stop at a red light, and couldn't string two words together or offer anything else in the way of even simulated intelligence. Others didn't think that even the chess win was so amazing. MIT linguist Noam Chomsky scoffed that a computer beating a grandmaster at chess was about as momentous "as the fact that a bulldozer can lift more than some weight lifter." It was simply another case in the long history of technology, he argued, of humans inventing machines that could perform highly specialized tasks with great efficiency. Specialization did not intelligence make.

Chomsky seemed to have a point. Deep Blue was no Hal. Over the course of many decades, chess computing had not actually enabled computers to think very much like humans at all. "Turing's expectation was that chess-programming would contribute to the study of how human beings think," says Jack Copeland, director of the Turing Archive for the History of Computing at the University of Canterbury. "In fact, little or nothing about human thought processes has been learned from the series of projects that culminated in Deep Blue."

Thinking like humans, though, had never really been the intention of the AI community. That had been Turing's original dream, but the practical consensus from the very beginning was to suss out a new kind of intelligence. And in fact, they had done just that. As the twenty-first century began, machines were able to make all sorts of intelligent actions that went far beyond mere calculations. "There are today hundreds of examples of narrow AI deeply integrated into our information-based economy," explains Ray Kurzweil, author of *The Age of Spiritual Machines*. "Routing emails and cell phone calls, automatically diagnosing electrocardiograms and blood cell images, directing cruise missiles and weapon systems, automatically landing airplanes, conducting pattern-recognition-based financial transactions, detecting credit card fraud, and a myriad of other automated tasks are all successful examples of AI in use today."

Add to that list: speech recognition, hazardous-duty robots, swimming pool antidrowning detectors, the Mars *Sojourner* explorer vehicle, and bits and pieces of most contemporary cars, televisions, and word processors. Looking at it under the hood, machine-based intelligence may look entirely different from human intelligence, but it *is* intelligence, proponents argue. "Believe me, Fritz is intelligent," Frederic Friedel, cofounder of ChessBase software, says of one of his company's most popular programs. "It is a *kind* of intelligence. If you look at anyone playing against a computer, within minutes they say things like, 'Oh God, he's trying to trap my Queen,' and 'Tricky little bloke,' and 'Ah, he saw that.' They're talking about it as if it is a human being. And it *is* behaving exactly like someone who's trying to trick you, trying to trap your Queen. It seems to smell the danger."

In other words, it passes the Turing test. In front of the curtain, it displays what seem like the actions of a very smart human being, even though, behind the curtain, its mechanics are in no way attempting to mimic the functions of the human brain. The AI community has already succeeded in substituting computers for functions formerly thought to require human intelligence, which implies that (1) we need to broaden our understanding of intelligence, and (2) the smart machines *are* coming. "This machine intelligence is completely different from what people thought it would be," says Friedel. "We have to acknowledge that intelligence, like life forms, has incredible variety. We [in the chess community] are the first to see a completely different form of intelligence. But we all have to understand it is coming." Friedel continues:

Can you imagine in ten or twenty years having judges who are made of silicon? I'm sure somebody will come along and say, "Wait a minute, does this thing know anything about justice, about human feeling, about human dignity? It knows nothing about that. It is only doing a billion statistical analyses per second—brute force statistical analysis. Of course it cannot possibly pass judgment over human beings!" Which is valid. Except—what happens if most people say, "You know, I want to go to the silicon one, because the humans are not good enough. These machines are better."

The smart machines are coming. Garry Kasparov, leader of the humans, did not maintain his exuberance and cloak of invincibility through the rest of his 2003 match against Deep Junior. After his victory in Game 1 and respectable draw in Game 2, he ran into trouble. Game 3 saw Kasparov again playing a fearless and ingenious game (as White) for a long while, then making a mistake and having to resign. This evened the match score, with three games to go. Game 4 was another tough contest, which eventually tilted toward Deep Junior and forced Kasparov into fighting for a draw. Game 5 seemed to find a dispirited Kasparov without much fight in him; he settled for a draw in just nineteen moves.

Then came Game 6, watched by an estimated 200–300 million people around the world on the sports network ESPN2. For a while, Kasparov did not disappoint. He played a stunning and creative game, eking out what commentators considered a potentially winning position. But then, shockingly, he requested a draw. The audience was dumbfounded. The great Kasparov had caved to the pressure of an awesome and near-flawless opponent. Afterward it became clear from his comments that as badly as Kasparov wanted to win, he wanted more badly not to lose; the machine's consistency and intelligence had spooked him, he admitted. Knowing that any tiny mistake would be ruthlessly exploited by the computer, he was simply unwilling to take that risk in front of such a large audience. So he settled for a draw—in the game and the match.

The symbolic message was unmistakable: Without actually mimicking the function of the human brain, well-designed computers could now perform some extraordinarily complex tasks as well as, if not better than, human beings. Whether or not we would ultimately call such machines "intelligent" would be far less relevant than what tasks we would actually allow them to perform.

THE IMMORTAL GAME

Moves 22 and 23 (Checkmate)

THERE'S A FAMOUS SAYING in chess: "You had a won game, but I won the game." A *won game* refers to a board position in which one player has an advantage such that, given flawless play by both sides through the end of the game, that player will win. But— fortunately—even among chess experts, imperfection reigns, and won games are frequently lost. Out of ignorance or under great time pressure or simple exhaustion, people frequently make obvious and not-so-obvious blunders, and a winning position will slip away. Human frailty helps to ensure that chess between mortals will always be interesting.

When one player closes in on the other player's King, the pressure rises. The defender becomes desperate, of course, not to lose. The attacker wants desperately not to blow it. And the best answers are rarely obvious.

It was extraordinary enough that Anderssen was even on the attack. He was, after all, two Rooks and a Bishop down. Even more amazing, his position actually looked good, as long as he could maintain offensive momentum. But how would he press his attack?

22. Qf6+

(White Queen to f6; *check*)

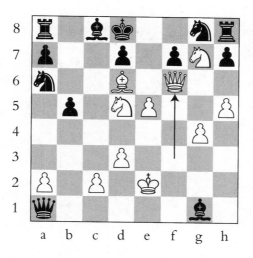

It was time for Anderssen's final surprise, his *immortal* flourish. He'd already sacrificed three major pieces; now, as much for the thrill as the tactical advantage, it seemed, he also let go of his Queen. Putting Kieseritzky in check, Anderssen offered up his Queen to Kieseritzky's g8 Knight.

22. . . . N×f6
(Black Knight captures Queen at f6)

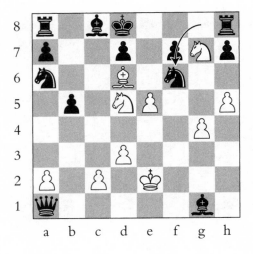

Once again, Kieseritzky took the offer. But in doing so he brought his Knight out of a critical position and . . .

23. Be7++

(White Bishop to e7; *checkmate*)

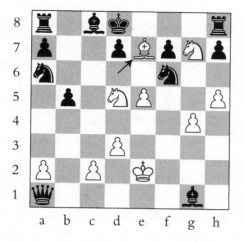

. . . allowed Anderssen to checkmate with his Bishop.

So ended the casual masterpiece forever to be admired by patzers and grandmasters alike. "In this game," Wilhelm Steinitz later wrote, "there occurs almost a continuity of brilliancies, every one of which bears the stamp of intuitive genius." The brilliance of the win was also immediately recognized by Kieseritzky, the loser, who, at the expense of his own ego, quickly arranged to telegraph it back to Paris and personally annotate it for publication in his own chess journal, *La Régence*. "This is not the right move," he remarked about his own move 8. After Anderssen's move 11, Kieseritzky observed that "from this moment, White plays better." But he reserved his most pregnant comment for his move 17. . . . Qxb2 (Black Queen captures Pawn at b2). "The taking of this Pawn and the attack against the two Rooks don't produce the result that one would have hoped." His final published note on the game comes just one stroke later, after Anderssen's move 18. "*Coup de grâce*," Kieseritzky writes, "that renders null all the efforts of the adversary. This game was conducted by M. Anderssen with remarkable talent." Broadcasting his own brutal loss was a testament to Kieseritzky's humility, his respect for Anderssen, and his devotion to the game.

For all its subsequent durability, the game itself lasted just under an hour. This puportedly casual encounter behind them, both men returned their full attention to the remaining three and a half weeks of the grueling seven-week international tournament which had brought them to London in the first place. This was the spotlight event chess lovers from all over the world were following breathlessly, game by game, move by move. All the sensational chess talents of the world were present—an unprecedented gathering—and the onlookers naturally expected landmark-quality play. But brilliance cannot be scheduled or predicted, and this extended clash of the chess titans turned out to be somewhat of a letdown. Most of the eighty-five tournament games were of no lasting consequence. As master player and analyst Andy Soltis would observe over a century later, they were "forgettable."

Instead, what emerged as the tournament's central drama was Adolf Anderssen's surprising triumph. Continuing on from his casual brilliance at the Divan, the underdog Anderssen dominated the tournament as well, twice more defeating Kieseritzky along with many of the other masters. It was the beginning of an extraordinary streak: in his seven subsequent tournaments, Anderssen won six, including two other elite international tournaments—London in 1860 and Baden-Baden in 1870. In hindsight, his astonishing performance against Kieseritzky at the Grand Divan was his quick debut as one of the most extraordinary chess minds of all time. He also came to be universally regarded as a fine human being. When Anderssen died in 1879, his obituary in the German chess newspaper *Deutsche Schachzeitung* ran nineteen pages long.

Life was not as kind to Kieseritzky, who would forever carry the moniker "Immortal Loser." Upon returning home to Paris from his three consecutive losses to Anderssen, he was soon forced to fold his failing chess magazine as he struggled with his finances and his health. He died in a Paris mental hospital in 1853, just two years after his loss in the Immortal Game. He had no money to his name. No one in the chess world contributed to give Kieseritzky a decent burial. No one stood by his grave.

THE NEXT WAR

Chess and the Future of Human Intelligence

"WE LEARN BY CHESS," wrote Benjamin Franklin in 1786, "the habit of not being discouraged by present bad appearances in the state of our affairs, the habit of hoping for a favorable change, and that of persevering in the search of resources."

It was only about a month after I began researching the deep history of chess's entanglement with the human mind that I realized this wasn't just a story about our past, but also one about our future. We have always needed to learn good habits, and we always will. In August 2002, ABC News *Nightline* featured a profile of Eugene Brown, an ex-con whose chance encounter with chess in prison had become a part of his personal salvation. Through the game he learned discipline, focus, patience, and persistence. After his release, Brown made it his mission to use chess as a tool to rescue disadvantaged youths before they got into serious trouble. He opened up a youth recreation center called Chess House. "When I came out [of prison]," Brown said, "I was carrying chess with me. Everywhere I was going, I had a board, and I was teaching people: There's three phases to a chess game—the opening, the middle and the end, and you have to put them all together to win. You just don't win in the opening. That's what I was trying to do when I went into that bank. I was trying to win in the opening. I was trying to get instant results. . . . You keep making bad moves, you're going to get checkmated. And on the street, it ain't checkmate. It's your life. It's a wheelchair. It's incarceration."

One striking thing about Brown's story was that it did not seem ridiculous. The producers at ABC News, and subsequently their viewers, found it interesting and not at all bizarre that this sixth-century Persian war game, with pieces named after medieval European figures and rules that have not substantially changed for more than five hundred years, would give a down-and-out American in the twenty-first century some insight into his own flaws and a philosophy on how to repair them. In the era of Xbox and PlayStation, chess was no longer the most popular game around, but it was still very much a part of the fabric of our culture, and even seemed to be enjoying yet another popular resurgence. Membership in the United States Chess Federation was at an all-time high. Sales of chess sets in Britain were booming. The game was attracting a storm of attention on the Internet—with upwards of 100 million games played online annually. There were also large swells in urban and suburban youth competition, and among trendsetters. Will Smith, Don Imus, Bill Gates, Julia Roberts, Sting, and Salman Rushdie all played. Madonna was taking lessons. Arnold Schwarzenegger, prior to his California governorship, established a permanent chess table in his movie set trailer, with one chair labeled "Loser" and the other—his—labeled "Winner." The improvisational rock band Phish had recently made history by arranging the two most populous chess games ever: the band versus its entire 15,000-person audience. Each side collectively offered one move per show (the audience voted during intermission), stretching out each game for several weeks. The band won the first game, the audience the second.

Part of the game's modern appeal, in a world increasingly interconnected in finance and culture, might be its universality. By the late twentieth century, the western European standardized form of the game had long since spread to every part of every continent, including all of Africa and South America, and had even overtaken the older *chatrang/shatranj* in its original quarters: India, Iran, Russia, and the Arab nations.

Most important of all, though, the game was becoming an integral part of school life in many nations, including the United States. A grow-

ing number of school systems were even making it a part of their cur-
ricula. In New York City, where I live, chess had recently worked its
way into the classrooms of 160 public schools. It was also widely taught
in private schools, where competition was fierce for the most sought-
after instructors. To witness this growing school–chess connection,
knowing the game's profound history, was nothing short of surreal.

"GOOD MORNING, CLASS." In a well-lit classroom in the
Sheepshead Bay neighborhood of Brooklyn, roving chess instructor
Nicholas Chatzilias introduced himself to a group of curious, well-
disciplined eight-year-olds. The large, rectangular room on the second
floor of Public School 52 had three computers in the corner, a row of
shallow coat closets on the east wall, and a table full of snacks and small
plant aquariums at the far end. Nestled close to the blackboard, nineteen second graders were arranged in four desk clusters. Chatzilias gently set his plastic poster-tube case against a table, picked up a piece of
chalk, and wrote his name up on the board.

"You can call me Mr. Nicholas," he told the group. A longtime amateur chess competitor, Chatzilias was now being paid to teach his passion by the New York-based Chess-in-the-Schools foundation. He
taught weekly chess classes in five different public schools and super-
vised their after-school chess clubs. Of the wide range of elementary,
middle, and junior high kids that Chatzilias would be working with this
semester, this youngest group would perhaps be the most challenging—
and yet, at the same time, the most promising. At their tender age, they
could only so quickly learn the nuances of the game. Once they took to
it, though, the benefits could be extraordinary. Contemporary studies
were helping to establish with modern scholarship what Benjamin
Franklin and others had been saying for centuries about chess's wide
range of intellectual and character benefits. The earlier the kids started,
the better. Chess literacy was like its own unique language: anyone
could learn it, but the very youngest players could hardwire it directly
into their brains.

Bringing chess into school classrooms was an experiment with roots in mid-twentieth-century Russia that began to catch the attention of Western educators in the late 1960s. In the mid-1970s, studies in Belgium and Zaire suggested that chess could improve students' spatial, numerical, and verbal abilities—as well as overall cognitive development. Other promising studies followed from Hong Kong, Venezuela, New Brunswick, Pennsylvania, and Texas. With each new study came an increasing number of communities inclined to give chess a try. After all, schools are not only supposed to impart knowledge; they're also supposed to teach kids *how to learn*, to instill curiosity and critical thinking skills. "It's the finest thing that ever happened to this school," remarked one New York City principal. A Florida superintendent echoed that sentiment: "Chess has taught my students more than any other subject," he said. "I used to teach for schools in the poor neighborhoods and that's why I came here," explained Maria Manuri, an educator working with a Toronto-based program called Chess'n Math. "With chess, you can learn all kinds of things. It's not just concentration, not just logic, it's everything. It's how to lose, how to win, how to be social. In schools today there's no ethics anymore. Chess can teach that to you too."

Indeed, researchers were finding that chess might help kids with skills far beyond math and logic. "Chess can enhance concentration, patience, and perseverance," concluded the University of Sydney's Peter Dauvergne, "as well as develop creativity, intuition, memory, and most importantly, the ability to analyse and deduce from a set of general principles, learning to make tough decisions and solve problems flexibly." At Memphis State University, Dianne Horgan investigated the cognitive mechanisms involved. She came away with a few powerful conclusions:

1. *More learning longer.* Chess teaches children to sharpen their information evaluation skills, and to build those skills for a longer period of time—to keep their "acquisition and revision processes active."

2. *More efficient learning.* Chess training and tournaments require

an unusual amount of "process feedback"—not just acknowledging that something has gone wrong after a lost game, but having to learn what went wrong. Honing feedback skills could have wide implications for future development.

3. *More self-perception.* Serious chess training improves "calibration," the correlation between a person's ability and that person's perception of his or her ability. (In the general population, calibration skills are poor.) Improving calibration can greatly enhance the value of feedback.

Chess was obviously not the only way to give the young brain a tune-up. But schools needed an array of tools to help them consistently produce disciplined, curious, persistent minds. The world is awash in information, scientific nuance, and fragmentation of culture and perspectives. Failure to deliver at least a basic education has greater consequences than ever before.

In New York, Chess-in-the-Schools, formerly known as the American Chess Foundation, had been offering free instruction to underprivileged New York City students since 1986. By 2005, thanks largely to support from New York philanthropist Lewis Cullman, they had a $4 million annual budget supporting fifty instructors in 160 schools. "Chess is not a game of luck," the foundation declared in its mission statement. "Children who practice and develop skills will reap rewards. The confidence they develop extends to other areas of their academic and emotional lives. . . . Our program has proven to be a cost-effective way to inspire and empower children to succeed, one move at a time."

Even after learning so much about chess's potential impact on the mind, I was still highly skeptical of this notion of actually importing the game directly into our school classrooms. At a time when public education was in such disrepair, did chess really deserve to be a priority agenda item? Wouldn't students' time and energy perhaps be better spent elsewhere? I wanted to witness this firsthand. Mr. Nicholas invited me to sit in on his class.

"Can anyone tell me how old chess is?" he asked his young students. "How long has it been around?"

Hands shot up with wild guesses.

"Eighteen years?"

"Thirty-eight?"

Obviously, Chatzilias wasn't expecting a correct answer from second graders. Rather, this was his opening gambit in a strategy to demonstrate how truly special and set apart the game was. None of his ambitious plans would go anywhere unless he could really get these kids hooked. They had to fall in love with the game.

"Here are some other games I'm sure you've heard of," he said, writing their names on the blackboard.

> Gameboy _____ years old
> Monopoly _____ years old
> Baseball _____ years old
> Chess _____ years old

For fun, he invited guesses about the age of each familiar game. Then he filled in the blanks with the real answers.

> Gameboy __15__ years old
> Monopoly __75__ years old
> Baseball __150__ years old
> **Chess __1,400__ years old**

"So chess is much, much older than all these other games. Why do you think people have been playing chess for so long? What's so good about it?"

Hands shot up.

"Because it's fun!"

"It is fun," Mr. Nicholas agreed. "It's lots of fun. It's my favorite game. I've been playing chess for twenty-five years and I'm going to continue to play it my whole life. Can you tell me some of the things you already know about chess?"

Everyone, it seemed, had something to offer.

"You have to think before you move the pieces."

"You can't play without the King."

"You have to take turns."

"There's a Queen."

"There's a Knight—it looks like a horse."

"It can take a whole day to move just one piece."

It can take a whole day to move just one piece. The line caught me by surprise and stuck in my head. It seemed to me that its implications were enormous for any eight-year-old to consider. If a player could spend all day pondering all of her options and trying to choose the smartest move, if a simple board game could draw that much energy and time, if thinking could be that complicated and consequential, then thinking carefully must be just about the most important activity a person could do for herself. Before even learning how to play, these kids had already tapped into one of chess's essential truths.

After working through some more history, the names and moves of each piece, and an introduction to chess notation, the fun could finally begin. Opening his large plastic poster tube, Mr. Nicholas unfurled a giant vertical demonstration chessboard and hung it in front of the blackboard. Every eight-year-old eye opened a little bit wider. From far away, the board looked like a simple flat piece of paper with a green-and-white checkered pattern painted on. Up close, though, one could see that it had small slots cut into the bottom of each square to hold the flat felt demonstration pieces. One by one, the kids got to practice putting pieces on the board, responding to Mr. Nicholas's coordinates. Naomi placed a Pawn on h4. Alicia put a Knight on f6. Thomas put a Queen on a3.

Giggles and murmurs ebbed and flowed as each student stood up to study the board and eventually place his or her piece. The group became especially keyed up when someone made a mistake. Mr. Nicholas had to shush them a few times, and was once compelled to play his trump card. "The faster we can get through a lesson," he said, "the sooner we get to play."

Decorum was essential, and not just because it moved the lesson along more smoothly, but also because it was an important aspect of the lesson itself. The millennium-old tradition of chivalrous chess play was a crucial part of the attraction for Chatzilias and other instructors. It helped introduce the dynamic of tough but friendly competition at a very early age, and dovetailed with one of the school's essential missions. In a sense, all schooling in the United States was an elaborate training session for the free-market, democratic, meritocratic, modern, bloodless warfare that would dominate their adult lives.

Mr. Nicholas offered a much simpler expression of this idea to his second graders. "We're going to shake hands before we play," he said, "and shake hands after we play."

Within a few weeks the second graders were indeed shaking hands and playing chess—sort of. Once a week they would break into pairs, set up the pieces, and move them around the board. But these were eight-year-olds—the play was not always conventional. Bishops would sometimes glide straight up and down the board; Pawns would sometimes stride diagonally without the necessary capture. Checks were sometimes ignored, or illegally resolved. Many of the young players seemed to make a move almost as fast as they could think of one.

It was a healthy start, predictable, and even uplifting. But this was not the thrilling majesty of chess. Watching Chatzilias explain *check* over and over again, I felt a little sorry for him. He and his older brother Alexis, an even more competitive player, had spent their teens and twenties immersed in chess games and problems, studying past masters, becoming more and more nuanced, battling one another over and over. ("I've never beaten him—not once," he said. "That is still my goal in chess.") Now he was "Mr. Nicholas," his days filled with shushing kids and correcting illegal Knight moves. It felt a little bit like watching a skilled Impressionist teach paint-by-numbers.

At least that was how *I* felt as I watched him on our first few days together—Chatzilias himself didn't show any disappointment or regret. To the contrary, I could tell he felt blessed to introduce very young children to his cherished game. But I asked him if he didn't also sometimes feel a little smothered, or just plain bored, spending all his time in such an elementary chess mode.

He raised his eyebrows and smiled. "You haven't seen my older kids play yet. You haven't seen my chess club."

CHESS CLUB was by invitation only. Every Friday afternoon, right after school, thirty of the most ambitious players from Mr. Nicholas's third, fourth, and fifth grade classes ambled into the large teacher's lounge on the first floor to focus on the fine points of the game. After a few minutes of snack time and some school-is-finally-over unwinding, the kids got ready to concentrate deeply for the rest of the afternoon.

Chatzilias set up his hanging demonstration board, just as he had in each classroom during the school day. But this time he immediately arranged the pieces into a complex chess molecule, consulting a chess history book for the precise arrangement.

"Mate in twenty-two moves," he said with an arch smile.

This sounded like a joke. Difficult chess problems typically require the problem solver to arrange checkmate in one or a handful of moves. Finding a mate in twenty-two moves seemed far beyond a manageable problem. Certainly this was not a challenge that a ten-year-old, even an ambitious one, could solve on the spur of the moment.

In fact, though, the challenge was authentic, much easier than it first appeared, and well suited to this group. It turned out that after the first few creative moves, White simply had to establish a simple pattern of moves that would push the Black King into a corner and, on move 22, checkmate him. Working together, after a few misses, the kids got it. There was no sign of obsession or anger or antisocial impulsiveness. These were kids being kids in the most uplifting sense possible, working together in innocence and fun on a difficult project.

Chatzilias was working in the context of the huge volume of modern chess knowledge and a panoply of styles. Over the previous half century, chess masters had advanced the game with one more great evolutionary step. Developed over several decades and known as Synthesis or New Dynamism, this style—or amalgamation of styles—was an effort to integrate the highly effective but seemingly contradictory advances from the previous decades—to bring together Steinitz's Scientific approach with the Hypermodernists' contrarianism and adventurous spirit. They did this by adopting a philosophy of organic play—"whatever happens," American grandmaster Reuben Fine would say, "flows naturally out of the position." Well versed in the broad varieties of play, a master of synthesis could be ready for anything with a full quiver of arrows.

But Chatzilias didn't spend much time on broad theory. He preferred to get into problem solving. His second challenge this afternoon was the evocatively titled Frankenstein-Dracula Variation, a favorite of his and his brother's. The name came from the hair-raising and bloodthirsty nature of the position that both players would find themselves in after just a few moves. Chatzilias set up the problem and put it to the group. 1. e4 c5 2. Nc3 Nf6 3. Bc4—and then Black lunges for the e Pawn with his Knight (3. . . . Nxe4!). Now White is tempted to take the Black Knight with 4. Nxe4, but that would be falling into Black's trap. Black would follow with 4. . . . d5, forking White's Bishop and Knight and securing an excellent stronghold in the center. So White instead moves 4. Qh5, threatening mate in one move. What is Black's only effective response? The most enthusiastic students were bunched up close near the board, and as ideas occurred a hand would shoot up and a voice would shout—"Pawn g6?"

Mr. Nicholas smiled. "No—that doesn't work, because Queen e5, check, and pin of the King and Rook." He demonstrated by quickly moving pieces across the large board for everyone to see. He paused to make sure everyone understood what he had just done, then moved the pieces back to the original position.

Everyone seemed to keep up but me. I sat about halfway back in the long room, at first just drinking in the happy energy of ten- and eleven-year-olds. Then I tried to follow Mr. Nicholas's moves on the board, but couldn't quite stay with it. Not everyone in the room was shouting out clever ideas on how to solve each problem, but enough of them were that I had trouble following it all. In contrast to the earlier second grade classroom lessons, Mr. Nicholas now moved the pieces rapidly, and skipped all the romantic mythology ("the Knight's job is to protect the castle"). Instead, he talked in dense chess notation. The kids seemed to follow it with the same intuition and boundless energy of a summer swim game. I felt old and distant, too arthritic to move quickly around the water.

Emotionally, at least, I was very much present. There was no way to avoid becoming swept up in this club's effervescent optimism and warmth: the dedication of young children to such a serious enterprise, the camaraderie between passionate teacher and ambitious students. It was overwhelming and infectious. Something profound was taking place in this large room, and it was impossible not to be moved by it.

These kids spoke the language. It seemed to come natural to them. They were serious and full of energy. They were focused and ready to solve problems. When they paired up and started to play, about thirty minutes into the afterschool session, they somehow managed to be serious chess competitors and exuberant kids at the same time. At Mr. Nicholas's insistence, they recorded all the moves of each game on a sheet of paper for future analysis. The room was quiet, but not somber.

Seeing all this, I finally got it—what chess and other hyper-stimulating thinking tools could do for these kids, and for all of us. We face in our modern, splintered world not only a crisis in education, but more pointedly a crisis of understanding—of thought and of willingness to engage in thought. We live in an age where the intellectual challenges are unprecedented; just to be an effective consumer one has to be able to navigate a hundred half-truths and advertising tricks every day. Ironically, in our information age, truth is harder to come by because it is so surrounded by facts, slick presentations, and tools of distraction.

One common response to our splintered, postmodern, slippery-truth age is not to think but to instead fall back on a fixed set of beliefs, a strict ideology. In consequence, we have—inside the United States and worldwide—a growing schism between enlightened, skeptical, thinking individuals and close-minded, fundamentalist ideologues. We are also literally in a war that is rooted in these differences. We must fight a real war with real weapons, of course. But we must also address the underlying schism. The single greatest danger to ourselves and future generations is to stop thinking, and it behooves us to do anything we can to encourage spinning, skeptical minds. To do this, we will need powerful thought tools like chess that help our minds expand, grow comfortable with abstraction, and learn to navigate complex systems.

As Mr. Nicholas walked from table to table quietly asking individual kids about certain moves, I realized that I was suddenly looking at chess in a whole new way. Through the eyes of these kids, I could see that one could learn the game without surrendering to the oppressive weight of its limitlessness. Being serious at chess didn't require abandoning the fun; it didn't require solitary neuroticism; it didn't even require putting up with the coldness and nastiness of aggressive adult players. Like a young chef learning only the basics of simmer and sauté, one could apply oneself to the elementary principles and thrive in that challenge, even knowing that there were—and would always be—entire levels of play beyond one's ability. I could be serious about chess on my own terms, approaching the study of it as a joyful exploration rather than a chore.

"Suddenly I see it all," I actually wrote in my notes. "I could learn to love chess."

CODA

A MYSTERY THAT WILL quite likely never be solved can nonetheless still be a rich vein of inquiry. In Europe every few years, a small group of chess historians from all over the world gathers together to hash over the perpetual obscurities of the game's origins and other ancient questions. In November 2003 I was invited to attend their Berlin conference. For two days, we met in a large room in Berlin's Kunstbibliothek (Art Library), directly across the street from the aging Philharmonie concert hall. There were lectures on Philidor and Chinese chess pieces, and remembrances of recently deceased chess historians Ricardo Calvo and Kenneth Whyld. I muddled through a presentation of my own, which I called "Patzers and Progress: Chess as a Thought-Tool Through the Ages." Some heads nodded in appreciation; others shook gently at a few sloppy historical errors. Near the conference's end, there was a fascinating presentation on zugzwang, the paradoxical endgame phenomenon wherein the player moving can only worsen his position. Zugzwang is to be avoided at all costs, because once entered, the game is lost. The demonstration came from Yuri Averbakh, the legendary Russian grandmaster and expert in ancient chess problems who, at this group's 1993 conference in Amsterdam, had announced that he had finally solved as-Suli's thousand-year-old Diamond chess problem.

On my way back home from Berlin, I made two stops. The first was in Ströbeck, the tiny German "Chess Village" where the game has been a defining feature for many centuries. Legend has it that a prince was exiled to the Ströbeck prison tower in 1011; there he taught his guards chess, who subsequently taught the rest of the town and all passersby. Since then, Ströbeck has been a monument to chess's endurance, a Mecca for serious players and a model for chess instruction in and out of the classroom. Of my countless chess losses in the course of researching this book, none was as fun as being swiftly taken apart by the leonine Josef Cacek, Ströbeck's former mayor and the founder of its rich chess museum.

My second stop was at Simpson's on the Strand, the still-thriving upscale pub and restaurant in London that had hosted the Immortal Game a century and a half before. Simpson's had long since ceased to be a serious chess haunt, but it held on to many artifacts from its glory days. The stairwell to its basement pub was crowded with chess drawings, boards, pieces, cartoons, and score sheets. For anyone who cares about the game, walking down these stairs is like a trip back in time to chess's

golden age. I don't know that there's any place on earth where one can get a more resonant sense of what chess meant to the culture of nineteenth-century Europe.

It was also a place of unexpected personal revelation. At the very bottom of the staircase, I looked up to see a vivid sketch from 1886 of the sixteen world's greatest chess players attending a tournament in London. In the very center, looking over my right shoulder, was the first close-up image I had ever seen of my grandmother's grandfather, Samuel Rosenthal.

He seemed to be staring into infinity.

ACKNOWLEDGMENTS

BOOKS, I HAVE LEARNED, begin with essential and unexpected sparks. I'd like to begin by gratefully acknowledging those who helped kick off this long project. Watching the illusionist Ricky Jay in a live performance one evening in New York, I found myself captivated by his blindfolded "Knight's tour"—moving a Knight to every square on the chessboard without looking and without landing on any square twice. By chance, I saw around this same time an episode of the television show *West Wing* that prominently featured ancient Indian chess sets and deployed the game as a metaphor for real-world military and diplomatic finesse. With considerable tact, the show's writer Aaron Sorkin simultaneously evoked the game's medieval resonance and its contemporary relevance. It got my mind whirring.

But the real *eureka* moment came when I stumbled onto an illuminating paragraph in *Tikkun* by the writer Daniel Schifrin. It began

> The game of chess—with its richness, complexity and barely suppressed violence—is an extraordinary metaphor for the human condition. Some of the most important fiction writers and poets of the last two centuries—Nabokov, Borges, Tolstoy, Canetti, Aleichem, Eliot, and others—have fully recognized the uncanny ability of a chess game to represent the contradictions, struggles, and hopes of human society.

Immediately I knew I wanted to tell that story in nonfiction form. I contacted my literary agent and decade-long collaborator, Sloan Harris, who, true to form, instantly understood the concept better than I did. Bill Thomas at Doubleday, the masterful editor of my previous book *The Forgetting*, welcomed me back with enthusiasm and a towering vote of confidence that every writer should have at the start of a long project.

My next lucky move was to make contact with medieval literary scholar Jenny Adams, now at the University of Massachusetts, who quickly became my academic benefactor—dispensing much raw material and sage advice. Even as she worked on her own book about part of chess's history, Jen was the model of the heartening side of academia—generous, scrupulous, wise.

As my research began in earnest, I came into contact with a legion of other well-established chess historians—some professional, some amateur, all serious and generous: Michael Negele, Tomasz Lissowski, Ernst Strouhal, Ken Whyld, Myron Samsin, Jean-Louis Cazaux, Bill Wall, Hans Ree, Mark Weeks, Ralf J. Binnewirtz, Jurgen Stigter, Egbert Meissenburg, Paul Harrington, Andy Ansel, Kurt Landsberger, Carmen Calvo, José A. Aarzón, Govert Westerveld, Edward Winter, Kevin Brook, David Li, Lawrence Totaro, and Gerhard Josten. Marilyn Yalom was, like me, venturing into chess history for the first time, and aiming for a general audience; rather than throw up a defensive block, she was helpful and encouraging. Thanks also to two impressive chess-history collectives, the Ken Whyld Association and the Initiative Group Königstein; and to Stephen Zietz and the rest of the staff at the extraordinary John G. White Collection at the Cleveland Public Library.

As the book's broad scope became clearer, I was propelled into a wide array of other specialized fields. Thanks to Kate Ohno at the Yale University Library and Roy Goodman at the American Philosophical Society (in Philadelphia) for important assistance with Benjamin Franklin. For help in better understanding Duchamp, thanks to Allan Savage and Andrew Hugill. Anna Dergatcheva helped with Nabokov; Nancy Mandlove with Borges. Steven Gerrard was immensely important with respect to Locke and Wittgenstein.

Critical insight into the ancient Islamic Empire came from Anne Broadbridge and Alex Popovkin. For specifics on Persia, I am grateful to Bo Utas, Antonio Panaino, Josef Wiesehöfer, and especially Ahmad Ashraf at Columbia University's *Encyclopaedia Iranica* project. Roman Kovalev helped with medieval Russia; Leonard Kress with Poland. For help with Spanish history, I am indebted to Govert Westerveld, José Antonio Garzón, and Josep Alio. Barbara Wolff was a great help at the Albert Einstein Archives in Jerusalem. In London, Simpson's general manager Robin Easton supplied valuable history. Jimmy Weir and Jon Shenk pitched in from Afghanistan. For my visit to Ströbeck, Germany, many thanks to my generous hosts: Susanne Heizmann, Josef Cacek, Renate Krosch, and Rudi Krosch.

Crucial text translations came from Danielle Vasilescu, Eric Berlow, and Victoria Lesser (French); from Sara Ogger (German); from Malgorzata Marjanska-Fish and Paul Fish (Polish); and from the vastly underappreciated Russian scholar Gersh Kuntzman.

Fleshing out Harold Murray's life required a team which included the *British Chess Magazine*'s Paul Harrington, Peter Gilliver, and Niko Pfund at the Oxford University Press, and Hilary Turner, Geoffrey Groom, and Greg Colley at Oxford's Bodleian Library. I had important help with the Immortal Game from Stephen Hubbell and A. J. Goldsby. Thanks to John Fernandez and Frederic Friedel for helping a neophyte wade through the Kasparov–Deep Junior match.

Needless to say, I am extremely grateful to Chess-in-the-Schools in New York City for their extensive cooperation with this book. Particular thanks to Marley Kaplan, Ella Baron, Reginald Dawson, and of course Nicholas Chatzilias. I also want to thank Robert Ferguson, at the American Chess School, who supplied much important source material on chess and education. Joan Dubois from the U.S. Chess Federation kindly gave me permission to adapt their text "Let's Play Chess."

Thanks, in addition, to Aodhnait Donnelly, Bill Price, Donald Jackman, Shaul Markovitch, Robert Cooper, Craig Hamilton, Margaret Freeman and the Coglit List, David Joyce, Edward Sandifer, Adrian Kok, Alan Borwell, Alex Kraaijeveld, Marc Rotenberg, Ben Rubin,

David Glenn Rinehart, the *Atlantic Monthly*'s Lucie Prinz, my twenty-year science guru Eric Berlow, the Feilers & the Benders, the Wunsches, Andrew Kimball, Andrew Shapiro, Steve Silberman, Richard Gehr, Roy Kreitner, Jeremy Benjamin, Linda Hirsch, and Richard Shenk.

I am indebted to my cousin Claire Heymann, the family archivist, for helping me become better acquainted with the life and legend of Samuel Rosenthal. Another cousin, Ian Cohn, gave me a look at the long-lost, and well-preserved, watch. It did not disappoint.

Samuel Rosenthal's watch.

The watch, it turns out, was a gift to Rosenthal from his chess club mates, team members in a grueling year-long correspondence match between the cities of Paris and Vienna in 1884–85. I will surely never know what it feels like to play world-class chess, but I do know the exhilaration of a solitary pursuit being transformed into a collective effort. Over three years' time, Bill Thomas and Sloan Harris deftly kept me on the right course. Kurt Hirsch was there first, last, and in between, and I hope he will take much pride in the result.

I am also very grateful to readers and critiquers of various drafts: Mitch Stephens, Jordan Goldstein, Joanne and Sidney Cohen, Jon Shenk, Bonni Cohen, Tom Inck, Katharine Cluverius, Kendra Harpster, Stephen Hubbell, Michael Strong, Andras Szanto, Steven Johnson, Sarah Williams, Josh Shenk, Peggy Beers, Michael Negele, and David Booth Beers.

Lastly, and mostly, my thanks and incalculable love to Alex, Lucy, and Henry.

Appendix I

THE RULES OF CHESS

Chess is a game for two players, one moving the White pieces and the other moving the Black pieces. At the beginning of the game, the pieces are set up as pictured below.

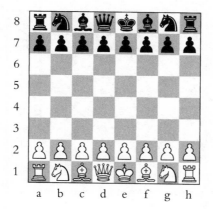

These hints will help you to remember the proper board setup:

1. Opposing Kings and Queens sit directly opposite each other.
2. The square in the lower right-hand corner is a light one ("light on right").
3. The White Queen goes on a light square, the Black Queen on a dark square ("Queen on her color").

White always moves first, and then the players take turns moving. Only one piece may be moved at each turn (except for "castling," a special move explained below). The Knight is the only piece that can jump over other pieces. All other pieces move only along unblocked lines. You may not move a piece to a square already occupied by one of your own pieces, but you can capture an enemy piece that stands on a square where one of your pieces can move. To capture, simply remove the enemy piece from the board and put your own piece in its place.

THE PIECES AND HOW THEY MOVE

The Queen

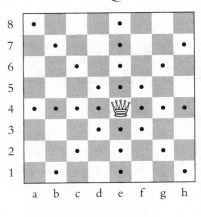

Possible Queen moves

The Queen is the most powerful piece. She can move any number of squares in any direction—horizontal, vertical, or diagonal—if her path is not blocked. She can reach any of the squares with dots in this diagram.

The Rook

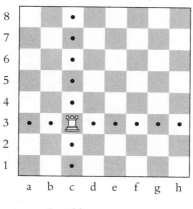

Possible Rook moves

The Rook is the next-most-powerful piece. The Rook can move any number of squares vertically or horizontally if its path is not blocked.

The Bishop

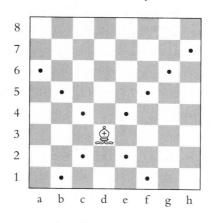

Possible Bishop moves

The Bishop can move any number of squares diagonally if its path is not blocked. Note that this Bishop starts on a light square and can reach only other light squares. At the beginning of the game, each player has one "dark-square" Bishop and one "light-square" Bishop, and each Bishop remains on its same-color squares throughout the game.

The Knight

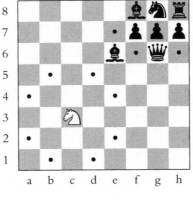

Possible Knight moves

The Knight's move is special: it is the only piece that can hop over other pieces on its way to a new square. Think of the Knight's move as an *L*. It moves two squares horizontally or vertically and then makes a right-angle turn for one more square. The Knight always lands on a square opposite in color from its original square.

The King

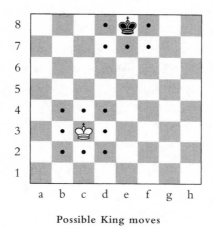

Possible King moves

The King is the most important piece. When he is under attack ("check"), the defending player must immediately attempt to secure his safety. If he is unable to escape ("checkmate"), his whole army loses and the game is over. The King can move one square in any direction—for example, to any of the squares with dots in this diagram. (An exception is castling, explained later.)

The Pawn

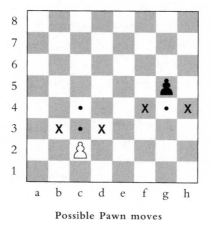

Possible Pawn moves

The Pawn moves straight ahead (never backward), but can only capture diagonally. It normally moves one square at a time, but on its first move it has the option of moving forward one or two squares. In the diagram, the squares with dots indicate possible destinations for the Pawns. The White Pawn is on its original square, so it may move ahead either one or two squares. The Black Pawn has already moved, so it may move ahead only one square at a time. The squares on which these pawns may capture are indicated by an X.

If a Pawn advances all the way to the opposite end of the board, it is immediately "promoted" to any piece of the player's choosing—usually a Queen. (It may not remain a Pawn or become a King.) Pawn promotion makes it possible for each player to have more than one Queen or more than two Rooks, Bishops, or Knights on the board at the same time.

SPECIAL MOVES

Castling

Castling is a special move that lets a player move two pieces at once—the King and one Rook. In castling, the King moves two squares to his left or right, toward one of his Rooks. At the same time, the Rook involved hops over the King toward the center of the board and lands on the square beside him (see illustrations below). In order to castle, neither the King nor the Rook involved may have moved before.

The King may not castle out of check, into check, or through check. Further, there may not be pieces of either color between the King and the Rook involved in castling. Each player may castle only when conditions allow and only once during a game.

Castling is often a very important move because it allows you to place your King in a safe location and also allows the Rook to become more active. When the move is legal, each player has the choice of castling Kingside, Queenside, or not at all, no matter what the other player chooses to do.

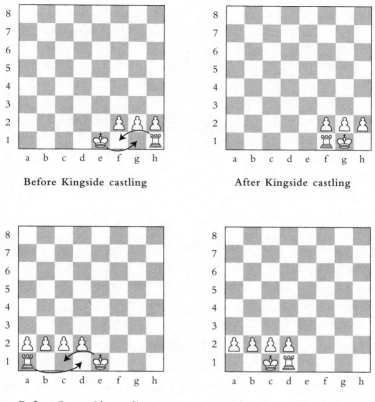

Before Kingside castling

After Kingside castling

Before Queenside castling

After Queenside castling

En Passant

This French phrase means "in passing," and refers to a special type of Pawn capture that occurs when one player moves a Pawn two squares forward as if to avoid capture by the opponent's Pawn. The capture is made exactly as if the player had moved the Pawn only one square forward.

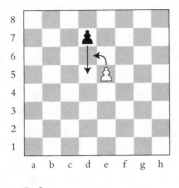
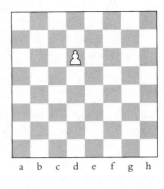

Before en passant capture   After en passant capture

In the diagram on the left, if the Black Pawn moves up two squares, the White Pawn has the option of capturing the Black Pawn en passant. Such capture must take place immediately after the Black Pawn's two-square move.

About Check and Checkmate

The one and only true goal in a game of chess is to checkmate your opponent's King. If the King is attacked ("put in check"), it must get out of check immediately. If there is no way to get out of check, the position is a "checkmate," and the side that is checkmated loses.

A player may not put his own King into check. When a King is put into check, there are three possible ways of escape:

1. Capturing the attacking piece.
2. Moving a piece between the attacker and the threatened King (impossible if the attacker is a Knight).
3. Moving the King away from the attack.

If a checked player can do none of these, he is checkmated and loses the game.

If a King is not in check, but that player can make no legal move with any of his remaining pieces, the position is called a stalemate and the game is scored as a draw, or tie.

(Adapted from "Let's Play Chess" with permission from the U.S. Chess Federation.)

Appendix II

THE IMMORTAL GAME (Recap)

AND FIVE OTHER
GREAT GAMES FROM HISTORY

THE IMMORTAL GAME
ADOLF ANDERSSEN VS. LIONEL KIESERITZKY
JUNE 21, 1851
LONDON

1. e4

(White King's Pawn to e4)

1. . . . e5

(Black King's Pawn to e5)

2. f4

(White King's Bishop Pawn to
f4)

2. . . . e×f4

(Black King's Pawn captures
White Pawn on f4)

3. Bc4

(White King's Bishop to c4)

3. . . . Qh4+

(Black Queen to h4; check to
the White King)

4. Kf1

(White King to f1)

4. . . . b5

(Black Queen's Knight Pawn to
b5)

5. B×b5

(White Bishop captures Black
Pawn on b5)

5. . . . Nf6

(Black Knight to f6)

6. Nf3

(White Knight to f3)

6. . . . Qh6

(Black Queen to h6)

7. d3

(White Queen's Pawn to d3)

7. . . . Nh5

(Black Knight to h5)

8. Nh4

(White Knight to h4)

8. . . . Qg5

(Black Queen to g5)

9. Nf5

(White Knight to f5)

9. . . . c6

(Black Pawn to c6)

10. g4

(White Pawn to g4)

10. . . . Nf6

(Black Knight to f6)

11. Rg1

(White Rook to g1)

11. . . . c×b5

(Black Pawn takes Bishop at b5)

12. h4

(White Pawn to h4)

12. . . . Qg6

(Black Queen to g6)

13. h5

(White Pawn to h5)

13. . . . Qg5

(Black Queen to g5)

14. Qf3

(White Queen to f3)

14. . . . Ng8

(Black Knight returns to g8)

15. B×f4

(White Bishop takes Pawn on f4)

15. . . . Qf6

(Black Queen to f6)

16. Nc3

(White Knight to c3)

16. . . . Bc5

(Black Bishop to c5)

17. Nd5

(White Knight to d5)

17. . . . Q×b2

(Black Queen captures Pawn at b2)

18. Bd6

(White Bishop to d6)

18. . . . B×g1

(Black Bishop captures Rook on g1)

19. e5

(White Pawn to e5)

19. . . . Q×a1+

(Black Queen captures Rook on a1; *check*)

20. Ke2

(White King to e2)

20. . . . Na6

(Black Knight to a6)

21. N×g7+

(White Knight captures Pawn on g7; *check*)

21. . . . Kd8

(Black King to d8)

22. Qf6+

(White Queen to f6; *check*)

22. . . . N×f6

(Black Knight captures Queen at f6)

23. Be7++

(White Bishop to e7; *checkmate*)

OTHER LEGENDARY GAMES

True chess aficionados revel in the "brilliancy" of many hundreds of games over the past century or more. Here are just a handful of superb games. Each can be played out move by move online at TheImmortalGame.com.

1. Bobby Fischer's "Game of the Century"

In 1956 thirteen-year-old Fischer defeated top player Donald Byrne (brother of eventual *New York Times* chess columnist Robert Byrne) in a contest that stunned commentators quickly dubbed the Game of the Century. Like the Immortal Game, Fischer's game also featured a number of prominent sacrifices—including Fischer's Queen.

According to the online encyclopedia *Wikipedia*, Fischer (Black) demonstrates in this game "brilliance, innovation, improvisation and poetry. Byrne (playing white), after a standard opening, makes a minor mistake on move 11, moving the same piece twice (wasting time). Fischer pounces, with strong sacrificial play, culminating in an incredible Queen sacrifice on move 17. Byrne captures the Queen, but Fischer more than compensates by taking many other pieces. The ending is an excellent demonstration of pieces working together to achieve a checkmate."

Donald Byrne vs. Robert James Fischer
October 17, 1956
New York

1. Nf3 Nf6
2. c4 g6
3. Nc3 Bg7

Fischer has opted for a defense based on Hypermodern principles: he's inviting Byrne to establish a classical Pawn stronghold in the center, which Fischer hopes to undermine and transform into a target. Fischer has fianchettoed his Bishop—moved it to the long diagonal of the board—so it can attack the a1–h8 diagonal, including its center squares.

4. d4 O-O

Fischer castles, concentrating on protecting his King immediately.

5. Bf4 d5
6. Qb3 d×c4
7. Q×c4 c6
8. e4 Nbd7
9. Rd1 Nb6
10. Qc5 Bg4

At this point, Byrne's pieces are more developed, and he controls the center squares. However, Fischer's King is well protected, while Byrne's is not.

11. Bg5?

Here Byrne makes a mistake—he moves the same piece twice, losing time, instead of developing another piece.

11. ... Na4!!

Fischer cleverly offers up his Knight, but if Byrne takes it with N×a4, Fischer will play N×e4, and Byrne then suddenly has some terrible choices.

12. Qa3 N×c3
13. b×c3 N×e4!

Byrne declined to take the Knight on move 12, so Fischer tries again by offering material to Byrne, in exchange for a much better position that is especially dangerous to White: an open e-file, with White's King poorly protected.

14. Bxe7

Byrne wisely decides to decline the offered material.

14. ... Qb6

15. Bc4 Nxc3!

16. Bc5 Rfe8+

17. Kf1 Be6!!

The move by Fischer that made this game famous. Instead of trying to protect his Queen, Fischer counterattacks with his Bishop and sacrifices his Queen.

18. Bxb6 Bxc4+

Fischer now begins a series of discovered checks, picking up material.

19. Kg1 Ne2+

20. Kf1 Nxd4+

21. Kg1 Ne2+

22. Kf1 Nc3+

23. Kg1 axb6

This move by Fischer takes time out to capture a piece, but it doesn't waste time because it also threatens Byrne's Queen.

24. Qb4 Ra4

25. Qxb6 Nxd1

The Game of the Century
after 17. . . . Be6!!

Fischer has taken a Rook, two Bishops, and a Pawn as compensation for his Queen; in short, he has gained significantly more material than he's lost. In addition, Byrne's remaining Rook is stuck on h1 and it will take precious time to free it, giving Fischer an opportunity to set up another offensive. Byrne has the only remaining Queen, but this will not be enough.

26. h3 R×a2
27. Kh2 N×f2
28. Re1 R×e1
29. Qd8+ Bf8
30. N×e1 Bd5
31. Nf3 Ne4
32. Qb8 b5
33. h4 h5
34. Ne5 Kg7

Fischer breaks the pin, allowing the Bishop to attack as well.

35. Kg1 Bc5+

Now Fischer "peels away" the White King from his last defender, and begins a series of checks that culminate in checkmate. In this interesting series of moves, Fischer shows how to use various pieces together to force a checkmate.

36. Kf1 Ng3+
37. Ke1 Bb4+
38. Kd1 Bb3+
39. Kc1 Ne2+
40. Kb1 Nc3+
41. Kc1 Rc2++ (Black checkmates White.)

(Adapted from an annotation written by David A. Wheeler, with help from Graham Burgess, John Nunn, and John Emms's *The Mammoth Book of the World's Greatest Chess Games* [Carroll & Graf, 1998]; Robert G. Wade and Kevin J. O'Connell's *Bobby Fischer's Chess Games* [Doubleday, 1972]; and James Eade's *Chess for Dummies* [IDG, 1996]. Online at *http://www.dwheeler.com/misc/game_of_the_century.txt*.)

2. Paul Morphy's "Opera Game"

This legendary game from 1858 was played during a performance of *Norma* in a private box very close to the stage in the Italian Opera

House in Paris. The legendary American player Paul Morphy played White; two strong European amateurs—the German Duke of Brunswick and the French Count Isouard—played Black as a team.

PAUL MORPHY VS. DUKE OF BRUNSWICK AND COUNT ISOUARD
PARIS, 1858

1. e4 e5
2. Nf3 d6
3. d4 Bg4?
4. dxe5 Bxf3
5. Qxf3 dxe5
6. Bc4 Nf6
7. Qb3 Qe7
8. Nc3

White prefers fast development to winning material.

8. ... c6
9. Bg5 b5?
10. Nxb5!

Morphy chooses not to retreat the Bishop, which would allow Black to gain time for development.

10. ... cxb5
11. Bxb5+ Nbd7
12. O-O-O

The combination of the Bishop's pin on the Knight and the open file for the Rook will lead to Black's defeat.

12. ... Rd8
13. Rxd7 Rxd7
14. Rd1 Qe6

Compare the activity of the White pieces with the idleness of the Black pieces.

15. Bxd7+ Nxd7

16. Qb8+!

    Morphy finishes with a stylish Queen
sacrifice.

16. . . . N×b8

17. Rd8++

(Annotations from *http://en.wikipedia.org/*
wiki/Opera_game.)

The Opera Game after
14. . . . Qe6

3. Wilhelm Steinitz's "Battle of Hastings"

Arguably the most exciting game in one of the most important chess
tournaments in history, this contest pitted the aging former world
champion Wilhelm Steinitz against the tournament leader Curt von
Bardeleben. The play was evidently so intense, and the loss so devastating, that von Bardeleben fell apart at the end and could not finish in a
sportsmanlike way.

WILHELM STEINITZ VS. CURT VON BARDELEBEN
HASTINGS, ENGLAND, 1895

1. e4 e5

2. Nf3 Nc6

3. Bc4 Bc5

4. c3

    So far, all of the moves have been natural developing moves.
White's fourth move furthers central control and the support of a
Pawn on d4.

4. . . . Nf6

5. d4 e×d4

6. c×d4 Bb4+

7. Nc3 d5

8. e×d5 N×d5

9. O-O

Steinitz has safeguarded his King and is now threatening to win a piece on d5, so Black is forced to do something about it. This game shows a familiar theme: one side leaves his King in the center too long, while the other side crashes through with the pieces and forces a checkmate. Moral: do not swap the e Pawns before your King is safe.

9.   . . . Be6

10. Bg5

Another strong move restricting Black's choice of reply. White has completed his development and at the same time has made an aggressive move. Black now retreats his Bishop.

10. . . . Be7

11. B×d5

White begins a set of exchanges because he has spotted that afterward the Black King will be stuck in the middle of the board.

11. . . . B×d5

12. N×d5 Q×d5

13. B×e7 N×e7

14. Re1 f6

15. Qe2

Although Qa5+ was a good alternative, Steinitz preferred Qe2, probably because it was simpler. White now threatens mate and the winning of the e7 Knight, so Black's choice of reply is very limited. White is now in a position to decide on Black's moves as well as his own, and that makes life much easier!

15. . . . Qd7

16. Rac1

Simple chess: Black's pieces are still tied down defending the e7 Knight, so White gets on with his development. Black should now have played 16. . . . Kf7, after which no variation clearly wins for White. It is quite common in chess that one side's moves do not actually give him an advantage with best play, but they give the opponent a problem in that he continually has to find the best move just to survive. At last, Black slips and plays:

16. ... c6

17. d5

This is the key move to the next stage of the attack: all of the White pieces are pointing at the Black King, but to deliver the killer blow, the Knight needs to join in the fun. The idea is that the Knight has to get to the e6 square (which White is controlling) and the only way to do this is by enabling the Knight to use d4. This Pawn move is known as a clearance sacrifice. Black, of course, captures the Pawn.

17. ... c6×d5

If White's Pawn had been allowed to stay on d5, that would have added further dangerous threats.

18. Nd4

This Knight is heading for e6, where it will command many key dark squares in the heart of Black's position and make it very difficult for Black to coordinate his pieces.

18. ... Kf7

At long last, Black unpins the e7 Knight.

19. Ne6

It is hard for Black, even with his extra Pawn, to make any headway in this game because the White pieces have so much control over the board.

19. ... Rhc8

Black sensibly tries for exchanges.

20. Qg4

A marvelous move: having got his Knight onto e6, Steinitz is now homing in on the squares it attacks with other pieces, in this case the g7 Pawn.

20. ... g6

21. Ng5+

This is another very fine move, and the only one which maintains

After 20. Qg4

the White advantage. Black is in check and an attack is discovered on his Queen. This means that he must play 21. . . . Ke8 to avoid instant defeat.

21. . . . Ke8

22. R×e7+

Steinitz has created a fantastic position in which all of White's pieces are under attack and they will remain so for several moves, but none can be taken.

22. . . . Kf8

23. Rf7+

White continues to walk the tightrope. Black has only one sensible reply:

23. . . . Kg8

24. Rg7+

White's Rook still cannot be captured because White then captures the Queen with check. Black cannot go to f8 either, because 25 N×h7+ would then force him to capture the Rook with his King (25. . . . Ke8 would be met with 26 Q×d7 mate) and all Black's pieces would be taken.

24. . . . Kh8

25. R×h7+

Having got so far, this move seems pretty obvious. The Rook cannot be captured for all of the reasons given before, so let's steal a Black Pawn. More importantly, it opens another route to the Black King.

25. . . . Kg8

Von Bardeleben now realized what was in store for him, effectively mate in ten moves. Rather than suffer this indignity or resign, he simply left the playing hall and did not come back. This left Steinitz to demonstrate to spectators how the game would be finished:

26. Rg7+ Kh8

27. Qh4+ K×g7

28. Qh7+ Kf8

29. Qh8+ Ke7

30. Qg7+ Ke8
31. Qg8+ Ke7
32. Qf7+ Kd8
33. Qf8+

And now we see why the White Rook needed to stay on the c-file.

33. ... Qe8
34. Nf7+ Kd7
35. Qd6 mate.

Even though von Bardeleben was unsporting and deprived Steinitz of the pleasure of playing this game through to the end, Steinitz was awarded the tournament's Brilliancy Prize anyway.

(Adapted from the Peter Walker Chess Coaching Pages, online at *http://coach ing.chesspod.com/coaching/games/steinitz1.html*.)

4. Rubinstein's "Polish Brilliancy"

One of the undisputed greatest chess games of all time, this tour de force of Akiba Rubinstein displays both his artistry and combinatorial genius. "There is nothing like seeing this game for the first time—or the second, third, or tenth time!" wrote Irving Chernev in *The Golden Dozen*.

GERSH ROTLEWI VS. AKIBA RUBINSTEIN
DECEMBER 1907
LODZ, POLAND

1. d4 d5
2. Nf3

This one move accomplishes three very important things: (1) most importantly, it controls the center; (2) it develops a piece; and (3) it prepares the possibility of Kingside castling by White.

2. ... e6

A good and natural move. Black guards the center, prepares Kingside castling, and also is ready to play the Pawn break—c5, attacking the center.

3. e3 c5

4. c4 Nc6

5. Nc3 Nf6

6. dxc5

Today we know that this move is premature. White goes for the immediate isolation of Black's Queen Pawn. The best move, according to modern theory, is 6. a3! a6. (See W. Korn and N. de Firmian, *Modern Chess Openings,* 14th ed., for more details on this "Tarrasch Defense" opening.)

6. ... Bxc5

Material balance.

7. a3 a6

This gives Black's Bishop on c5 a "hidey-hole" on a7, prepares b7-b5, and blunts the worst effects of a possible b2-b4-b5 advance by White. Additionally this is an excellent waiting move. Rubinstein's handling of this opening is nearly flawless.

8. b4 Bd6

A good aggressive move, and a nice gambit of a Pawn (which White cannot immediately accept).

9. Bb2

White fianchettos his Queen's Bishop, as will Black.

9. ... O-O

Very nice. Black continues his development, and offers a gambit (which White should not take).

10. Qd2

This move is not well thought out. The Queen will soon be a target in the open Q-file. She may have been better off on c2.

10. ... Qe7

Black develops and offers a gambit at the same time.

11. Bd3

White develops—he possibly does not wish to exchange Pawns and change the Pawn structure, opening lines for Black. But White loses at least two tempi with this move, especially in combination with his previous inaccuracies.

11.   . . . dxc4

12. Bxc4 b5

Black gains space and prepares to fianchetto his Queen's Bishop. This is nice, as he gains a move, and forces White to retreat the cleric at c4.

13. Bd3

Pointing at the Black King and trying to block the d-file.

13.   . . . Rd8

14. Qe2 Bb7

15. O-O Ne5

Favorably breaking the symmetry.

16. Nxe5 Bxe5

17. f4

White tries to block the key b8–h2 diagonal. (He also gains some space.)

17.   . . . Bc7

18. e4

This opens up the game at a time when only Black can profit from an open game.

18.   . . . Rac8

To the casual observer, the position seems approximately equal. But this is deceiving, as both of White's Rooks have yet to move. Irving Chernev writes: "Rubinstein brings up the reserves. This sort of move always reminds me of Blackburne's advice, 'Never commence your final attack until your QR is in play.' "

19. e5

White thinks he is closing attacking avenues, but he is actually opening lines. Grandmaster Andy Soltis writes: "This makes the game a textbook case of what happens when a player pushes his Pawns too far and opens diagonals leading to his King. Better was 19. Rac1."

19. ... Bb6+

Getting on a new diagonal with a gain of time.

20. Kh1 Ng4!

At first glance, this appears to be a blunder. (Black will soon have practically all of his pieces under attack.) In fact, though, this move is the grand beginning of one of the most beautiful and titanic combinations ever played.

21. Be4

White tries blocking the long diagonal. A reasonable move, considering the situation. It seems to be the best, under the circumstances.

21. ... Qh4

22. g3

Now it seems Black has run out of moves. But the following refutation of White's position is one of the most beautiful in all of chess.

22. ... Rxc3!!

A truly wonderful Queen sacrifice.

23. gxh4

White takes the Queen. But there is little choice at this point.

23. ... Rd2!!

This is one of the most beautiful and surprising moves in all of chess literature. The idea is to deflect the Queen away from the defense of the Bishop on e4. Note that four of the five Black pieces are hanging.

24. Qxd2 Bxe4+

25. Qg2 Rh3!

Another thunderbolt. There is no reply to such a move. White resigns.

After 23. ... Rd2

(Adapted from an annotation of A. J. Goldsby, which relied on references to Irving Chernev's *The Golden Dozen: The 12 Greatest Chess Players of All Time* [Oxford University Press, 1976]; Reuben Fine's *The World's Great Chess Games*

[Dover/D. McKay Books, 1976]; Burgess, Nunn, and Emms's *The Mammoth Book of the World's Greatest Chess Games* [Carroll & Graf Books, 1998]; and Andy Soltis's *The 100 Best Chess Games of the 20th Century* [McFarland Books, 2000]. Online at *http://www.geocities.com/lifemasteraj/rotle-rubin_1.html*.)

5. One of Kasparov's Finest

Garry Kasparov, considered by many to be the best player in the history of chess, has produced many a game that has stunned and exhilarated serious players. Occasionally one game stands out above the rest. This contest, from his longtime rivalry with former world champion Anatoli Karpov, is one such game. It is considered by many to be one of the most brilliant games ever played.

ANATOLI KARPOV VS. GARRY KASPAROV
LINARES, SPAIN, 1993

1. d4 Nf6
2. c4 g6
3. Nc3 Bg7
4. e4 d6
5. f3 O-O
6. Be3 e5
7. Nge2 c6
8. Qd2 Nbd7
9. Rd1

Karpov prefers to castle on the Kingside. Kasparov will now devote all his energy, and a fair amount of material, to making sure he never does.

9. ... a6
10. dxe5 Nxe5

In his pregame preparations, Karpov likely dismissed this response because of the inevitable loss of the d6 Pawn. Kasparov's intuition tells him that his active pieces combined with White's lack of development give him a strong initiative. Besides, 10. . . . dxe5 11. c5! would allow White to clamp down on the Queenside, which is not the kind of positional confrontation one wants to start with Karpov.

11. b3 b5

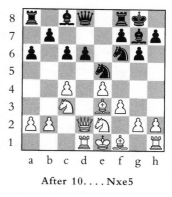

After 10. . . . Nxe5

The seeds of a long-term combination are taking root. In reality, Black's tenth move pushed him upon this path. Trying to play solidly with 11. . . . Ne8? now succeeds only in sabotaging Black's game.

12. cxb5

Karpov goes for it. While I admire his courage, I question his judgment. The text opens the a-file to Black's benefit, ensuring him excellent piece play for his lost d6 Pawn. The worst thing that can ever happen to Black is a four-versus-three Pawn ending.

12. . . . axb5

13. Qxd6 Nfd7

The crucial point in Black's scheme. Exchanging Queens promises nothing, while 13. . . . Qe8? leaves Black's pieces cloistered. The sacrificial 13. . . . Qa5?? 14. Qxe5 Nd5 15. Qxg7+ Kxg7 16. exd5 is a disaster for Black. With the text, Kasparov envisions . . . Qd8-a5 (where the Queen belongs) to be followed by . . . b5-b4 and . . . Bc8-a6. Black's threats would quickly pile up. Karpov, therefore, feels the need to regain control of events by making a move that undermines the fundamental nature of his position: his solid Pawn formation.

14. f4 b4

A brilliant move that is timed beautifully. The plausible 14. . . . Ng4 15. Bd4 falls in line with White's plans to neutralize Black's active pieces.

15. Nb1

Poor Karpov is being hounded into a corner. Dazzling tactics abound.

15. ... Ng4
16. Bd4 B×d4
17. Q×d4 R×a2

Now the game is over. If 18. Q×b4? Ne3 with the twin threats ... N×d1 and ... Nc2+ is killing. On top of everything else, Black's pieces have picked up more mobility, while White's are rooted to their original squares.

18. h3 c5
19. Qg1 Ngf6
20. e5 Ne4
21. h4 c4

Black continues in the same style as he started the game. His position is so good that quiet moves like 21. ... Qe7, preparing ... Nb6 and ... Be6, should suffice. But Kasparov wants to strike while the iron is hot. The text envisions ... Qa5 and ... Nd7 c5, which is crushing. Black's position is so good, I've spent some time trying to make 21. ... N×e5!? work, e.g., 22. R×d8 R×d8 23. f×e5 Rb2, but have concluded the sacrifices are unnecessary.

22. Nc1 c3

In the heat of battle Kasparov goes overboard. He clearly missed the simple 22. ... Rb2 23. Qd4 c3! 24. Q×e4 c2, winning. The answer for this oversight is one that I've experienced in my own games. You see a trap that your opponent has set for you. Being a crafty player yourself, you naturally show your own cunning by avoiding the trap. But had you looked closer at the "trap," you would have seen that it actually works out in your favor. Kasparov saw Karpov's trap and so blocked out a simple win! Now in order to win, Kasparov has to find a truly wonderful combination.

23. N×a2 c2
24. Qd4 c×d1Q+
25. K×d1 Ndc5
26. Q×d8 R×d8+

APPENDIX II   2 7 9

27. Kc2 Nf2

White resigns. Here Karpov happily watched his flag fall to save him from playing 28. Rg1 Bf5+ 29. Kb2 Nd1+ 30. Ka1 N×b3 mate, a gruesome finish. While Karpov never really made it out of the opening, it's only Kasparov who has ever shown us how to handle him.

Appendix III
BENJAMIN FRANKLIN'S "THE MORALS OF CHESS"

(First Published in *Columbian Magazine*, December 1786)

Playing at Chess, is the most ancient and the most universal game known among men; for its original is beyond the memory of history, and it has, for numberless ages, been the amusement of all the civilized nations of Asia, the Persians, the Indians, and the Chinese. Europe has had it above a thousand years; the Spaniards have spread it over their part of America, and it begins lately to make its appearance in these States. It is so interesting in itself, as not to need the view of gain to induce engaging in it; and thence it is never played for money. Those, therefore, who have leisure for such diversions, cannot find one that is more innocent; and the following piece, written with a view to correct (among a few young friends) some little improprieties in the practice of it, shews at the same time that it may, in its effects on the mind, be not merely innocent, but advantageous, to the vanquished as well as to the victor.

The Game of Chess is not merely an idle amusement. Several very valuable qualities of the mind, useful in the course of human life, are to be acquired or strengthened by it, so as to become habits, ready on all occasions. For Life is a kind of Chess, in which we have often points to gain, and competitors or adversaries to contend with, and in which there is a vast variety of good and ill events, that are, in some degree, the effects of prudence or the want of it. By playing at chess, then, we may learn,

I. Foresight, which looks a little into futurity, and considers the consequences that may attend an action; for it is continually occurring to the player, "If I move this piece, what will be the advantages of my new situation? What use can my adversary make of it to annoy me? What other moves can I make to support it, and to defend myself from his attacks?"

II. Circumspection, which surveys the whole chess-board, or scene of action, the relations of the several pieces and situations, the dangers they are respectively exposed to, the several possibilities of their aiding each other, the probabilities that the adversary may make this or that move, and attack this or the other piece; and what different means can be used to avoid his stroke, or turn its consequences against him.

III. Caution, not to make our moves too hastily. This habit is best acquired by observing strictly the laws of the game, such as, "If you touch a piece, you must move it somewhere; if you set it down, you must let it stand:" and it is therefore best that these rules should be observed, as the game thereby becomes more the image of human life, and particularly of war; in which, if you have incautiously put yourself into a bad and dangerous position, you cannot obtain your enemy's leave to withdraw your troops, and place them more securely, but you must abide all the consequences of your rashness.

And, lastly, we learn by chess the habit of not being discouraged by present bad appearances in the state of our affairs, the habit of hoping for a favorable change, and that of persevering in the search of resources. The game is so full of events, there is such a variety of turns in it, the fortune of it is so subject to sudden vicissitudes, and one so frequently, after contemplation, discovers the means of extricating one's self from a supposed insurmountable difficulty, that one is encouraged to continue the contest to the last, in hopes of victory by our own skill, or, at least, of giving a stale mate, by the negligence of our adversary. And whoever considers, what in chess he often sees instances of, that particular pieces of success are apt to produce presumption, and its consequent, inattention, by which more is afterwards lost than was gained by the preceding advantage, while misfortunes produce more care and attention, by which the loss may be recovered, will learn not to be too much discouraged by the present success of his adversary, nor to despair of final good fortune, upon every little check he receives in the pursuit of it,

That we may, therefore, be induced more frequently to chuse this beneficial amusement, in preference to others which are not attended with the same advantages, every circumstance which may increase the pleasures of it should be regarded; and every action or word that is unfair, disrespectful, or that in any way may give uneasiness, should be avoided, as contrary to the immediate intention of both the players, which is, to pass the time agreeably.

Therefore, firstly: If it is agreed to play according to the strict rules, then those rules are to be exactly observed by both parties; and should not be insisted on for one side, while deviated from by the other: for this is not equitable.

Secondly. If it is agreed not to observe the rules exactly, but one party demands indulgences, he should then be as willing to allow them to the other.

Thirdly. No false move should ever be made to extricate yourself out of a difficulty, or to gain an advantage. There can be no pleasure in playing with a person once detected in such unfair practices.

Fourthly. If your adversary is long in playing, you ought not to hurry him, or express any uneasiness at his delay. You should not sing, nor whistle, nor look at your watch, nor take up a book to read, nor make a tapping with your feet on the floor, or with your fingers on the table, nor do any thing that may disturb his attention. For all these things displease; and they do not shew your skill in playing, but your craftiness or rudeness.

Fifthly. You ought not to endeavour to amuse and deceive your adversary, by pretending to have made bad moves, and saying you have now lost the game, in order to make him secure and careless, and inattentive to your schemes; for this is fraud, and deceit, not skill in the game.

Sixthly. You must not, when you have gained a victory, use any triumphing or insulting expression, nor show too much pleasure; but endeavour to console your adversary, and make him less dissatisfied with himself by every kind and civil expression, that may be used with truth, such as, "You understand the game better than I, but you are a little inattentive;" or, "You had the best of the game, but something happened to divert your thoughts, and that turned it in my favour."

Seventhly. If you are a spectator while others play, observe the most perfect silence: For if you give advice, you offend both parties; him, against whom you give it, because it may cause the loss of his game; him, in whose favour you give it, because, though it be good, and he follows it, he loses the pleasure he might have had, if you had permitted him to think till it occurred to himself. Even after a move or moves, you must not, by replacing the pieces, show how it might have been played better: for that displeases, and may occasion disputes or doubts about their true situation. All talking to the players, lessens or diverts their attention, and is therefore unpleasing: Nor should you give the least hint to either party, by any kind of noise or motion. If you do, you are unworthy to be a spectator. If you have a mind to exercise or show your judgement, do it in playing your own game when you have an opportunity, not in criticising, or meddling with, or counselling the play of others.

Lastly. If the game is not to be played rigorously according to the rules above mentioned, then moderate your desire of victory over your adversary, and be pleased with one over yourself. Snatch not eagerly at every advantage offered by his unskillfulness or inattention; but point out to him kindly, that by such a move he places or leaves a piece in danger and unsupported; that by another he will put his King in a dangerous situation, &c. By this generous civility (so opposite to the unfairness above forbidden) you may, indeed, happen to lose the game to your opponent, but you will win what is better, his esteem, his respect, and his affection; together with the silent approbation and good will of impartial spectators.

SOURCES AND NOTES

In my research, I relied on hundreds of text and electronic sources, and scores of individuals. Three books stood out for their constant usefulness:

H. J. R. Murray. *A History of Chess*. Oxford University Press, 1913.

Richard Eales. *Chess: The History of a Game*. Facts on File, 1985.

David Hooper and Kenneth Whyld. *The Oxford Companion to Chess*. Second edition. Oxford University Press, 1992.

Sources for specific quotes and information in particular chapters are as follows:

EPIGRAPH
xiii Caliph Ar-Radi was walking: Murray, *History of Chess*, p. 200.

PROLOGUE
xv When eleven-year-old Marcel Duchamp: Calvin Tomkins, *Duchamp: A Biography* (Henry Holt, 1996), is the definitive work on Marcel Duchamp. I also relied on Andrew Waterman's essay "The Poetry of Chess," in Burt Hochberg, *The 64-Square Looking Glass* (Times Books, 1993); Hans Ree, *The Human Comedy of Chess* (Russell Enterprises, 1999); and Ernst Strouhal, *Acht X Acht* (Springer, 1996).

xvi "Chess holds its master": The Einstein quote comes from the foreword to Johannes Hannak, *Emanuel Lasker: Biographie eines Schachweltmeisters; mit einem Geleitwort von Albert Einstein* (S. Engelhardt, 1952). Despite Einstein's stated opposition to chess, he did play. One recorded game shows him handily defeating his famous physicist colleague Robert Oppenheimer. An animated version of the game can be viewed online at *chessgames.com/perl/chessgame?gid= 1261614.*

INTRODUCTION

1 Large rocks, severed heads: The Baghdad battle scene and much of the context of that period come from Volumes 31 and 32 of *The History of al-Tabari,* originally written in the ninth century and published in English translation by the State University of New York Press. Gaston Wiet, *Baghdad: Metropolis of the Abbasid Caliphate* (University of Oklahoma Press, 1971), was also helpful, as was *The Internet Medieval Sourcebook,* an online resource edited by Paul Halsall at the Fordham University Center for Medieval Studies (*ford ham.edu/halsall/sbook.html*).

2 "O Commander of the faithful": This exchange is taken from Murray, *History of Chess,* p. 197.

3 The ancient Greeks had *petteia* and *kubeia*: Roland G. Austin, "Greek Board Games," *Antiquity,* September 1940, pp. 257–71, is fascinating reading. The article is available online at *http://web.archive.org/web/200410240145 29/gamesmuseum.uwaterloo.ca/Archive/Austin.*

6 "Here is nothing less": Alfred Kreymborg, "Chess Reclaims a Devotee," in Hochberg, *The 64-Square Looking Glass.*

7 orthodox enemies to stamp it out: The list of religious figures who have tried to outlaw chess comes partly from Bill Wall's "Religion and Chess," online at *geocities.com/siliconvalley/lab/7378/religion.htm.*

Iraq's current most powerful Islamic authority, Grand Ayatollah Ali al-Sistani, has completely forbidden chess. From his list of General Rules: "503. It is *harām* [absolutely forbidden] to play chess, regardless of whether or not the play is with betting. It is also *harām* to play chess through computerized instrument, if there are two players involved in it. Based on obligatory precaution, one must refrain from it, even if just the computer is the other player." See *sistani.org/html/eng/menu/2/books/2/inside/51.htm.*

CHAPTER I

13 "When Sissa had invented chess": Murray, *History of Chess,* p. 211.

13 It is said that in ancient India: Murray, *History of Chess,* pp. 212, 213.

14 The annals of ancient poetry: Norman Reider, "Chess, Oedipus, and the

Mater Dolorosa," *International Journal of Psychoanalysis* 40 (1959), pp. 320–33, contains a comprehensive summary of chess-origin myths.

14 Pythagoras, the ancient mathematician: Eales, *Chess*, p. 15.

14 The Greek warrior Palamedes: Victor A. Keats, *Chess in Jewish History and Hebrew Literature* (Magnes Press, 1995), pp. 132, 133.

14 the great medieval rebbe: Joseph Jacobs and A. Porter, "Chess," *Jewish Encyclopedia* (1901–06), now online at *jewishencyclopedia.com*.

15 Myths, said Joseph Campbell: Campbell, "The Impact of Science on Myth," *Myths to Live By* (Penguin, 1993).

16 One story portrays two successive Indian kings: Murray, *History of Chess*, p. 210.

16 One tale, known as "The Doubling of the Squares": Murray, *History of Chess*, p. 218. "The calculation is undoubtedly of Indian origin," Murray writes. "It would appear to have also been a favorite calculation among the Muslims . . . to illustrate the different systems of numeration."

More on chess and math

There is some evidence that the actual chess moves were designed according to an ancient mathematical key code. The *Chatrang-namak* included a mythical tale of the invention of *chatrang* by a group of sixth-century Indian wise men as a provocation to their Persian rivals. Along with a hoard of gold, pearls, elephants, and camels sent as conditional tribute, the *chatrang* board and unarranged pieces were presented to King Nushirwan of Persia *with no instructions on how to play*. Instead, it came with this message:

> SINCE YOU BEAR THE TITLE "KING OF KINGS" AND ARE KING OVER ALL US KINGS, IT IS [EXPECTED] THAT YOUR WISE MEN SHOULD BE WISER THAN OURS.
>
> IF NOW YOU CANNOT DISCOVER THE INTERPRETATION OF THE *CHATRANG*, PAY US TRIBUTE AND REVENUE.

The king was given three days to comply.

For two days, there was an eerie silence, as the game seemed to stump everyone in his court. Finally, on the third and final day, a nobleman named Wajurgmitr figured it out in perfect detail. Not only that: he also played and defeated the Indian king's ambassador in twelve straight games. "And there was great joy throughout the whole land."

On the surface, chess in this story is clearly a substitute for war, a new method for settling disputes according to wits rather than brute force (perhaps because the Indians considered themselves militarily inferior but intellectually superior).

But it also suggested a second, hidden meaning. How could even the wisest of wise men possibly deduce the rules to a totally unfamiliar game without a single clue as to its sources or methods? That would be like asking someone to come up with street-by-street driving directions by studying a blank piece of paper instead of a road map. It simply wasn't possible. According to the logic of the story, there had to be some sort of hidden clue allowing the puzzle to be solved.

This remained a riddle for chess historians until the 1970s, when three of them—Germany's Reinhard Wieber, Yugoslavia's Pavle Bidev, and Spain's Ricardo Calvo—stumbled onto ancient references to an eight-by-eight "magic square" that also, inexplicably, contained chess pieces.

A widespread feature of ancient civilizations in Egypt, India, China, and elsewhere, the magic square is a matrix of numbers positioned in such a way that every row, every column, and every diagonal adds up to the same sum. They can be any size—three by three, four by four, five by five, and so on. An example:

8	3	4
1	5	9
6	7	2

The symmetry of such squares conveyed a mystical quality, and suggested a hidden, cosmic truth. For that reason they were immensely popular in a world that possessed few reliable facts about the universe. Magic squares were used widely to probe the unknowable and explore the relationships among numbers.

They also apparently had something to do with the creation of chess, a game that contains no numbers at all but turns out to contain an uncountable number of mathematical expressions.

In separate examinations of an eight-by-eight magic square from a medieval Arab text, Wieber, Bidev, and Calvo discovered that the ancient moves of chess fit eerily into it. "Increasingly, through mathematical investigation," concluded Calvo, "it would appear as though the rules of chess are somehow miraculously present in this numerological arrangement. The inventor or inventors of chess must have used this pre-existent numerological arrangement (the 'genetic code of chess,' as Prof. Bidev put it) before deciding how to institute the various moves of the different chess pieces upon the board."

The moves of chess, in other words, appeared to be originally de-signed according to a particular number scheme, an old magic square. As fantastic as it seemed, this theory that chess had a master "genetic code" rooted in numerical mysticism also neatly solved the mystery of the King Nushirwan puzzle, where the Persians had been given no instructions on how to play the game. If the Persians in the story were able to uncover a hidden magic square that dictated a veiled mathematical superstructure of chess, then the story made perfect sense. Such a key code *could* enable someone to deduce the moves of each piece. It would be extremely dif-ficult, but not impossible—precisely the dynamic suggested by the story. This explanation instantly transformed the Indian-Persian legend from a mystical tale into a plausible piece of history.

Sources: Ricardo Calvo, "Mystical Numerology in Egypt and Meso-potamia," online at *goddesschess.com/chessays/calvonumerology.html*. See also Pavle Bidev, "Geschichte der Entdeckung des Schachs im magischen Quadrat und des magischen Quadrat im Schach," *Schachwissentschaftliche Forschungen*, January 5, 1975.

18 "Understanding [is] the essential weapon": Murray, *History of Chess,* p. 152.

18 one of the oldest books mentioning the game: The *Karnamak-i Artakhshatr-i Papakan* (Book of the deeds of Ardashir, son of Papak), written near 600, mentions an already popular game called *chatrang*. Murray, *History of Chess*, p. 149. Subsequently, the Persian poem *Chatrang-namak* (The book of *chatrang*)—circa 650–850—explicitly describes the game in some detail. Murray, *History of Chess*, pp. 150–52.

The Indian text *Harshacharita*, written in about 625, is the earliest reliable mention of *chaturanga* as the Sanskrit antecedent of *chatrang*. It also names the *ashtapada* as the sixty-four-square board the game was played on. "Under this monarch," boasted King Harsha's biographer about his ruler's reign of peace and stability, "only bees quarrel in collecting dews; the only feet cut off are those in metre; only *ashtapadas* teach the positions of the *chaturanga*." *Chaturanga* also meant "army" or "army formation." Its use in *Harshacharita* had a double meaning, the point being that during the reign of the powerful and wise King

Harsha, the only wars fought—or even trained for—were those fought on a chessboard. An ideal society indeed.

19 "Chess was the companion and catalyst": Strouhal, *Acht X Acht*, footnote 20.

19 The early Islamic chess master: Murray, *History of Chess*, p. 338.

19 "Chancellor of the Exchequer": "The Dialogue concerning the Exchequer" (late twelfth century), in Ernest F. Henderson, *Select Historical Documents of the Middle Ages* (George Bell and Sons, 1910), online in *The Internet Medieval Sourcebook* at *http://www.fordham.edu/halsall/source/excheq1 .html*.

19 in Dante's *Paradiso*: *Paradiso*, Canto 28.

THE IMMORTAL GAME: MOVE 1

23 "When one plays over a game by a fine technician": Anthony Saidy, *The March of Chess Ideas* (McKay Chess Library, 1994), p. 6.

For biographical information on Anderssen and Kieseritzky and the game itself, I relied on Robert Hübner, "The Immortal Game," *American Chess Journal*, no. 3 (1995), pp. 14–35; F. L. Amelung, *Baltische Schachblätter* 4 (1893), pp. 325–26, as cited in Hübner above and in personal correspondence by Michael Negele, of the Ken Whyld Association; Bill Wall, "Adolf Anderssen (1818–79)," online at *geocities.com/siliconvalley/lab/7378/andersse .htm*; and "Lionel Kieseritzky," *chessgames.com/perl/chessplayer?pid=15970*.

For chess analysis of the Immortal Game, I relied on Lionel Kieseritzky, firsthand annotation of the game in his journal *La Régence*, July 1851; Hübner, "The Immortal Game," pp. 14–35; Irving Chernev, *1000 Best Short Games of Chess* (Fireside, 1955); Chernev, *The Chess Companion* (Simon & Schuster, 1973); Graham Burgess, John Nunn, and John Emms, *The Mammoth Book of the World's Greatest Chess Games* (Carroll and Graf, 1998); Lubomir Kavalek, chess column, *Washington Post*, July 2003; David Hayes, "The Immortal Game," online at *logicalchess.com/resources/bestgames/traditional/game13parent.html*; David A. Wheeler, analysis, online at *dwheeler.com/misc/immortal.txt*; S. Tartakower and J. Du Mont, *500 Master Games of Chess* (Dover Publications, 1975); David Levy and Kevin O'Connoll, *The Oxford Encyclopedia of Chess Games* (Oxford University Press, 1981); Ron Burnett and Sid Pickard, *The Chess Games of Adolph Anderssen, Master of Attack* (Pickard and Son, 1996); Reuben Fine, *The World's Great Chess Games* (Dover, 1983); A. J. Goldsby, analysis, online at *geocities.com/lifemasteraj/a__ander.html*; "Anderssen, A-Kieseritzky, L,

London, 1851: Mate the Uncastled King-Part I," online at *brainsturgeon.com/iversen/000415a.htm*; and Stephen Hubbell, in a reenactment of the game, spring 2005.

27 They anticipated a caliber of chess: Andy Soltis, *The Great Chess Tournaments and Their Stories* (Chilton Book Co., 1975), p. 3.

CHAPTER 2

29 "Acquire knowledge": Sir Abdullah Suhrawardy, *The Sayings of Muhammad* (Citadel Press, 1990), p. 94.

30 "The [board] is placed between two friends of known friendship": Murray, *History of Chess*, p. 184.

30 "The skilled player places his pieces": Murray, *History of Chess*, p. 184.

30 A list of prominent players: Sa'id ibn al-Musayyib, of Medina, an Arab who played in public; Sa'id ibn Jubair, a Negro, who excelled in blindfold play; Az-Zuhri, the great lawyer of the Umayyad period; Hisham ibn Urwa, another blindfold player, whose three granddaughters Safi'a, A'isha, and 'Ubaida also played chess; and Al-Qasim ibn Muhammad, grandson of the Caliph Abu-Bakr. Murray, *History of Chess*, pp. 191, 192.

30 "I keep you from your inheritance": Murray, *History of Chess*, p. 194. "The chess allusion is perfectly certain," he writes, "for *baidaq* has no other meaning than that of chess [Pawn]." The poet's allusion also refers to the phenomenon of Pawn promotion.

30; 32 allowable under Islamic law: Murray, *History of Chess* pp. 187–91. "Images" and "lots": the respective Arabic terms are *ansab* and *maisir*.

31 A Guide to Shatranj: Information and some direct text taken from *chess variants.org/historic.dir/shatranj.html*. Another excellent resource is *history.chess .free.fr/shatranj.htm*.

The image of two players is from *Shahnameh* (The epic of kings), by the great Persian poet Ferdowsi Tousi (935–1020). Scanned from Strouhal, *Acht X Acht*, p. 195.

33 Ceramic chess set from twelfth-century Iran: Anna Contadini, "Islamic Ivory Chess Pieces, Draughtsmen and Dice," *Islamic Art in the Ashmolean Museum*, Part One, edited by James Allan (Oxford University Press, 1995), p. 111, online at *goddesschess.com/chessays/contadinil.html*.

33 "The empress into whose place": Murray, *History of Chess*, p. 164.

34 the first true Islamic Renaissance: Husain F. Nagamia, "Islamic Medicine: History and Current Practice," online at *iiim.org/islamed3.html*; Ted

Thornton, "The Abbasid Golden Age," online at *nmhschool.org/tthornton/ mehistorydatabase/abbasid_golden_age.htm*; "Islam and Islamic History in Arabia and The Middle East," online at *islamicity.com/mosque/ihame/Sec7.htm*; Jens Høyrup, "Sub-Scientific Mathematics: Observations on a Pre-Modern Phenomenon," *Measure, Number, and Weight: Studies in Mathematics and Culture* (State University of New York Press, 1994).

35 there were just five *aliyat*: Jabir al-Khufi, Rabrab, Abu'n-Na'am, al-Adli, and ar-Razi. Murray, *History of Chess*, p. 197.

35 One particular al-Adli problem: Bill Wall, online at *geocities.com/ SiliconValley/Lab/7378/aladli.htm*.

THE IMMORTAL GAME: MOVE 2

40 from the Italian *gambetto*: First introduced by Ruy Lopez, according to G. T. Chesney, encyclopedia entry, 1911, online at *http://21.1911encyclopedia .org/C/CH/CHESS.htm*.

40 colorful names to various opening sequences: Murray, *History of Chess*, p. 39.

CHAPTER 3

43 Despite appearances to the contrary: Principal sources are Neil Stratford, *The Lewis Chessmen and the Enigma of the Hoard* (British Museum Press, 1997); and Michael Taylor, *The Lewis Chessmen* (British Museum Press, 1978). Also useful was J. L. Cazaux's history site: *http://history.chess.free .fr/lewis.htm*. The description of dune formation was informed by a personal communication with Hans Herrmann, University of Stuttgart. Additional facts on the Isle of Lewis come from Patti Smith at the Stornoway Tourist Information Center. *Uig* is pronounced *oo-eeg*. Irving Finkel quote from BBC website: *news.bbc.co.uk/1/shared/spl/hi/entertainment/03/british_museum_treasures/ html/9.stm*.

46 Fortunately, such doggedness was second nature to Harold Murray: Obituary of Harold Murray in *British Chess Magazine*, August 1955; Harold Murray, unpublished "Autobiography of Chess Play" (Bodleian Library, Oxford University, H. J. R. Murray Papers, Volume 73, p. 216, SC49132–3); "Dictionary milestones: A chronology of events relevant to the history of the OED," online at *oed.com/public/inside/timeline.htm*; Marilyn Yalom, *Birth of the Chess Queen: A History* (HarperCollins, 2004).

More on H. J. R. Murray

A History of Chess, by Harold James Ruthven Murray, was published by Oxford University Press in 1913. Murray covered the first 1,400 years of the game's history in crystallized, definitive detail. It was Murray who chronicled the role of Harun ar-Rashid, the *Chatrang-namak*, and the tale of Indian King Balhait. It was Murray who relentlessly tracked down the problems of al-Adli, who translated the romantic poetry of Marie de France, who exhaustively collected and interpreted virtually everything there was to know about the game at that time. Murray's book is, in fact, in some ways too complete. At nine hundred pages of small (and even smaller) print, with large sections in Latin, German, and French (with smatterings of Chinese, Japanese, Arabic, and Greek), innumerable chess diagrams and annotated games, pages and pages of ur-text romantic medieval poetry, hundreds of chess problems (and their solutions), a river of footnotes, and extensive catalogues of ancient manuscripts, *A History of Chess* is truly not a book for casual consumption. It provides historians with an exhaustive catalogue of chess's more than twelve million hours of existence, but for the lay reader it does not effectively tell chess's story or convey its meaning.

Reading through it for the first time, poring through its footnotes and bottomless index, was for me at once a thrill and a vexing frustration, like suddenly being able to see a gigantic photograph of the planet earth in unprecedented detail—but only from one inch away, through a magnifying glass. The assemblage of facts was magnificent, leaving me desperate to back up a few steps and view them in more meaningful components. The irony was that this clearly definitive book was inadvertently obscuring much about chess's history—and human history. In logging the voluminous facts of the game, it left out much of the context, and in so doing concealed chess's majesty and true importance. And yet no one could seriously imagine chess history without it, or easily conceive of what its pioneer author went through to compile it. As he began his work at the end of the nineteenth century, Murray had no specialized chess libraries at his disposal as we do today in Cleveland, Princeton, and The Hague. There was no central game database. Source material was scattered, hidden, and/or recorded in forgotten languages. Even at Oxford, the center of the academic universe, compiling a serious chess history was a career-long undertaking. We should all be grateful for Murray's perseverance. Imagine piecing together the trail of a Red Knot Sandpiper from Tierra del Fuego, at the southern tip of South America, to the Arctic Circle by following its droppings. You could do it, but only if it meant that much to you; only if you were willing to devote much of your life to the task.

47 By 900, Muslim armies controlled: W. C. Brice, *An Historical Atlas of Islam*, as found on *princeton.edu/~humcomp/dimensions.html*; map at *ccat.sas.upenn.edu/~rs143/map5.jpg*.

47 In 1005 the Egyptian ruler al-Hakim: Murray, *History of Chess,* p. 203.

48 Persian Muslim nicknamed Ziriab: Ricardo Calvo, "*The Oldest Chess Pieces in Europe,*" presentation to the Initiative Group Königstein (Amsterdam, December 2001), online at *goddesschess.com/chessays/calvopieces.html*; Hans Ree, *The Human Comedy of Chess: A Grandmaster's Chronicles* (Russell Enterprises, 2001) (Ree notes that in the twenty-first century Ziriab is still a well-known figure in the Andalusian region of southern Spain); Yalom, *Birth of the Chess Queen,* p. 11.

49 Not long after this: This is apocryphal, from Jerzy Gizycki, *A History of Chess* (Abbey Library, 1972), p. 15.

49 "It is a paradoxical but well-established fact": Eales, *Chess,* p. 42.

50 The medieval French historian Robert de St. Remi: Murray, *History of Chess,* p. 419.

50 Tracking chess's migration . . . to a Swiss monastery by 997: Yalom, *Birth of the Chess Queen,* p. 16.

50 to northern, Christian-controlled Spain by 1008: Eales, *Chess,* p. 43; Murray, *History of Chess,* p. 405. (Murray says perhaps 1010.)

50 to southern Germany by 1050; and to central Italy by 1061: Murray, *History of Chess,* p. 418.

50 By the early twelfth century . . . ensconced in the culture of medieval chivalry: Yalom, *Birth of the Chess Queen,* p. 52; Eales, *Chess,* p. 53.

50 The very first mention of the chess Queen: Yalom, *Birth of the Chess Queen,* pp. 19–26.

50 the introduction of dark and light checkered squares: first mentioned in Einsiedeln manuscripts, according to Murray, *History of Chess,* p. 452.

51 Finally, the game's name shifted: Murray, *History of Chess,* p. 400.

51 The medieval historian Alexander Neckam: Murray, *History of Chess,* p. 502.

51 "There was a *demand* for a game like chess": Eales, *Chess,* p. 48 (italics mine).

51 In the twelfth century: W. L. Tronzo, "Moral Hieroglyphs: Chess and Dice at San Savino in Piacenza," *Gesta* 16, no. 2, pp. 15–26.

53 *Liber de moribus*: This is one of the early titles appended to a translation of Cessolis's work, which probably had no formal title to begin with. Source: Jenny Adams, personal communication.

54 the twelfth century had seen an "early Renaissance": "In the early 12th Century," writes historian Norman Cantor, "it was becoming more apparent every day that knowledge was power . . . many of the most brilliant minds of the new generation that came to maturity about 1100 set off for the new cathedral schools to participate in the intellectual revolution." Cantor, *The Civilization of the Middle Ages* (HarperCollins, 1994).

55 *Liber de moribus* used the chess metaphor: "Language normally grows by a process of metaphorical extension; we extend old names to new objects. (In fact, someone has happily called metaphors 'new namings.')" C. Brooks and R. P. Warren, *Modern Rhetoric* (Harcourt Brace Jovanovich, 1979).

55 "Before the *Liber*": Jenny Adams, *Power Play: The Literature and Politics of Chess in the Late Middle Ages* (University of Pennsylvania Press, 2006).

57 Thus chess, now with many different names: Murray, *History of Chess*, pp. 455–56.

58 "The wearingness which players experienced": Eales, *Chess*, p. 69.

58 If it landed on "1": Anne Sunnucks, *The Encyclopaedia of Chess* (St. Martin's Press, 1976), p. 97. "The use of the dice reduces the necessity for thought and the formation of a plan of campaign, but it destroys the liberty of play which is so closely associated with the differentiation of each piece, and ruins the real entity of chess." Murray, *History of Chess*, p. 454.

The Immortal Game: Move 3

60 For one shilling and sixpence: Personal visit to Simpson's Divan, and personal correspondence with Robin Easton, general manager of Simpson's. "£4.84 in the year 2002 has the same 'purchase power' as £0, 1s, 6d in the year 1851." John J. McCusker, "Comparing the Purchasing Power of Money in Great Britain from 1264 to Any Other Year Including the Present" (Economic History Services, 2001), online at *eh.net/hmit/ppowerbp*.

Chapter 4

67 "This Century, like a golden age": *historyguide.org/earlymod/lecture1c.html*.

69 you'll have to trust the number crunchers on this: *http://mathworld* *.wolfram.com/Chess.html.*

70 "barely thinkable": Stefano Franchi, "Palomar, the Triviality of Modernity, and the Doctrine of the Void," *New Literary History* 28, no. 4 (1997), pp. 757–78.

70 The estimated total: I. Peterson, "The Soul of a Chess Machine: Lessons Learned from a Contest Pitting Man against Computer," *Science News*, March 30, 1996.

71 "I understand you," replied the queen: Yalom cites Christopher Hibbert, *The Virgin Queen: Elizabeth I, Genius of the Golden Age* (Addison-Wesley, 1991).

71–72 "I thinke it ouer fond": *Basilicon Doron*, London, 1603. William Poole, "False Play: Shakespeare and Chess," *Shakespeare Quarterly* 55, no. 1 (2004), p. 62.

72 In 1550 Saint Teresa: Saint Teresa of Ávila, *The Way of Perfection*, Chapter 16, translated by E. Allison Peers (Image, 1964), online at *ccel.org/t/teresa/way/ cache/way.txt.* "I hope you do not think I have written too much about this already," she writes, "for I have only been placing the board, as they say. You have asked me to tell you about the first steps in prayer; . . . even now I can hardly have acquired these elementary virtues. But you may be sure that anyone who cannot set out the pieces in a game of chess will never be able to play well, and, if he does not know how to give check, he will not be able to bring about a checkmate."

72 In 1595 English courtier Sir Philip Sidney: Poole, "False Play: Shakespeare and Chess."

72 Cervantes used it: *Don Quixote*, Part 2, Chapter 12.

72 The English playwright Thomas Middleton: Jenny Adams, in personal correspondence. The play was extraordinarily popular, one of the first plays ever to have a continuous run. Adams also points out that Middleton also used chess to represent a rape in his play *Women Beware Women*. Adams cites T. H. Howard-Hill's edition of the play (Manchester University Press, 1993).

73 political cartoonists: See cartoon on p. 299. See also *http://www.chessbase* *.com/columns/column.asp?pid=166.*

73 law firms: See *http://goodwinproctor.com.*

73 technology consultants: Allarus.

73 the U.S. Army would adopt: The Army "Psyops" unit uses chess in its insignia:

A 1991 political cartoon by Pancho
from the French newspaper *Le Monde*.

73 John Locke: *Essay Concerning Human Understanding*, Chapter 13, Sections 8 and 9.

74 "The whole world is like a chess-board": Eales, *Chess*, p. 65. Eales also suggests that the bag metaphor encouraged peasants to be patient for greater rewards in the afterlife.

75 Chess, as James Rowbothum suggested: From Poole, "False Play: Shakespeare and Chess."

THE IMMORTAL GAME: MOVES 4 AND 5

79 Kieseritzky's earlier wins in 1844 and 1847 were against, respectively, John Schulten in Paris and Daniel Harrwitz in England.

CHAPTER 5

87 Along with just about everyone else: H. W. Brands, *The First American: The Life and Times of Benjamin Franklin* (Anchor Books, 2000); *The Papers of Benjamin Franklin* (Yale University Press, 1959); Benjamin Franklin, *The Morals of Chess* (Passy, 1779); *The Autobiography of Benjamin Franklin* (1793), online at *earlyamerica.com/lives/franklin/*; Ralph K. Hagedorn, *Benjamin Franklin and Chess in Early America* (University of Pennsylvania Press, 1958).

89 Thomas Jefferson tells a similar story: Jefferson to Robert Welsh, 4 December 1818, supplied by Kristen K. Onuf, Monticello Research Department, online at *monticello.org/reports/quotes/chess.html*.

90 "In the Age of Reason": Larry Parr and Lev Alburt, "Life Itself," *National Review*, September 9, 1991.

91 "He seldom goes to bed till day-break": John Conyers, "Annual Register for the year 1767," *Characters* (1800), online at *humanities.uchicago.edu/homes/VSA/Conyer.html*.

91 In 1754, the Jewish philosopher Moses Mendelssohn: Daniel Johnson, "Cold War Chess," *Prospect*, no. 111 (June 2005), *www.tiea.us/5195.htm*.

92 Mendelssohn's last written work: From "Controversy with Jacobi over Lessing's Alleged Pantheism," online at *plato.stanford.edu/entries/mendelssohn/#7*.

92 Admirers frequently worked to pair him with good players: Names from Bill Wall, *geocities.com/SiliconValley/Lab/7378/prez.htm*.

92 Of Jefferson, a friend wrote: Ellen Wayles Coolidge Letterbook, p. 37 (1853), supplied by Kristen K. Onuf, Monticello Research Department, online at *monticello.org/reports/quotes/chess.html*.

94 "I call *this* my opera": Hochberg, *The 64-Square Looking Glass*, p. 7.

96 His standing was such: "Chess: The Fickle Lover," online at *angelfire.com/games/SBChess/Morphy/fickle.html*.

96 playing two games simultaneously while blindfolded: Seven years later, he pushed it to three blindfold games at once.

96 Dating all the way back: So says John B. Henderson, in his column "The Scotsman," at *http://www.rochadekuppenheim.de/heco/ar0203.html*. Murray, on the other hand, says that the Muslim Borzaga was possibly the first exponent of the art of blindfold play, circa 1265. *History of Chess*, p. 192.

96 Philidor, it was said: Henderson, "The Scotsman," at *rochadekuppenheim.de/heco/ar0203.html*.

98 In his memoirs, Rousseau: *The Confessions of Jean-Jacques Rousseau*, Book 7, online at *etext.library.adelaide.edu.au/r/r864c/book7.html*.

THE IMMORTAL GAME: MOVES 6 AND 7

99 the evolution of chess play: In fact, one of the great masters of the early twentieth century, Richard Reti, suggested that every player's personal learning curve in chess instinctively repeats chess's evolutionary path. "Such evolution," he offered, "has gone on, in general, in a way quite similar to that in which it goes on with the individual chess player, only with the latter more rapidly." Furthermore, Reti provocatively declared, "[in] the development of the chess mind we have a picture of the intellectual struggle of mankind."

100 Even after Philidor: With his novel approach, Philidor was one of the earliest players to advocate a *closed game*—one in which Pawns are not exchanged early on, but instead work toward a united and formidable front. This was in contrast to the *open game*, the universally popular style of Pawn exchanges or sacrifices that forced vertical openings in the fence of Pawns and encouraged a quicker, more aggressive contest.

CHAPTER 6

107 the Café de la Régence: George Walker, "The Café de la Régence, by a Chess-player," *Fraser's Magazine* 22 (July to December 1840).

107 his underling opponents frequently found it inconvenient to win: Thierry Libaert, *Revue du Souvenir Napoléonien*, no. 424 (1999), p. 55. Conveyed by Peter Hicks, Fondation Napoléon.

107 exiled to the tiny island of St. Helena: St. Helena measured 122 square kilometers (47 square miles). The story finally came to light in 1928, during an

A chess set designed for Napoleon, with cannons for Rooks. From the treatise *Nuovo giuoco di scacchi ossia il giuoco della guerra* (Genova, 1801), by Francesco Giacometti, online at *chessbase.com/columns/ column.asp?pid=166.*

exhibition of Napoleonic artifacts. Source: Mike Fox and Richard James, *The Complete Chess Addict* (Faber & Faber, 1987).

110 "There's all sorts of anecdotal evidence": Emma Young, "Chess! What Is It Good For?" *Guardian*, March 4, 2004.

111 the British public became fascinated: "The London Correspondence Match," online at *bm3.pwp.blueyonder.co.uk/ecchist2.htm*. Between 1834 and 1836 Paris and London competed in another high-profile correspondence match, which Paris won.

111 That event fed interest: Adolf Anderssen later said that he learned chess strategy from another William Lewis book, *Fifty Games between Labourdonnais and McDonnell* (1835).

112 Travel and long-distance communication were cheaper: *brynmawr.edu/library/speccoll/guides/travel/europe.html*.

112 timed to coincide with a major international fair in the same city: The five-and-a-half-month festival of industrial and culture offerings from around the world attracted some six million visitors to London's Hyde Park. The chess competitors gathered about a mile away, at the St. George Club at Cavendish Square.

112 "Comfort is not particularly high": From an old article translated and reprinted on *avlerchess.com/chess-misc/Translate_a_Finnish_Article_on_London_1851_182037.htm*.

113 In 1103 the knight Pierzchala: Jerzy Gizycki, *A History of Chess* (Abbey Library, 1972), p. 31.

113 In 1564 a mock-epic poem, *Chess*: The poem, by Jan Kochanowski, paraphrased an earlier effort by the Italian poet Marco Girolamo Vida. Source is Prof. Edmund Kotarski at *monika.univ.gda.pl/~literat/autors/kochan.htm*.

113 a major Polish revolt against Russian rule: "During the Polish uprising, the Jews suffered, as always, at the hands of both sides: the [Russian] Cussaks who suppressed them and the revolutionaries who demanded money from the Jewish community." Dr. Kasriel Eilender, *A Brief History of the Jews in Suwalki*, *http://www.shtetlinks.jewishgen.org/suwalki/history.htm*. (I have altered the punctuation in this quote for clarity.)

114 In 1884–85, Rosenthal led a Paris team: Carlo Alberto Pagni, *Correspondence Chess Matches between Clubs 1823–1899*, Vol. 1 (1996).

114 In 1887 he was awarded: Tadeusz Wolsza, *Arcymistrozowie, mistrzowie, amatorzy: Slownik biograficzny szachistów polskich, tom* 4 (Wydawnictwo, 2003).

114 Rosenthal was said by Wilhelm Steinitz: He had chess columns in *Le Monde Illustré* and *Republique Française*. Steinitz said Rosenthal averaged 20,000 francs per year in the last thirty years of his life (Hooper and Whyld, *Oxford*

Companion to Chess). That amounts to $57,670 in 1991 U.S. dollars. (Average exchange rate in this period was 5.15 francs per dollar. One U.S. dollar in 1875–1900 equates to $14.85 in 1991 U.S. dollars, so 20,000 nineteenth-century francs = $3,883.50 nineteenth-century dollars = $57,670 1991 dollars. Sources: *nber.org/databases/macrohistory/contents/fr.html*, *nber.org/databases/macro history/rectdata/14/m14004a.dat*, and *http://web.archive.org/web/2004112408 5221/http://www.users.mis.net/~chesnut/pages/value.htm.*)

114 Both soldiers and players: From obituary in French newspaper, September 1902.

115 Though for three decades: He won the first French chess championship in 1880. See *http://www.logicalchess.com/info/history/1800–1899.html.*

115 he "reigned supreme as the leader of Parisian chess": *Chicago Tribune*, October 12, 1902, p. 12.

115 he managed to beat legendary players: chessgames.com database has all actual games.

116 Franklin, who had described chess as battle without bloodshed: Papers of Benjamin Franklin, XXXII, p. 54.

CHAPTER 7

124 A number of chess masters: Alfred Binet, *Mnemonic Virtuosity: A Study of Chess Players,* translated by Marianne L. Simmel and Susan B. Barron (Journal Press, 1966); S. Nicolas, "Memory in the Work of Binet, Alfred (1857–1911)," *Année Psychologique* 94 (no. 2), pp. 257–82; Douwe Draaisma, *Metaphors of Memory: A History of Ideas about the Mind* (Cambridge University Press, 2000); Howard Gardner, *Frames of Mind: The Theory of Multiple Intelligences* (Basic Books, 1993); F. Galton, "Psychology of Mental Arithmeticians and Blindfold Chess-Players" (Review of Alfred Binet, *Psychologie des grands calculateurs et joueurs d'échecs*)," *Nature* 51: 73–74; O. D. Enersen, *Alfred Binet, whonamedit .com/doctor.cfm/1299.html*; René Zazzo, "Alfred Binet (1857–1911)," *Prospects: The Quarterly Review of Comparative Education* 23, no. ½ (1993), pp. 101–12.

127 Binet's original hypothesis might: W. G. Chase and H. A. Simon, "The Mind's Eye in Chess," *Visual Information Processing: Proceedings of the 8th Annual Carnegie Psychology Symposium* (Academic Press, 1972); Herbert A. Simon and Jonathan Schaeffer, "The Game of Chess," *Handbook of Game Theory*, edited by R. J. Aumann and S. Hart, vol. 1 (Elsevier, 1992); M. E. Glickman and C. F. Chabris, "Using Chess Ratings as Data in Psychological Research" (Unpublished article, 1996, available at *http://www.wjh.harvard.edu/~cfc/Glickman 1996.pdf*); D. Regis, "Chess and Psychology"; Fernand Gobet, "Chess,

Psychology of," *The MIT Encyclopedia of the Cognitive Sciences*, edited by R. A. Wilson and F. C. Keil (MIT Press, 1999); N. Charness, "The Impact of Chess Research on Cognitive Science," *Psychological Research-Psychologische Forschung* 54, no. 1, pp. 4–9: Helmut Pfleger and Gerd Treppner, *Chess: The Mechanics of the Mind* (David & Charles, 1989); William Bechtel and Tadeusz Zawidzki, *Biographies of Major Contributors to Cognitive Science*, online at *mechanism. ucsd.edu/~bill/research/ANAUT.html*; "Brief survey of psychological studies of chess," online at *jeays.net/files/psychchess.htm*; K. Anders Ericsson, "Superior Memory of Experts and Long-Term Working Memory," online at *http://web. archive.org/web/20041019073517/http://www.psy.fsu.edu/faculty/ericsson/ ericsson.mem.exp.html*.

130 young chess luminaries like Fischer and Waitzkin: Michael J. A. Howe, Jane W. Davidson, and John A. Sloboda, "Innate Talents: Reality or Myth?" *Behavioral and Brain Sciences*, no. 21 (1998), pp. 399–442; "Nature vs. Nurture in Intelligence," online at *wilderdom.com/personality/L4-1IntelligenceNatureVs Nurture.html*; D. R. Shanks, "Outstanding Performers: Created, Not Born? New Results on Nature vs. Nurture," *Science Spectra*, no. 18 (1999); K. Anders Ericsson and Neil Charness, "Expert Performance—Its Structure and Acquisition," *American Psychologist* 49, no. 8 (August 1994), pp. 725–47.

130 "He has become a fine player at a very young age": Tom Rose, "Can 'old' players improve all that much?" online at: *chessville.com/Editorials/Roses Rants/CanOldPlayersImproveAllThatMuch.htm*. Rose adds: "Of course he still had to do the hard work. With the same advantages many would not make such good use of them."

CHAPTER 8

141 "Chess-play is a good and witty exercise": Robert Burton, *The Anatomy of Melancholy*.

142 For about a decade: Hooper and Whyld, *Oxford Companion to Chess*, p. 395.

142 "He approached the structure and dynamics": Anthony Saidy, *The March of Chess Ideas* (David McKay, 1994), pp. 14–15. Steinitz himself said, "Chess is a scientific game, and its literature ought to be placed on the basis of the strictest truthfulness, which is the foundation of all scientific research."

143 For a time, he was confined to a Moscow asylum: *The Steinitz Papers: Letters and Documents of the First World Chess Champion*, edited by Kurt Landsberger (McFarland & Co., 2002).

143 **In 1779 the accomplished French physician:** Franklin's response is not recorded.

143 **"A nameless excrescence upon life":** H. G. Wells, *Certain Personal Matters* (1898), quoted in Norman Reider, "Chess, Oedipus, and the Mater Dolorosa," *International Journal of Psychoanalysis* 40 (1959), p. 442.

143 **The tally included:** for Gustav Neumann, see Hooper and Whyld, *Oxford Companion to Chess*, p. 270; for Johannes Minckwitz, see *geocities.com/silicon valley/lab/7378/death.htm*; for George Rotlewi, see *chessgames.com/perl/chess player?pid=10262*; for Akiba Rubinstein, see Anne Sunnucks, *The Encyclopaedia of Chess* (St. Martin's Press, 1976), p. 414; for Carlos Torre-Repetto, see *chessgames.com/perl/chessplayer?pid=12991*, for Aron Nimzowitsch, see Hans Kmoch, "Grandmasters I Have Known: Aaron Nimzovich (1886–1935)," online at *chesscafe.com//text/kmoch02.txt* (additional material online at *chessgames .com/player/aron_nimzowitsch.html?kpage=1*); for Raymond Weinstein, see Sam Sloan, "I Have Found Raymond Weinstein," online at *samsloan.com/weinste .htm*; for Bobby Fischer, see Rene Chun, "Bobby Fischer's Pathetic Endgame," *Atlantic Monthly* (December 2002). I found Rene Chun's article on Fischer to be comprehensive, but also mean-spirited and grossly insensitive to the cruel realities of mental illness. Long after Chun establishes beyond any doubt that Fischer is crippled by mental illness, he rhetorically piles it on, ridiculing Fischer for his bizarre behavior.

146 **"Most of his novels":** Personal e-mail with Anna Dergatcheva.

147 **Sigmund Freud's biographer and protégé:** Alexander Cockburn, *Idle Passion: Chess and the Dance of Death* (Simon & Schuster, 1974), pp. 22–23.

147 **While Freud himself apparently never considered:** Sigmund Freud, "Further Recommendations in the Technique of Psycho-Analysis," *Collected Papers*, vol. 2 (1913), p. 342.

148 **In 1937 Isador Coriat:** Isador Coriat, "The Unconscious Motives of Interest in Chess," based on a paper read before the Boston Psychoanalytic Society, October 12, 1937, online at *psychoanalysis.org.uk/chess.htm*.

148 **In 1956 Reuben Fine's:** Reuben Fine, *The Psychology of the Chess Player* (Dover, 1956).

149 **Writer, psychiatrist, and serious chess player:** Charles Krauthammer, "The Romance of Chess," in Hochberg, *The 64-Square Looking Glass* (Times Books, 1993).

149 **A third plausible route to chess madness:** Gizycki, *A History of Chess*, pp. 259–61.

THE IMMORTAL GAME: MOVES 12–16

151 the leading Spanish player Lucena: These are paraphrases, not quotes from Lucena.

CHAPTER 9

163 A Nazified version of chess called *Tak Tik*: Author's direct observations of the game in Ströbeck chess museum.

164 After slipping in and out: Andrew Soltis, *Soviet Chess, 1917–1991* (McFarland & Co., 2000), p. 7.

164 When the Germans captured France in 1940, Alekhine agreed: Bill Wall, online at *geocities.com/SiliconValley/Lab/7378/nazi.htm*.

164 There are persistent claims: *Nardshir* appears in the Kethuboth 61b tractate of the Babylonian Talmud. The Alexander Kohut quote is from Victor A. Keats, *Chess in Jewish History and Hebrew Literature* (Magnes Press, 1995), p. 26, also online at *mynetcologne.de/~nc-jostenge/keats.htm*.

165 Abraham ibn Ezra, the Spanish poet: Keats, *Chess in Jewish History*.

166 World champion Wilhelm Steinitz: There is some question about whether he was educated in a yeshiva.

166 Tarrasch and Lasker became such bitter rivals: J. O. Sossnitsky cites Soltis, *The Great Chess Tournaments and Their Stories* (Chilton Book Co., 1975).

167 six pro-Nazi essays: Brian Reilly, distinguished editor of the *British Chess Magazine*, was the one to actually see Alekhine's Nazi letters. He reported it to several people in the field, but was later reluctant to see himself credited for this. In his reluctance he inadvertently cast some confusion on the matter. The chess historian Edward Winter definitively puts the issue to rest with a juxtaposition of letters and conversations collected on his "Chess Notes Archives" page, online at *chesshistory.com/winter/winter06.html*.

167 the first ever official team sporting event for the USSR: Denker–Botvinnik, USA–USSR Radio Match, 1945.

1. d4 d5 2. c4 e6 3. Nc3 c6 4. Nf3 Nf6 5. Bg5 dxc4 6. e4 b5 7. e5 h6 8. Bh4 g5 9. Nxg5 hxg5 10. Bxg5 Nbd7 11. exf6 Bb7 12. Be2 Qb6 13. O-O O-O-O 14. a4 b4 15. Ne4 c5 16. Qb1 Qc7 17. Ng3 cxd4 18. Bxc4 Qc6 19. f3 d3 20. Qc1 Bc5+ 21. Kh1 Qd6 22. Qf4? Rxh2+! 23. Kxh2 Rh8+ 24. Qh4 Rxh4+ 25. Bxh4 Qf4

168 One pithy illustration: Bill Wall, online at *geocities.com/SiliconValley/Lab/7378/nazi.htm*.

168 Russia had a special relationship with chess: I. M. Linder, *Chess in Old Russia* (Michael Kühnle, 1979), p. 62.

169 "Marx adored chess": Daniel Johnson, *Prospect*, no. 111 (June 2005), online at *tiea.us/5195.htm*.

169 "grew angry when he lost": Maksum Gorky, *V. I. Lenin* (first published 1924), online at *marxists.org/archive/gorky-maxim/1924/01/x01.htm*.

169 Russian prime minister Alexander Kerensky: Gizycki, *A History of Chess*, pp. 169, 170.

169 Not long after the 1917 takeover: Larry Parr and Lev Alburt, "Life Itself," *National Review*, September 9, 1991.

169 "Take chess to the workers": Soltis, *Soviet Chess*, p. 25.

169 "The Bolsheviks' motives": *Checkmate*, BBC Radio 4, online at *http://72.14.207.104/search?q=cache:cIllTNvUY5wJ:www.bbc.co.uk/radio4/ discover/archive_features/22.shtml+The+Bolsheviks%27+motives+ for+promoting+chess+were+both+ideological+and+political,+Daniel+King&hl=en& client=firefox-a*.

169 By 1929, 150,000 serious amateur players: Soltis, *Soviet Chess*, p. 82.

170 "a dialectical game": Taylor Kingston, "Recounting the Course of Empire," cited by Soltis, *Soviet Chess*, p. 25.

171 "Following every move": Italics mine.

171 "I had an adjourned game": Rene Chun, "The Madness of King Bobby," *Guardian*, online at *observer.guardian.co.uk/osm/story/0,6903,870785, 00.html*.

Bobby Fischer

172 "I'll never play in one of those rigged tournaments again": Chun, "The Madness of King Bobby."

172 "There were some agreed draws at Curaçao": Chun, "The Madness of King Bobby."

173 After a tournament in Yugoslavia: "Robert Fischer, The World's Greatest Chess Player," online at *chess-poster.com/great_players/fischer.htm*.

173 "If you were out to dinner with Bobby in the Sixties": The friend is Don Schultz. Source: Rene Chun.

174 "I told Fischer to get his butt over to Iceland": Rene Chun.

174 the match began: All Fischer–Spassky games are online at *chess-poster.com/great_games/fischer_spassky_en/game_1.htm*.

175 Spassky was world champion for a reason: Boris Spassky, Wikipedia, online at *onelang.com/encyclopedia/index.php/Boris_V._Spassky*.

175 Ironically, just as Fischer: Peter Nicholas and Clea Benson, "Files Reveal How FBI Hounded Chess King," *Philadelphia Inquirer*, March 31, 2005.

176 "Spassky stood on stage applauding": Archived online at: *http://web .archive.org/web/20041014080956/http://www.chessclub.demon.co.uk/culture/ worldchampions/fischer/fischer_spassky_match.htm.*

CHAPTER 10

185 "I always loved complexity": These two statements came from different interviews. The first sentence comes from Achille Bonito Oliva, editor of *The Delicate Chessboard: Marcel Duchamp: 1902/1968* (Centro Di, 1973). "With chess one creates beautiful problems" comes from Yves Arman, *Marcel Duchamp: Plays and Wins* (Galerie Yves Arman, 1984).

185 "As metaphor, model and allegory": Martin Rosenberg, "Chess Rhizome: Mapping Metaphor Theory in Hypertext," archived online at *http://web.archive.org/web/20041030015424/http://www.nwe.ufl.edu/sls/ abstracts/rosenberg.html.*

188 "All chess-players are artists": Calvin Tomkins, *Duchamp: A Biography*, p. 211.

188 Cuban sensation José Raul Capablanca: C. H. O. Alexander, *A Book of Chess* (Harper & Row, 1973), p. 52.

The Hypermodernists

"The essence of the Hypermodern philosophy was the affirmation of individuality of each position," writes Anthony Saidy, "and thus a rejection of the notion of the Scientific school that general rules always apply."

Not surprisingly, in its early years, Nimzowitsch's Hypermodern approach was considered so strange that it drew little response but deep skepticism. Only after he and others had proven its utility over and over again in tournaments were these ideas slowly welcomed into the canon of chess. In 1929 Nimzowitsch solidified his legacy with the book *My System*, which would garner a long-lasting reputation as eminently accessible and unusually full of energy.

188 "fear to struggle": Alexander Alekhine, "Aryan Chess and Jewish Chess," online at *www.hagshama.org.il/en/resources/view.asp?id=120.*

189 Records still exist of an Alekhine–Duchamp game: Alekhine played White: 1. e4 c5 2. d4 cxd4 3. Nf3 Nc6 4. Nxd4 Nf6 5. Nc3 d6 6. Bg5 Qb6

7. Bxf6 gxf6 8. Nb3 e6 9. Qf3 Be7 10. O-O-O a6 11. Qg3 Bd7 12. Qg7 O-O-O 13. Qxf7 Qxf2 14. Qh5 Rdg8 15. h4 Ne5 16. Kb1 Be8 17. Qh6 Rg6 18. Qc1 Rhg8 19. Nd4 Bf8 20. b3 Rg3 21. Nce2 Re3 22. g3 Bh5 23. Rh2 Qxh2 24. Qxe3 Bg4 25. Rd2 Qh1 26. Qf2 Nf3 27. Nxf3 Qxf3 28. Qg1 Qxe4 29. Qa7 Bxe2 30. Bxe2 Bh6 31. Rd4 Qh1+ 32. Rd1 Qe4 33. Qa8+ Kc7 34. Qxg8 Qxe2 35. Qxh7+ Kc6 36. Qd3 Qe5 37. g4 Bg7 38. Qd4 f5 39. Qxe5 dxe5 40. g5 e4 41. h5 e3 42. h6 Bf8 43. Rh1 f4 44. Kc1 f3 45. Kd1 Bb4 46. c3 Bxc3 47. Kc2 e2 48. Kxc3 White resigns.

191 "[It] would interest no chess player": Andrew Hugill, "Beckett, Duchamp and Chess in the 1930s," originally published online in 2000 at *Samuel-Beckett.net/hugill.html.*

191 Beckett published his second play: Deirdre Bair, *Samuel Beckett: A Biography* (Simon & Schuster, 1990), pp. 465–67.

191 "a King in a chess-game lost from the start": Beckett in a 1967 interview; see Paul Davies, "Endgame," *The Literary Encyclopedia* (2001), online at *http://www.litencyc.com/php/sworks.php?rec=true&UID=5366.*

191 other gloomy Beckett works: Wallace Fowlie noted Beckett's penchant for writing about the "impotence of man." Fowlie, *Dionysus in Paris* (Meridian Books, 1960), pp. 214–16.

192 "yes and chess": Timothy Cahill, "Deconstructing Duchamp: The Tang shows why the French innovator deserves his place at the pinnacle of 20th-century art," *Albany Times Union,* July 6, 2003.

CHAPTER 11

199 *2001: A Space Odyssey*: Chess experts will notice a very subtle—purposeful?—point in this scene. Hal doesn't tell the truth about the forced mate. The computer essentially intimidates the player into resigning.

200 supercomputer known as Deep Blue: All Kasparov–Deep Blue games online at *research.ibm.com/deepblue/watch/html/c.html.*

200 later charged that the rules: "Kasparov on Computer Chess History," lecture on April 20, 1999, at Annual Conference on High Speed Computing in Oregon.

200 the first "purely scientific match": CNN, online at *http://www.cnn.com/2003/TECH/fun.games/02/08/cnna.kasparov.*

202 Kasparov and his seconds possessed a copy: This according to personal correspondence with Owen Williams, press assistant to Kasparov. Williams clarifies: "Garry received a prototype or generic version of Junior in the summer of 2002 (July). The match was Jan/Feb of 2003. The Junior Team was able to change the program right up to the start of the match and even between matches."

205 after the Persian term *shah-mat*: Murray, *History of Chess*, p. 159.

205 The eleventh-century Azerbaijani poet Khagani: Khagani Shirvani, "The Ruins of Madain," translated by Tom Botting, online at *literature.aznet .org/literature/xshirvani/w2_xshirvani_en.htm*.

205 "Since Garry knows how the game ends": Anne Kressler, "Kasparov: The World's Chess Champion," *Azerbaijan International* 3, no. 3 (autumn 1995).

205 Kasparov held the world championship from 1985 to 2000: The world championship has been embroiled in controversy since the mid-1980s. The story is explained in About.com's "Reunification of the World Chess Title" (September 2002), online at *chess.about.com/library/weekly/aa091402a.htm*.

207 "Its play has been almost completely indistinguishable from that of a human master . . .": Mig Greengard, "Mig on Chess #185: Real Chess against a Virtual Opponent," online at *chessbase.com/columns/column.asp?pid= 160*. I have rearranged the order of these two quoted sentences without altering the meaning in any way, in order to make a smoother transition to the next part of the chapter.

207 popular American chess columnist Mig Greengard: "Mig on Chess #184: Junior in Deep Against Kasparov," online at *chessbase.com/columns/ column.asp?pid=159*.

208 Future British champion Harry Golombek: Andrew Hodges, *Alan Turing: The Enigma* (Walker & Company, 1983), p. 265.

209 games of perfect information: Paraphrase from Hodges, *Alan Turing*, p. 213.

210 Turing became perhaps the first person: Hodges, *Alan Turing*, p. 331.

210 "It could fairly easily be made": Hodges, *Alan Turing*, pp. 332–33.

210 "What we want is a machine": Jack Copeland, "What Is Artificial Intelligence?" May 2000, online at *alanturing.net/turing_archive/pages/Reference %20Articles/what_is_AI/What%20is%20AI03.html*.

210 Turing is today revered for his vision: "At the time," write Stefano Franchi and Güven Güzeldere, "most specialists in the field tended to consider [computers] just number-crunchers perennially devoted to solving differential equations." "Machinations of the Mind: Cybernetics and Artificial Intelligence from Automata to Cyborgs," in Stefano Franchi and Güven Güzeldere, eds., *Mechanical Bodies, Computational Minds: AI from Automata to Cyborgs* (MIT Press, 2005), pp. 15–149.

211 it managed to beat Champernowne's wife: Hodges, *Alan Turing*, p. 388.

211 Chess computing—and artificial intelligence (AI) itself: All of computer science would be built on binary thinking. Chess, that complex and resonant game of perfect information, would help them construct the building blocks. "While the Turing Test has served as the center of gravity in the last 50 years of research on language in AI," write Franchi and Güzeldere, "chess emerged and remained as another similarly important center of gravity in AI research on thought, or thinking. Chess and the Turing Test can be regarded as the central research paradigms of early AI research, being concerned with the two pillars of AI: thought and language." From "Machinations of the Mind."

211 Turing's counterparts across the Atlantic: Peter Frey, *Chess Skill in Man and Machine* (Springer-Verlag, 1983).

212 With Bishops, it would have needed three hours: Frederic Friedel, telephone interview.

213 a future computer examining moves: Ronald Rensink, "Computer Science Lecture 3: Computer Reasoning," Lecture outline for Cognitive Systems 200, University of British Columbia, online at *www.cogsys.ubc.ca/pdf.*

217 it would henceforth no longer be possible: Bart Selman, "Intelligent Machines: From Turing to Deep Blue and Beyond," Lecture outline for CIS300, Cornell University, 2005, online at *http://www.cis.cornell.edu/courses/cis300/2005sp/Lectures/12%20-%20Artificial%20Intelligence.pdf.*

217 David Levy into a draw: "Man vs. Machine: History of the Battle," online at *http://web.archive.org/web/20040613231751/http://www.x3dworld.com/x3dEvents/Archives/chessMVM/MvMHistory.html.*

218 MIT linguist Noam Chomsky scoffed: Scott Sanner et al., "Achieving Efficient and Cognitively Plausible Learning in Backgammon," *Proceedings of the Seventeenth International Conference on Machine Learning* (July 2000), pp. 823–30, online at *http://www.cs.toronto.edu/~ssanner/Papers/ICML2000.pdf.*

218 "In fact, little or nothing about human thought": Philosophy scholars Stefano Franchi and Güven Güzeldere take this point one step further, arguing that chess computing and related pursuits have proven to be an enormous distraction from what should have been a more humanistic approach to artificial intelligence. "Early AI's focus on logical-analytical problem-solving skills . . . tended to eliminate these other components as peripheral to a proper understanding of intelligent human behavior," they write. "It is this radical stance taken by early AI that generated an almost total disinterest in any analysis of the material conditioning of the thought processes, starting from the material embodiment of the mind. At a time in the development of Western philosophy when many authors focused their attention on the peculiar relationships that obtain, below the level of consciousness, between bodily actions and the sur-

rounding environment, AI research moved exactly in the opposite direction."
"Machinations of the Mind."

218–19 "There are today hundreds of examples": Ray Kurzweil, "A myopic perspective on AI," published on KurzweilAI.net, September 2, 2002, online at *http://www.kurzweilai.net/meme/frame.html?main=memelist.html?m=3%23532.*

220 Then came Game 6: "Kasparov & Deep Junior Fight to 3–3 Draw!" online at *http://www.thechessdrum.net/tournaments/Kasparov-DeepJr.*

THE IMMORTAL GAME: MOVES 22 AND 23 (CHECKMATE)

222 As with many top-level chess games, the end of the Immortal Game was likely not played out on the board. It was reported in the journal *Baltische Schachblätter* in 1893, that after Kieseritzky played move 20. . . . Na6, Anderssen announced the final inevitable moves to checkmate, and Kieseritzky yielded.

225 "In this game": The entire quote from Steinitz is interesting: "In this game, there occurs almost a continuity of brilliancies, every one of which bears the stamp of intuitive genius, that could have been little assisted by calculations, as the combination-point arises only at the very end of the game." Larry Parr, "The Kings of Chess: A 21-Player Salute: Karl Ernst Adolf Anderssen," online at *worldchessnetwork.com/English/chessHistory/salute/kings/anderssen.php.*

226 the onlookers naturally expected landmark-quality play: Soltis, *The Great Chess Tournaments and Their Stories* (Chilton Book Co., 1975), p. 3.

226 Most of the eighty-five tournament games: Soltis, *Great Chess Tournaments*, p. 14. All final match scores of the 1851 tournament are available online at *mark-weeks.com/chess/v1lon-ix.htm.*

226 He died in a Paris mental hospital: Bill Wall, "The Immortal Game," online at *geocities.com/siliconvalley/lab/7378/immortal.htm.*

CHAPTER 12

228 Membership in the United States Chess Federation: Paul Hoffman, "Chess Queen: At 22, Jennifer Shahade is the strongest American-born woman chess player ever," *Smithsonian Magazine*, August 2003.

228 Sales of chess sets in Britain were booming: In Britain, one chess set manufacturer reported that recent sales were twice what had been forecast. Stephen Moss, "Chess: the new rook'n'roll? Madonna's influence has helped

the game become cool," *Guardian*, November 20, 2004, online at *guardian.co
.uk/uk_news/story/0,3604,1355581,00.html*.

228 upwards of 100 million games played online annually: Frederic Friedel
reports 49 million games per year on playchess.com. Personal correspondence.

228 Arnold Schwarzenegger: "Judgment day for chess players," chessbase.com,
May 8, 2003, online at *chessbase.com/newsdetail.asp?newsid=1100*.

228 The improvisational rock band Phish: "What does chess have to do with
Phish?" online at *phish.net/faq/chess.html*.

228 the game was becoming an integral part of school life: Cindy Kranz,
"Chess offers children a challenge, a chance," *Cincinnati Enquirer*, April 2, 2003.

230 In the mid-1970s, studies in Belgium and Zaire: Johan Christiaen,
"Chess and Cognitive Development," doctoral dissertation, Belgium, 1976,
English language edition prepared for the Massachusetts Chess Association
and American Chess Foundation by H. Lyman, 1981; Albert Frank and
W. D'Hondt, "Aptitudes and Learning Chess in Zaire," *Psychopathologie
Africaine* 15, no. 1, pp. 81–98; Robert Ferguson, Jr., "Chess in Education
Research Summary," paper presented at the Chess in Education: A Wise Move
conference, Borough of Manhattan Community College, New York, January
1995, online at *http://www.gardinerchess.com/publicationsbenefits/ciers.pdf*.

230 Maria Manuri: Phone interview.

230 Peter Dauvergne: Peter Dauvergne, "The Case for Chess as a Tool to
Develop Our Children's Minds," in "The Benefits of Chess in Education: A
Collection of Studies and Papers on Chess and Education," compiled by
Patrick S. McDonald, Youth Coordinator for the Chess Federation of Canada,
online at *http://www.psmcd.net/otherfiles/BenefitsOfChessInEdScreen2.pdf*.

230 Dianne Horgan: Dianne D. Horgan, "Chess as a Way to Teach
Thinking," *Teaching Thinking and Problem Solving*, vol. 9 (1987).

236 Over the previous half century: Saidy, *The March of Chess Ideas* (McKay
Chess Library, 1994).

236 Frankenstein-Dracula Variation: Tim Harding, "Frankenstein and
Dracula at the Chessboard," online at *http://www.chesscafe.com/text/kibitz01.txt*.
The Frankenstein-Dracula Variation is 1. e4 e5 2. Nc3 Nf6 3. Bc4 N×e4!?; as
cited by Eric Schiller in his book *The Frankenstein-Dracula Variation in the Vienna
Game*.

ACKNOWLEDGMENTS

241 an episode of the television show *West Wing*: Episode 58, "Hartsfield's
Landing," originally broadcast February 27, 2002.

INDEX

Page numbers in italics refer to illustrations.